What Your Colleagues A

The vast experience and knowledge of the authors in efforts is a major strength of this book, as is the focus for organizational change and for the education of hu book offers is its emphasis on making education "hu to improve society.

Karen L. Tichy, Assistant Professor of Educational Leadership
Saint Louis University, MO

Self-understanding and self-regulation are foundational skills to support autonomous learners and are fundamental for working in socially embedded environments in the real world or online. This comprehensive book provides insights, tools, and strategies for deeper, healthier learning systems.

Mark Sparvell, Senior Manager, Microsoft

The book really hits the mark. The best thing about it is the in-depth discussion of systems. It is with great pleasure that I read and reread this book. It delivers a good combination of big vision with specific strategies and techniques.

Jeff Beaudry, Professor, Educational Leadership
University of Southern Maine, Portland, ME

This is just what we need in our district. This engaging book will help change teams support their systems to effectively measure deeper learning. Readers will be drawn in by great examples from around the globe of educators putting students first. This energizing book calls us to take action for all of our students today and for our future.

Charisse Berner, Director of Teaching and Learning (Curriculum)
Bellingham Public Schools, WA

This book is a guide for all teachers, principals, and stakeholders in education who are aware that learning should be deep and contribute to humanity. It nails down what learning should be about with structured examples, exercises, and tools that, when applied, will lead to deeper learning for everyone.

Baukje Bemener, Research Consultant, NPDL New Measures Leader
Turning Learning, Amsterdam, Netherlands

Measuring Human Return is a great summary of the work that is being done in our region with schools that have embraced deeper learning. When school systems have the support to embrace systemic change and teachers have the support to design deeper learning experiences for their students, everyone succeeds! Our classrooms need this support so that our students gain the necessary global competencies that will prepare them for the world today and tomorrow! This is *the work* we all need to embrace in our schools.

Pam Estvold, Assistant Superintendent, Teaching and Learning
Northwest Educational Service District 189, Anacortes, WA

To our families and our learners—
poipoia te kākano kia puawai.

Measuring Human Return

Understand and Assess What Really Matters for Deeper Learning

Joanne McEachen

Matthew Kane

FOR INFORMATION:

Corwin
A SAGE Company
2455 Teller Road
Thousand Oaks, California 91320
(800) 233-9936
www.corwin.com

SAGE Publications Ltd.
1 Oliver's Yard
55 City Road
London EC1Y 1SP
United Kingdom

SAGE Publications India Pvt. Ltd.
B 1/I 1 Mohan Cooperative Industrial Area
Mathura Road, New Delhi 110 044
India

SAGE Publications Asia-Pacific Pte. Ltd.
3 Church Street
#10-04 Samsung Hub
Singapore 049483

Publisher: Arnis Burvikovs
Development Editor: Desirée A. Bartlett
Editorial Assistant: Eliza B. Erickson
Production Editor: Melanie Birdsall
Copy Editor: Will DeRooy
Typesetter: C&M Digitals (P) Ltd.
Proofreader: Wendy Jo Dymond
Indexer: Amy Murphy
Cover and Interior Designer: Gail Buschman
Marketing Manager: Sharon Pendergast

Icons throughout the text are courtesy of
The Learner First, 2018

Printed in the United States of America

ISBN 978-1-5443-3082-2

This book is printed on acid-free paper.

18 19 20 21 22 10 9 8 7 6 5 4 3 2 1

Contents

Appendices: The Learner First Tools

Visit the companion website at
resources.corwin.com/MeasuringHumanReturn
to download these tools.

Preface

THE DEPTH OF HUMANITY

When students and educators talk about **deeper learning**, we're talking about developing the range of learning outcomes that are truly important not only in school but over the course of our lives. We're talking about *humanity*—where we are now, where we want to be, and what we need to learn and be able to do to get there. No matter where we are in the world, the outcomes that matter are the **deeper learning outcomes:** self-understanding, knowledge, competency, and connection. These outcomes support us to connect with and contribute to the lives of others and the world in meaningful and fulfilling ways. They support us to succeed and to help others do the same.

Our school systems' mission or purpose statements often speak to the deeper learning outcomes and education's role in developing them. These statements beg the question, "What's actually being done to develop them?" As students, parents, teachers, school and school-system leaders, and other diverse community members—as *learning partners*—we're looking for ways to more purposefully and intentionally develop the full range of outcomes we value. We'll get there with measurement. It's the only way to know whether what we're doing is right for our learners, and what's measured is what we focus on and assess. It's easy to design assessments that tell us what students *know*. What's more challenging is assessing and subsequently measuring whether that knowledge—combined with self-understanding, key learning competencies, and strong connections with others and the world—supports students to learn, create, act, and succeed. It may be difficult, but it's important—emphasizing what's easy to measure over the full range of important outcomes ignores who learners are and how they can advance the world. Said differently, *it ignores what makes them human.*

The measurement framework introduced and described in this book reflects a deeper understanding of our learners and their needs. If we want our students to lead meaningful and fulfilling lives, we have to focus on all the outcomes that contribute to meaning and fulfillment. And if we want to know whether learners are successfully developing those outcomes, we have to measure their progress. The same can be said of educators' and system leaders' development of the *capabilities* and *practices* that make deeper learning outcomes a reality. Taking a more authentic, formative, and inquiry-driven approach to professional and system learning will ensure our action plans are centered on students' needs and driven by a commitment to collaborative change. Throughout these pages, we'll help you develop your capacity to measure and develop the deeper learning outcomes, capabilities, and practices mentioned earlier, and we'll illuminate the role of the *change team* process as the vehicle for fostering and spreading deeper learning throughout school systems and beyond. The deepest levels of learning aren't achieved in isolation. We can all do more for our learners, and we'll make the greatest impact if we do it *together*.

> **Part I: Capable Systems of Change** sets the stage for deeper learning and measurement with shifts in perspective and priorities that break from traditional assumptions about students, school systems, and the purpose of learning to arrive at a systemic, collaborative change team approach to making depth a reality.
>
> **Part II: Five Frames of Measurement** kicks off the exploration of a comprehensive measurement framework rooted in measuring *and* developing the outcomes, capabilities, and practices characteristic of a deeper learning system.
>
> **Part III: Authentic Inquiry Practice** dives deeper into the practices that will develop desired learning outcomes, exploring what deeper learning experiences and the outcomes they develop actually look like in schools and school systems and how you can promote them in your own context.

This book responds to the growing needs of students, parents, teachers, school and school-system leaders, and others globally who are looking to identify, assess, measure, and develop the outcomes that are important for learners. It features the following:

- **A new measurement framework** and collaborative **change team approach** centered on deeper learning outcomes and what enables their development
- **Measures, guides, and other tools** designed to help you foster, assess, and track deeper learning
- **Vignettes and examples** that demonstrate how deeper learning has been successfully implemented, assessed, and measured in diverse school and school-system environments
- **An ongoing case study** exploring one US school district's deeper learning journey at each stage of implementation
- Recurring **activities and reflections** that will support deeper learning implementation in your own context

The examples and approaches in these pages demonstrate where we are collectively with deeper learning, the specific practices that have gotten us there, and where and how we can continue to progress. What we're finding are students who not only are more engaged and active in their learning, but both want and are able to *use their learning to engage others* in ways that better their lives and communities. They're using who they are, what they know and can do, and their understanding of and connections with others in order to contribute back. That's meaningful and fulfilling, and what we're learning in partnership with others around the world informs and illuminates our framework for making these outcomes a reality—everywhere, and for everyone.

After reading this book, you'll be able to

- develop and measure deeper learning outcomes and the capabilities and practices that will bring them to life, at class, school, district, and school-system levels (depending on your role);
- set up a change team in your school or throughout your school system;
- leverage the inquiry process to better assess, design, implement, measure, reflect on, and deepen both student and professional learning;
- use measures and other tools to better assess your students, their needs, and their depth of learning, along with your own and your system's needs and levels of development; and
- understand the possibility and necessity of intentionally developing deeper learning outcomes that make a real difference in learners' lives and communities.

There's more to learning than what we see on the surface, and there's much more to our learners themselves. In order for education to develop and measure deeper learning outcomes, it has to match the depth of the humanity it serves. Start by celebrating your students and the fact that who they are, what they know and can do, and their connections with others and the world will determine what our world will become. If we support our learners to develop these outcomes, they'll bring them—*along with unknown wonders*—to life.

Part I

CAPABLE SYSTEMS OF CHANGE

Chapter 1

CHAPTER 1

FROM SURFACE TO DEEP

Deeper Learning in a Changing World

We all should celebrate our humanity. The depths of understanding and connection it allows for are bottomless, and the capacity it gives us for making a *collective* difference in others' lives and in the world exceeds that of anyone acting alone. Any individual can rise to great *heights*, but the *depths* we can reach together are greater.

Learning that reflects our humanity should be celebrated, too. We're talking about learning that's concerned not only with what we know but also with who we are, what we can do, and how our self-understanding, knowledge, and competencies come together to connect us at incredible depths of meaning, fulfillment, and contribution. Developing the outcomes that help us make a real and sustainable difference, now and in the future—that's **deeper learning**, and it's cause for celebration.

We realize that this isn't the sort of language traditionally used to describe education and its outcomes. It *should* be—it describes the full range of outcomes that actually matter for learners, now and throughout their lives. For us and for the students, educators, families, and communities with whom we continue to learn and partner, and, we would argue, *for all of us*, the outcomes that actually matter are those related to self-understanding, knowledge, competency, and connection. These **deeper learning outcomes** are the outcomes that are universally consistent with meaning and fulfillment, and they're the outcomes that help us connect with and contribute to our local and global communities. These outcomes are important, so education should develop them—all of them, and not just in mission or principle but through authentic and intentional **practice**.

When learning is deeper, we as educators can *feel* it. But in order to truly know whether students are developing any intended learning outcome, we have to *measure* it, too. **Measurement** provides an overall understanding of learning or development in relation to intended outcomes. When determined validly, individual measurements reflect the breadth of available **evidence**, synthesized to arrive at a fully informed decision or understanding. **Assessment** provides those individual points of evidence that combine to inform the measurement process. In this way, measurement relies on the strength and diversity of assessments that get at the heart of whatever we're trying to measure. Although the shortfalls of standardized assessments are well documented (Chappuis, Commodore, & Stiggins, 2017; Meier & Knoester, 2017), one of the most significant shortfalls concerns the *comprehensiveness* of what they can assess. Ultimately, they inform an incomplete picture of student performance, one that fails to account for who students are as individuals, what they can and hope to accomplish both as individuals and collectively, and what it really takes for every learner to be a successful and engaged citizen of the world. Focusing solely on narrowing measures of student success, in turn, narrows teaching and learning, limiting assessment practice along with students' opportunities for success.

The thinking and practice emerging to fill the gaps left by traditional teaching and learning are extraordinary. Powerful movements, including personalized (Kallick & Zmuda, 2017), project based (Larmer, Mergandoller, & Boss, 2015), 21st century (Bellanca & Brandt, 2010), social and emotional (Merrell & Gueldner, 2010), and culturally responsive (Hammond, 2015) learning, as a whole, respond to the importance of learning that's meaningful to the lives and identities of students and the importance of the outcomes that truly matter in today's rapidly changing and increasingly global communities. Individual interests and needs should shape each student's engagement with academic content, which requires educators to truly know and value every single learner as an individual. At the same time, personalized learning is only as valuable as the outcomes it develops, and so educators are working to determine the outcomes that matter and how to bring them to life. These complementary frameworks and approaches are shifting practice and making a difference for students, educators, and communities worldwide.

Deeper learning, as defined and explored in this book, is the collective aim of the movements mentioned above and the necessary aim of education because it's the global aim of humanity: to live in ways that are meaningful and fulfilling. This humanistic aim, as well as the framework of deeper learning outcomes, is only beginning to be explored in the context of education, but the people involved are developing, sharing, and spreading deeper learning and practice at an exciting pace. At The Learner First (thelearnerfirst.com), as founder and CEO (Joanne) and director of research and writing (Matthew), we the authors partner with school districts across America to identify, implement, and measure what's important for individual learners, cultivating cultures in which learning is continuous, centered on, and driven by students. Deeper learning doesn't happen in isolation—an inquiry-driven *change team process* connecting the different levels of our school systems illuminates the full picture of our students, our systems, and their needs, ensuring that what's important for learners is assessed, measured, and acted on. Our work with Michael Fullan, Joanne Quinn, and the New Pedagogies for Deep Learning (NPDL) global partnership currently engages some fifteen hundred schools in seven countries (Australia, Canada, Finland, the Netherlands, New Zealand, the United States, and

Uruguay) in developing and measuring deeper learning competencies, or the "6Cs"—character, citizenship, collaboration, communication, creativity, and critical thinking (Fullan, Quinn, & McEachen, 2017). What we're learning in partnership with these diverse districts and groups of schools informs our framework for making deeper learning a reality, wherever and whoever you are.

This book reflects the work of students, teachers, and other leaders throughout the world who are driving real outcomes for learners through a recognition of and commitment to depth. While we said that deeper learning is learning worth celebrating, it may be more appropriate to say that deeper learning *is* a celebration—the excitement displayed by students and their learning partners at the intersection of self-understanding, knowledge, competency, and connection could be called nothing less. This book continues the celebration by sharing the experiences of those who are embracing deeper learning.

In Part I, we introduce concepts that'll set the stage for the learning to come, examine the personal and systemic shifts that can bring deeper learning to life, and take an initial look at the power of change teams to spread deeper learning within school systems and beyond.

A Comprehensive Measurement Framework

The measurement and assessment of deeper learning require significant changes at all levels of our educational system, from the classroom level to the national level. Within the US educational system, each level represents a **system** in and of itself—a complex and connected body working, at its best, clearly and cohesively toward shared outcomes or ends. Whether you're a teacher, a principal, a district superintendent, or a higher administrator, with deeper learning, there's room for you to grow while still meeting your system's requirements and demands, *no matter what those requirements are.* In fact, deeper learning will help you meet them while also helping your learners achieve in exciting new ways. We should tell you up front that pursuing deeper learning isn't something you "do" here or there or every once in a while or as an add-on in addition to other pursuits. It's a true organizational *culture*, enhancing what you're already doing and enabling what you've always wanted to do. Anyone can lead this work by example—wherever you can, *go deeper*, and spread that depth throughout your system. Deeper learning begins with *you.*

It starts with shifts in thinking. Paving the way for deeper learning requires that you do away with certain biases and assumptions about the relationships between students, teachers, school and wider-system leaders, learning, and school systems. It requires a real understanding of your system and your students, as well as of how your system and everyone within it can best meet the needs of each individual learner (not the other way around). The

assumption-shatterers described later in this chapter will lead to deeper and more meaningful system-level focuses, namely, the five **system capabilities**:

1. **Understanding your system**
2. **Engaging learners, parents, and communities as real partners**
3. **Identifying and measuring what's important**
4. **Leading for deep and sustainable change**
5. **Creating a culture of learning, belonging, and high expectations for all**

We'll explain how anyone—truly, *anyone*—can strengthen these capabilities to foster deeper outcomes for learners.

All systems are capable of deepening learning—capable systems deepen learning for all. Since system-wide depth is the ultimate goal, educators need an impetus or vehicle for spreading learning within and beyond their system. Our recommended vehicles are **change teams**, formed within—and, ideally, between—schools, districts, and wider systems to bring stakeholders together to share practices, challenges, and ways forward at every point in the learning journey. Whether you start with a single district or even a single school, a change team is important because deeper learning is a partnership—between and among students, teachers, parents, school and wider-system leaders, community members, and all other **learning partners** committed to collectively improving students' outcomes. Throughout this book, we'll draw on the experiences of change teams in Burlington-Edison School District (in Washington State), focusing on how you can apply the lessons from their and others' deeper learning journeys in your own individual context.

When you share the idea of working to ensure deeper learning, you'll likely meet with questions such as "Why?" or "Why now?" from various learning partners. We suggest you respond with another question: "What outcomes are important for our learners?" In most school systems, certain outcomes that learning partners believe are important aren't being measured or intentionally developed. If you suspect that's the case in your system too, you can address the situation head-on by telling your learning partners, "We haven't been focusing on what's important, *but now we will*."

When asked what outcomes are important for learners, your learning partners will no doubt point to **self-understanding**, **knowledge**, **competency**, and **connection**—the very outcomes that determine humans' desire and ability to contribute to the lives of others and their communities in meaningful and fulfilling ways. Developing these outcomes means developing learners' capacity to use their learning to make a positive and sustainable difference in the world. Measuring these outcomes, then, is measuring **human return**.

It's one thing to identify these outcomes or even make them the explicit goals of your educational system, but it's another thing entirely to measure them.

Measuring an outcome helps you focus on and design methods of developing that outcome, and it's the only way to know what methods prove successful. If you don't know what's working, you won't improve your practice, and if you don't improve your practice, you won't improve learners' outcomes. You have to approach deeper learning with purpose and intention, and you have to continuously monitor your progress in bringing its outcomes to life. Measurement accomplishes all that and more. It gives you the language you need to (1) talk about deeper learning and how deeper learning can develop and (2) build the *capacity* to assess and develop it at any level of your school system. Furthermore it shows you what and how you need to assess in order to gather the evidence that measurement requires. This book will provide you with the *measures*, additional tools, and processes for bringing deeper learning to life no matter your role, location, or relation to your school system, along with a framework for authentic measurement practice comprising the **five frames of measurement**:

1. **Engagement**
2. **Development**
3. **Clarity**
4. **Inquiry**
5. **Depth**

We'll explore each of these frames of measurement using examples from individual schools and wider school systems that are moving toward deeper learning.

Collectively, your learning partners already know what's important for every learner. Your school or wider system simply needs to come together around what matters and then *act* on what you find. From there, you'll have the opportunity to identify, develop, build clarity around, and use measures of deeper learning aligned to learners and their needs.

Although measurement will be your lever for sustainable, student-centered shifts throughout your system, it operates within a wider inquiry process (adapted from Timperley, 2011) designed to focus all decisions on learners and their outcomes, transform the roles of students and other learning partners, and deepen instructional and other system-level practices. "Inquiry" describes the ubiquitous, continuous process of assessment, **design, implementation**, measurement, and **reflection and change** pervading every level of a deeper learning system and framing all activity within it. To present it another way, we like to think of inquiry as the process of designing and implementing assessments that support the development and measurement of learning, reflecting along the way, and changing practice as necessary. In the inquiry narrative, *assessments are both evidence and solutions*. They *evidence* where learners currently are with their learning and what they need in order to progress further. They're also the subsequent *solutions* designed and implemented to support learners to progress in the ways identified, and, through them, new evidence is collected about new learning levels and needs. In short, assessment evidence is what you'll use to measure your own and your students' development. And since what you'll be measuring is *deeper* than before, you'll need a deeper and more authentic approach to assessment, too.

That approach is **authentic mixed-method assessment** (AMMA), which describes the process of gathering the full range of evidence, both quantitative and qualitative, required to arrive at a fully informed understanding (measurement) of overall levels of progress and development (Davidson & McEachen, 2015). Most school systems' current emphasis on test scores and other limiting indicators of success promotes a form of single-narrative thinking, in which a narrow range of evidence is used to arrive at an understanding, or to measure an outcome, that's far more complex than any single indicator could fully describe. Using the example of a test score, a single data point won't tell you everything you need to know about whether a learner is succeeding, but it can serve as a useful and even important indicator that, when considered alongside others, informs a deeper understanding of overall levels of learning. With AMMA, those "others" take on a wider and more important role, and a lot of them are already at your fingertips: projects, assignments, conversations with students and their parents, surveys, tests, observations—what you *see*, *hear*, and *feel* every day in your school or school system evidences where you are and in which areas you need to improve. Right now, most of what we know about our learners isn't valued at higher levels of our school systems, and so it isn't captured and acted on in meaningful ways. But as long as we know what's important and have what we need to measure it, we can start to gather and act on this evidence with purpose and intention, developing the full range of outcomes that humanity values and that all learners need for success.

Measurement, assessment, and each of the other individual inquiry processes are *practices* that you can leverage to bring deeper learning to life. In relation to inquiry, what's important isn't simply that you engage in the process, but *how* you engage, with whom, in what physical and cultural conditions, and with what tools and technologies. As a complete and interconnected set, (1) **partnerships** with students, parents, and others; (2) natural and built learning **environments**; and (3) digital tools and other **technologies** join with (4) each individual inquiry process to comprise the **elements of authentic practice.** (You can find similar elements of deep learning design in Fullan, Quinn, and McEachen's 2017 book, *Deep Learning*.)

The elements of authentic practice embody proven ways of doing and being that are successfully developing deeper outcomes for students and system capabilities for professionals. We'll explore what they are in the context of professional practice by examining **deeper learning experiences**—any student-level learning experience that successfully develops and supports us to measure deeper learning outcomes—demonstrating how to engage students and other learning partners in equitable, personally relevant learning experiences *every day*, no matter the content or aim of the learning at hand.

CHAPTER 1

In reference to outcomes of learning, you may have heard this before or believed it to be true: "If it isn't measurable, it doesn't count." Let's flip that thinking: "If it's important, we *can* and *have to* measure it." To help you get there, this book includes the following measures and other tools:

- *Capability Rubrics* for measuring professional and system development of the five capabilities (Appendix A),
- a *Learning Development Rubric* for measuring systems' overall deeper learning progress (Appendix B),
- *Change Team Tools* for setting up and working within change teams (Appendix C),
- *Learning Progressions* for measuring students' development of deeper learning outcomes (Appendix D),
- *Authentic Inquiry Guides* to help you embed authentic practices in the cultural fabric of your school or wider system (Appendices E and F),
- a *Learning Experience Rubric* to help you measure the strength of practice embedded in individual learning experiences (Appendix G),
- an example *Oral Presentation Measure* designed by learning partners at Oakland Unified School District (Appendix H), and
- example *reading, math*, and *high school success measures* designed in partnership with Oklahoma City Public Schools (Appendix I).

online resources

Access the appendices at **resources.corwin.com/MeasuringHumanReturn**

We'll take a deep and formative look at these measures and other tools, their development, and how to leverage them within a continuous process of inquiry to bring deeper learning to life (see Figure 1.1).

As educators, we all want to use practices that will work best for *our* learners, and we know that what works in other educational settings won't necessarily work well in our own. Deeper learning and its underlying practices, however, differ from other approaches in an important way: they're universal. What's best for all learners are deeper learning outcomes, and as long as you're working to develop the same outcomes and capabilities, *practice applies*. We've seen this to be true, in the sharing of learning and practice between countries with educational systems that are dissimilar on the *surface* but aligned and connected on a much *deeper* level. Whether yours are Common Core or any other local or national standards, they'll go out of fashion before deeper learning outcomes do. Learners have standards, too, and they're more enduring than local or national ones. Both sets of standards are important, and we'll look at examples from schools and districts in the United States and elsewhere that are successfully meeting them in unison. Even with these as a guide, applying successful practice or implementing deeper learning in your own school or wider system will take a good deal of time and effort—after all,

Figure 1.1 • The Human Return Framework—An Authentic Approach to Deeper Learning

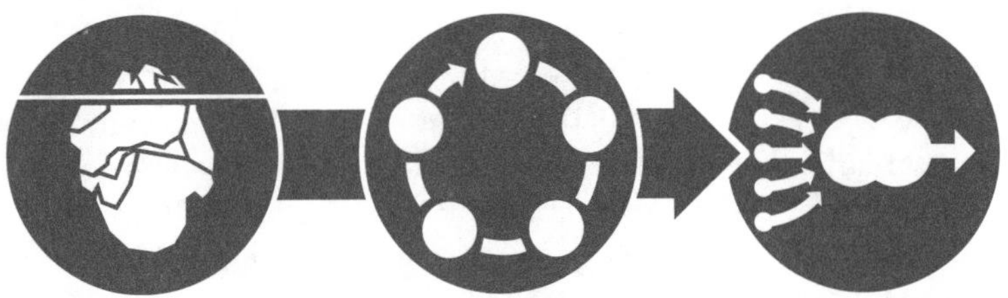

The Right Mix of Approaches	**Lifting Capabilities and Practice**	**Student Success**
Change levers at multiple levels of the system	*Measuring and developing what enables deeper learning*	*Measuring and developing deeper learning outcomes*
Five frames of measurement	Capability Rubrics	Self-understanding, knowledge, competency, and connection
Change teams	Learning Development Rubric	Learning Progressions
The inquiry process	Professional inquiry guides	Student inquiry guides
System capabilities	Learning Experience Rubric	Deeper learning experiences
Elements of authentic practice	Collaborative moderation	Contribution, meaning, and fulfillment

Source: The Learner First, 2018

each system, just like every learner, is different. But rather than emphasizing the differences, we'll support you to "put depth into practice," with reflections and activities designed to help you apply deeper learning and practice in any context. When it comes to deeper learning, the only differences that really matter are the differences that make your learners who they are—and the differences they can make in the world.

Putting Depth Into Practice

This is innovative work, and how to implement what you'll learn about in this book will require some thinking. For this reason, it's important that you slow down and reflect on your learning every step of the way. The reflections, prompts, and activities in the "Putting Depth Into

(Continued)

(Continued)

Practice" boxes throughout this book will support you through exactly that. Look out for these sections—they indicate opportune times to think about and act on what's been presented, where you and your system currently are in relation to best practice, and what you and your learning partners can do right now to bring deeper learning to life from whatever level of the school system you're working in. We'll offer valuable considerations along the way, we'll refer back to and build on previous activities, and even if you choose not to engage in some of the activities during your initial reading (some can't be completed in one sitting or, even, while sitting), they'll be here for you to revisit and build on all throughout your work. Know that the reflections are for everyone—if you're a school or school-system leader and a question is framed around instructional practice, think about what you can do to support teachers to take their practice deeper. If you're a teacher and a question is geared toward work at other levels of the school system, think about what you can do to influence those levels by spreading your own thinking and practice. If you're a parent or community member, think about what you can do every day, either inside or outside of school walls, to develop the outcomes that matter (in other words, to *take the walls down*). Deeper learning is a partnership—*it's best if done together*—and, in the same way, this book will have the greatest impact if you and others reflect on it together, deliberately and with collective purpose. Everyone wants their students to learn deeply. With the help of these activities, you and your learning partners can commit to doing the same.

Reflect

Take some time to reflect on what you've read so far. Are the deeper learning outcomes the outcomes you want your learners to develop? If so, what do you need in order to commit to developing them? Think about your understanding of measurement and assessment and their roles in the deeper learning process. Where do you perceive opportunities for deeper measures of learning and for more authentic assessment practice? Are you open to learning from and with systems and learning partners all over the world, collaborating to share and spread your own learning in order to deepen others', and celebrating your and your students' learning every step of the way?

The State of the System

The system is real. For those of us who have worked within an educational system, this reality makes itself known in a myriad of ways, and with varying degrees of force, throughout our daily practice. An outcome understood and shared at every level of a school system is more easily achieved than an outcome prioritized at anything less, and the deepest and most lasting change will always reflect a shifting *whole*. Why? No matter our level within a school system, its invisible hand guides us always to act in accordance with its self-interest. The interests of a school, for example, are most easily pursued if they align with the interests of the district, which, in turn, operates most effectively when aligned with the interests of the state, and so on up the line. If an objective is prioritized at your district level, you'll naturally be better supported to make it happen in your school. If there's no or little focus—or even conflicting focuses—in the levels above you, you'll be less supported to implement and sustain that independent interest. Given the preceding, we recommend that you adopt dual emphases: (1) doing everything you can for your learners no matter who you are or what your role is and (2) spreading your learning and practice to others. Luckily, and as will quickly become clear in your classroom, school, or wider system, deeper learning is infectious.

Those of us who have tried to *change* an educational system—not simply by words or policies but by working to shift the culture and underlying beliefs governing the way things are done—understand the challenges. It helps if you start by getting to know yourself and the system you work in, with the understanding that the system isn't the enemy. Get to know its invisible hand—*shake it*—and focus all your actions within it around who your learners are, what they really need, and how you can further deepen learning by encouraging others to focus on the same.

The modern US school system, ironically, is hardly modern. It's remarkably similar to what we've had for decades, despite the changes occurring all around it. Of all the reasons behind school systems' failure to progress (Koretz, 2009; Ravitch, 2011; Wolk, 2011), one of the most fundamentally damaging involves school systems' measures of success. In a traditional system, we wrongly accept that a certain percentage of students will fail, and those who succeed are those who demonstrate proficiency—or adequacy—on performance measures that don't get at the heart of real success. In this environment, school systems that work for learners work well only at supporting them to develop a small piece of what actually matters. Right now, performance in a series of regulated subjects and eventual high school graduation are invalid indicators of *deeper learning* and, therefore, of whether students are truly succeeding and will succeed later in life.

A lot is said in our school systems and communities about the importance of becoming "a contributing member of society" *after leaving school.* Yet our students will be best prepared to make those contributions if they begin making them *now*, partnering with their teachers, school and other system leaders, families, and communities every step of the way. Start small—deepen your thinking, and assess the effects of doing so on your practice—and aim big, measuring the combined effect of your changes in practice on your students' deeper learning outcomes. *Your students* are ready for deeper learning, so you have to be too. Get to know each of your students for who they really are, find out what excites them and what they're passionate about, and work to make their learning environments places where those passions are clearly reflected in the experiences you share. We've seen and illustrate in this book what deeper learning does for students and their learning partners. *It's worth sharing and spreading.* Go slow, and remember what you're working toward—every step is meaningful and a cause for celebration.

Take a second to think about the magnitude of the shifts described earlier and why they're so important. When we look at the financial crises that have impacted US and global communities over the past century, we're looking at the failure of *financial return*—what we *get back* from our investments—to amount to more than we've given. Said differently, we're looking at the failure of a system's measured outcome to better the outcomes of the individuals within it and to work for the people it was intended to serve. School systems that fail to measure and develop the range of outcomes that actually matter, or that fail to recognize why *they* even matter in the first place, are headed down the same path. Waiting until those systems crashed would be choosing to place our learners in the same position as so many in the midst of a financial crisis—without a job and at a loss for how the system was allowed to serve them so poorly.

Individual and collective success and advancement rely on *human return*—the human capacity to *contribute back* to the lives of others and to the world, fully realized at the intersection of deeper learning outcomes. Our contributions to one another's lives and the world take on many forms; they may affect a single person, or they may affect everyone. They're a function of self-understanding, knowledge, competency, and the human connection that reveals us to others and draws us into their lives, and when they come together for the betterment of life and the world they bring us meaning and fulfillment. *This is why we learn.* It's not only to prepare ourselves for the future but also to support one another in the here and now through the process of seeing ourselves, our progress, and our learning reflected in the lives of others and in the world.

Assumption-Shatterers

Think about what your educational system would look like if it actually worked for every one of your learners. Its self-interest would be their best interest. It would be dynamic, coherent, and responsive to their needs, drawing from a deeper understanding of who its learners are to inform the decisions made at all levels, from individual classrooms to boardrooms. The engagement of students, families, and communities as partners would effectively blur the line between "school" and "world" so that learners could explore and develop their identities, interests, and competencies with friends, teachers, parents, and others anywhere and at any time. The system would match the depth of the humanity it served, preparing its learners for a lifetime of fulfillment and contribution.

This isn't a "pie-in-the-sky" vision. These are outcomes you can achieve with your learners and your resources in *your* school system. All it takes to get deeper learning going is for one person to change her or his thinking. The following assumption-shatterers lay the foundation for systems in which the outcomes described earlier can be measured and realized. They're designed to take you and your learning partners deep below the surface of policies and programs and to help you question your beliefs and values, both as individuals and as a system (see the **cultural iceberg** in Figure 1.2). There's no doubt they'll be met with objections from some of your learning partners (and, in the following, we've included and responded to a likely objection to each), but these mindsets will be critical to your students' success. Individually and collectively, work to prevent such objections from keeping your school system from achieving what's best for your learners.

Figure 1.2 • The Cultural Iceberg

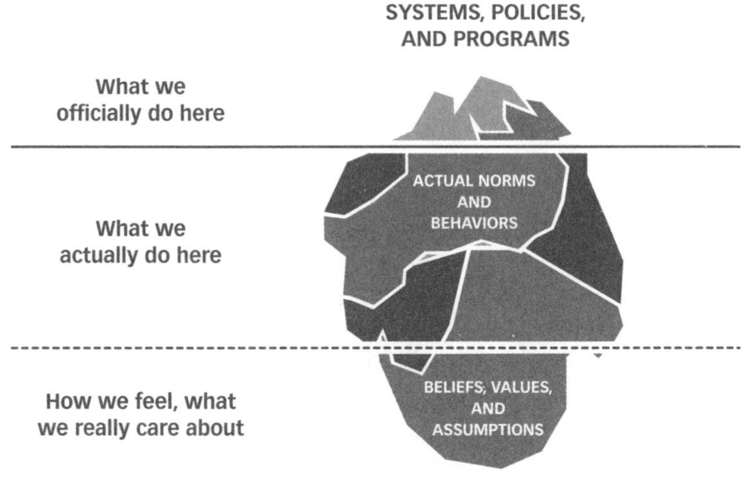

Source: The Learner First, 2018; adapted from Hall, 1976

Assumption-Shatterer 1: Learners aren't failing in the system—the system is failing learners. It's easy to fault low-performing students without considering what their "failure" actually indicates—the *system's* failure to meet their needs. While it's true that some of the factors contributing to an individual student's performance (e.g., poverty, health, and social challenges) are outside the system's immediate control, the hours that educators have with students each week represent a massive opportunity to focus on factors that *are* in their sphere of influence, including working collaboratively to develop the outcomes that paint an equitable picture of performance. Deeper learning shifts the focus away from attributing blame and onto designing the right mix of solutions together.

Yeah, but . . . sometimes low performance really *is* the student's fault.

The implication of this objection is that nothing within the school system's control could have been done to improve the learner's outcomes. In other words, *some students just can't succeed.* As long as success is measured on the range of outcomes that matter, however, that will never be the case. We can always do more to improve learners' outcomes, and we owe it to learners to ensure that we do.

Assumption-Shatterer 2: The only acceptable mindset is 100 percent success. Everyone working and learning in the system has to possess the unshakable belief that every learner *can* succeed and *will* succeed if we collectively work to develop the right outcomes, capabilities, and practices. Although it's common practice to accept and even celebrate 90 percent as a test grade or overall mark (regardless of whether what sits underneath that mark has assessed what's actually important for the learner), students aren't test questions. It can't be *acceptable* to do one out of every ten students "wrong."

Yeah, but . . . 100 percent success is statistically unachievable.

It's a mindset. Aiming for anything lower than 100 percent success implies that it's acceptable to expect a certain percentage of learners to fail—or even to *let* them—and to maintain that a system is working even though it doesn't work for everyone. Unless we as educators, leaders, and parents are willing to tell our learners how many of them *can* fail, then nothing we say, do, or believe should aim for anything less than total success.

> Adopting the 100 percent mindset—truly committing to the success of every student—is the most difficult and most important step in the process. But by focusing on the students who are least well served by the system and accepting that there is no such thing as student failure, only system failure, you shift from blaming them to accepting them. Learn their name and the story behind it. Know their interests. Know their strengths. Know their needs. Know their hopes and dreams. When we do that, we bring humanity into the system and care for them as human beings, not test scores.
>
> —**Rob Neu**, Former Superintendent, Oklahoma City Public Schools, United States

Assumption-Shatterer 3: Equal treatment leads to inequitable outcomes. Every single learner is different. Each has his or her own identity, knowledge, competencies, connections, and ideas about how to make the world a better place. Because these are constantly changing and developing, every learner should get what he or she actually needs at any given point, not what he or she doesn't need, won't need, or already has. Treating all students the same may not actually work for any of them, and it certainly won't work for all of them in the same way. Learning is deepest when it connects to who students are as individuals, where they are in their learning, and where they'd like to take it next. One size fits one.

Yeah, but . . . trying to personalize every student's learning is a fool's errand.

No one (we hope) would argue against the value and importance of caring about and getting to know learners as individuals. It's amazing how much our knowledge of others contributes to their learning and comprehension, and it starts with the little things we can do every day to drive learning home by more closely connecting it to our students and their interests. Students' engagement with a single assessment can take any number of forms—encourage and support your learners to give shape to their engagement. It's not about reinventing the wheel for every learner; it's about getting to know and acting on what gets your learners' wheels turning. These connections will go a long way toward developing learners' self-understanding, knowledge, and competencies.

Assumption-Shatterer 4: Focusing on the least-served learners creates shifts that benefit everyone. The learners struggling the most within an educational system provide us with the best lens for understanding how and in what ways it needs to change. What do we know and what do we need to learn about these students, and what does that tell us about why the system is failing them? There's increasing evidence of the power of deeper learning for those students who struggle the most in the traditional schooling system (Fullan et al., 2017). Why? Traditional outcomes are inequitable—they rely on a narrow set of typically knowledge-related indicators of success. These traditional outcomes aren't exclusively those that lead to meaning and fulfillment, and alone they're an appalling detriment to those learners whose capacity for success in life tragically outweighs and is undermined by their capacity for success in school. Deeper learning outcomes do away with that disconnect.

Yeah, but . . . let's not forget the learners who are already successful.

Our most-struggling learners will show us what we've been missing. Learning about who they are, what they're interested in, and why they haven't found success, and then changing our practice to better support their needs, can deepen learning for everyone. Such learners are the entry point through which we'll discover what it takes to bring deeper learning to life and begin to see and admire our learners for who they really are, after which it'll become impossible to view any of our students in any other light. In addition, students can "succeed" in a traditional assessment system without developing the outcomes that support them to succeed beyond it. Deeper learning benefits everyone, no matter their previous levels of success, because it transforms the very picture of success into one that's meaningful and sustainable for every learner.

Assumption-Shatterer 5: Systems can measure what matters for their learners. In large part, measures of learning are intended to tell us whether our learners are successful. The sad truth is that *traditional measurement practice is one of the most significant barriers to learners' success.* It doesn't tell us whether students are succeeding, because it fails to measure what constitutes real, meaningful success, and it doesn't encourage assessment that develops the complete range of important outcomes. The prevailing belief is that school systems can't measure a deeper set of outcomes, at least not in a valid or reliable way. *They can.* Measures are easier to create when you know what you're looking for, and they're easier to use when you have a firm grasp on assessment practice. The measurement framework introduced in this book will guide you through the ongoing process of developing and using measures of (1) the outcomes that matter and (2) the capabilities and practices that will enable those outcomes. It makes it possible for any school system—in fact, any level, "system," or individual within the wider school system—to assess and measure real success (discussed in Part II).

Yeah, but . . . my system isn't *ready* to measure deeper learning.

"We're not ready to measure and develop the outcomes that support you to contribute to the world in meaningful and fulfilling ways." If you wouldn't say that to a student, it's probably not in his or her best interest. Saying that an individual or system isn't ready for deeper learning is the same as saying that they aren't ready for improvement. That's never the case, no matter where we are on the "depth spectrum," because each and every one of us can always do more for our learners at any point in time. Deeper learning isn't about waiting for our schools or school-system requirements to catch up to this level of thinking; it's not about waiting for others to lead the work from above, either. It's about what each one of us can do individually and collectively, every single day, to deepen learning outcomes for our students. Measurement isn't something to build up to. It's something to build *on*, and it's a lever for getting deeper learning going.

Assumption-Shatterer 6: Students are partners in instructional practice. We mentioned that deeper learning changes the roles of students, teachers, parents, communities, and all other learning partners. It's important to note from the outset that with deeper learning, instructional practice and its elements—partnerships, environments, technology, and inquiry—extend to students as well, whose roles and responsibilities are consistent not only with *learning* but also with those once blanketed under *teaching* (McEachen, 2017). We refer to this as the diminishing division between teaching and learning, and it gives students the opportunity to leverage powerful practices in the development of their own and others' deeper learning outcomes.

Yeah, but . . . enhancing the role of the student diminishes the role of the teacher.

This objection couldn't be more mistaken. When students direct and take responsibility for their learning at this level of depth, the teacher's role becomes more important than ever. It's no longer enough to teach students to *know* or even to *learn*. In this model (or what may best be called a "deeper learning mindset"), teachers

- know and understand who all their learners are, what they know and can do, how they're connected with others and the world, and how to take their learning deeper;
- help design and implement assessments that support the measurement of deeper learning outcomes, supporting students through and providing them with engaging opportunities to explore learning areas of individual interest;

- leverage authentic practices in the direct development of learners' outcomes, enabling meaningful and engaging learning anytime, anywhere, and with anyone; and
- learn alongside and in partnership with their students and others every step of the way.

All the while, teachers instill in their learners the capacity and desire to *develop deeper learning outcomes in others*, the ultimate application of learning, which people achieve when they *use* their learning to teach, share, and contribute back. Deeper learning is facilitated not *for* learners but *by* learners, with others, and for the world.

Assumption-Shatterer 7: The journey to system-wide deeper learning is collaborative. Educators can't do it alone. Change processes that don't engage students, parents, and others as active partners in visualizing, describing, and driving the change won't create deep, sustainable, and systemic change. In addition to those of students, the roles of families and other community members will have to shift as well. Parents are experts on their children. They know who they are and what they're interested in, and at any given time they can offer invaluable support and insight into what may be impacting their child's learning and where there are opportunities for growth. Other members of the community want the best for children, too. They know what it takes to thrive in their community, and like parents, they hold the key to learning partnerships that'll directly enable learners' development of deeper learning outcomes. We can't confine learning to the classroom. If our systems work for our learners, it means that learning happens everywhere, with anyone, and at any time.

Yeah, but . . . they don't want to be involved, let alone know enough to make a difference.

"They" could be anyone from parents or community members to students or system leaders, with their involvement referring to anything from an individual project to the change team process. In the same way that every learner can succeed in a deeper learning system, any learning partner can be engaged by a system that works for them. If parents haven't been engaged in the past, don't assume it's because they don't care about their kids. Instead, look for new ways to show them that *you* care about their kids and their outcomes and that you truly value the parents' role in developing those outcomes. Breaking the constrictive barriers between school and world means welcoming "the world" and its multifarious expertise inside old education-drawn boundaries.

Even if you agree with these assumption-shatterers in principle, you're likely to object to some of their implications for practice. Whenever you catch yourself forming an objection, *consider its implications for learners' outcomes*. Checking your objections will go a long way toward ensuring that your interests don't conflict with learners' needs.

CHAPTER 1

I didn't want [The Learner First process] to work, because I wanted to stay the same. *I* wanted to stay the same, so I didn't want it to work. But every time I came to the [change team] meetings, I had to admit it worked.

[A parent and I] began to develop a different type of relationship, and one day I just talked to [her] and I said, "Look, you've got to do something different for your son, and I've got to do something different for your son, because it's not working." And we just had conversations, and we met sort of in the middle. We just started talking with each other. We found out that we had things in common. . . . We found out what [her son] liked to do.

He likes to draw. He wants to be an architect. He likes to design. He likes to study how things are made. I had never asked him that in class. As a matter of fact, when [I] came to the [change team] meeting, I said, "I'll be part of the change as long as I get to keep doing what I'm doing." And I am a pusher—I push the information, you receive it. You don't tell *me*; I'm telling *you*. You're the student; I'm the teacher. Well, that really wasn't working, so I became a receiver. Now it's push and pull; it's give and take. Now the mom waves at the end of the day from the car window. The son, the student—oh, he's not *my* son, but I feel like that—he escorts me down to my room sometimes with his arm. He still has bad days, but he enjoys school more [than he used to]. Because he enjoys it more, he gets to discover what he likes, and then I teach in the context of what he likes.

Right now, we're building a community. . . . I very seldom have a bad day at school.

—**Karen McNeely-Smith**, Teacher, Monroe Elementary, Oklahoma City Public Schools, United States

The quotation above illustrates the power of these assumption-shattering mindsets to help a teacher

- improve the outcomes of a struggling learner by recognizing a failure to meet his needs,
- collaborate with learning partners around the outcomes that matter,
- get to know the learner as an individual and personalize the learning around his interests and needs, and
- build a classroom community rooted in newfound understanding of what it takes to change learners' outcomes.

Changing is, of course, more challenging than staying the same. But when you see the effects of those changes on the lives of your learners, their families, and others, you'll never go back. You and your learning partners can put this depth of thinking into practice, and the system capabilities described in the following chapter are what will make it happen.

Putting Depth Into Practice

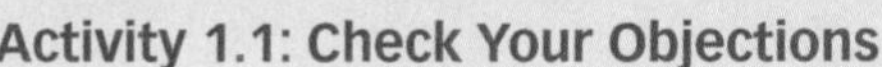

Activity 1.1: Check Your Objections

Whenever you find yourself objecting to a proposed change, ask yourself, "Does my objection *advance* or *inhibit* what's best for learners?" This simple question can do a lot to tell you whether your interests are aligned with your learners' needs. Always and everywhere, frame your own interests, wants, and needs in relation to learners' outcomes. For now, think about or write down the objections you or others might have in relation to each of the seven assumption-shatterers. Does the attitude behind each objection advance or inhibit what's best for your learners? What other objections, conflicting interests, or system constraints are preventing your students from deeper learning? In what ways, if any, might deeper learning outcomes be inhibited by your desire to stay the same?

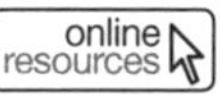

Access the appendices at
resources.corwin.com/MeasuringHumanReturn

Chapter 2

SYSTEM CAPABILITIES

CHAPTER 2

Shifting Priorities

The previous chapter's assumption-shatterers can pave the way for powerful shifts in behavior and practice that collectively enable deeper learning outcomes and, in the process, make the experience of working and being in an educational system much more enjoyable. Healthy systems—those in which deeper learning is fostered, developed, measured, and sustained for all—continuously develop the capabilities that best support students' development of deeper learning outcomes. In this chapter, we identify and explore five key system capabilities.

System Capabilities

1. **Understanding Your System**
   Developing a deeper, evidence-based understanding of your system, its learners, and the capabilities and conditions that enable valued outcomes
2. **Engaging Learners, Parents, and Communities as Real Partners**
   Connecting with students, parents, educators, and communities (learning partners) around who learners are and how they can contribute back
3. **Identifying and Measuring What's Important**
   Setting up a system of measurement rooted in learning-partner engagement and reliable, evidence-based practice
4. **Leading for Deep and Sustainable Change**
   Achieving real and sustainable outcomes with a continuous focus on learners and their needs and commitment to collective leadership and change
5. **Creating a Culture of Learning, Belonging, and High Expectations for All**
   Fostering an environment in which everyone is learning and in which every learner is genuinely known, celebrated, and expected to succeed

Figure 2.1 • Moving From Surface to Deep With the Five System Capabilities

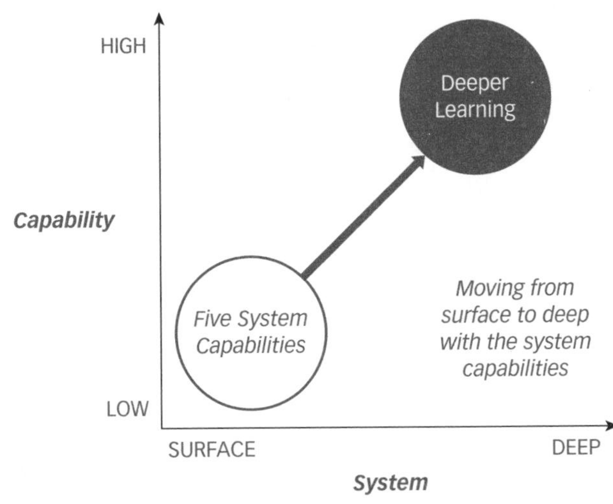

Source: The Learner First, 2018

CHAPTER 2

When we engage with, assess, and measure these capabilities, we're evidencing what we need to focus on collectively—what exactly do we have to do, *right now*, to support learners' development of deeper learning outcomes? The five capabilities reflect culture—who we are and what we believe as individuals and a system and how those identities and beliefs show up in practice and learning. Cultures of **capability** are marked not only by action but also by a clear and consistent understanding of the effects of every action on learners' outcomes: If an action or inaction is detrimental to learners' outcomes, we find a different route. If it's good for kids, we find a way to make it happen.

Let's dive into the five system capabilities, drawing on examples of learning partners globally who are finding ways to bring deeper learning to life. As we go, we'll help you use measures of your system's capabilities to better understand where you are now and in what areas you need to improve.

System Capability 1: Understanding Your System

While there are always shared similarities, every school system, like every learner, is different. No matter his or her position, every educator and system leader is charged with understanding the strengths, weaknesses, culture, and individual identities of his or her system. It's the only way to know where improvements can be made to deepen practice and, in turn, deepen outcomes.

Right now, many children in American schools are struggling. Their struggles may relate to

- language or other cultural considerations;
- challenges concerning a particular subject or content area;
- an inability to communicate or collaborate effectively with peers and other learning partners or to think critically and creatively to solve social and academic problems;
- a search for meaning, purpose, or identity; or
- other issues with their relationships, their communities, and their place in the world.

Education can and should alleviate these concerns, but far too often it adds to them. As long as this is the case for even a single learner, it's important that we all strive for greater depth and capability, both in our own practice and in our systems at large. Your efforts to understand your system and build your capacity to develop and measure what matters requires a focus on the following **dimensions**:

Dimensions of Understanding Your System

✓ Establishing clarity around the real causes of underachievement

✓ Developing a systemic professional learning strategy that addresses the real causes of underachievement

✓ Understanding what works best, for whom, and why

✓ Gathering meaningful, collective evidence in the system and in the community

The Capability Discussion Starters tool in Appendix C.1 includes questions to get you thinking about these dimensions and about the dimensions of the other capabilities. There may be questions you don't have answers to at this time (i.e., questions you don't have enough *evidence* to answer). That's okay—once you know what you're looking for, it's only a matter of coming up with ways to gather the evidence you need. Meaningful evidence gathering will help you establish clarity around the causes of underachievement; understand what works, for whom, and why; and then focus your professional learning opportunities around how to better meet each learner's needs. Evidence is important: it's what you need to inform the measurement *and* development of deeper learning outcomes and the capabilities that enable them.

You'll be engaging in deeper learning and practice all throughout your reading (and, hopefully, in between and long after), in partnership with other learners in school systems globally who are working toward the same outcomes. We'll follow the ongoing deeper learning journey of Burlington-Edison School District (BESD, introduced in Chapter 1) to inform and illuminate this framework for you every step of the way. Like any other school district, BESD has a unique set of learners and other learning partners, initiatives, and standards, but it serves as an example for all schools and other systems that wish to achieve the global outcomes consistent with contribution, meaning, and fulfillment. Take the time to learn with and from BESD, the other examples included throughout this book, and all other potential learning partners in your own system and beyond.

Let's continue our journey toward system-wide depth by developing a deeper understanding of BESD as a *system* and of its collective reasons for deeper learning. In the process, we'll help you develop a deeper understanding of your own system.

The cases in this book from BESD are informed by The Learner First's ongoing work with learning partners in BESD, the Northwest Educational Service District (NWESD), and beyond—especially by our interviews and conversations with Don Beazizo (athletic director); Brenda Booth, Tiffanee Brown, and Grant Burwash (instructional design team); Laurel Browning (superintendent); Tracy Dabbs (coordinator of technology and innovation); Bryan Jones, EdD (director of equity and assessment); K. C. Knudson (executive director of teaching and learning); Jim Logan (programmer/database analyst); Amy Reisner (principal); and Erica Tolf (consultant teacher).

A Recipe for Return: Models of Practice From BESD

Why Deeper Learning?

BESD comprises six schools (four K–8 schools, one P–6 dual-language school, and one comprehensive high school), serving some 3,700 students in Washington State. It operates within Northwest Educational Service District 189 (NWESD), a network of thirty-five public school districts in the state. Hoping to redesign and add depth to the way they engaged with district improvement, in 2013 BESD learning partners set out to involve the entire school district in designing a dynamic road map for achieving a more meaningful set of student and system outcomes (Figure 2.2). The road map centers on the district's mission, which is to educate each student for lifelong success. It starts with understanding what "success" really is, which, for BESD, started with a *promise*.

The district's promise to its students is to support every one of them to be respected, empowered, valued, connected, responsible, engaged, and collaborative. This is viewed as the foundation for students to aspire to learn, practice thoughtful citizenship, and sustain success both throughout school and over the course of their lives. BESD's systemic foundation, the core of who its learning

Figure 2.2 • **Burlington-Edison School District (BESD) Road Map**

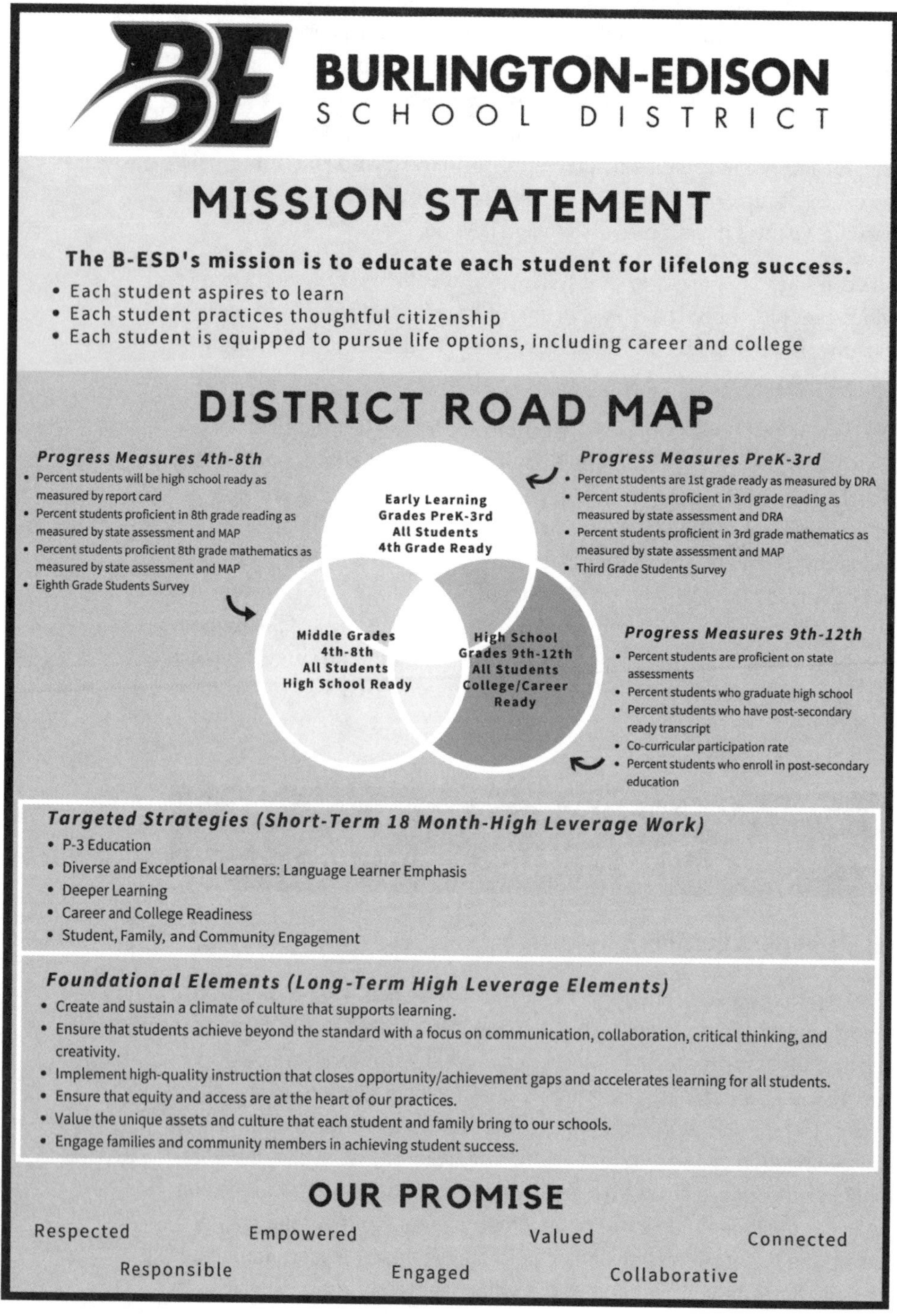

Source: Burlington-Edison School District (https://www.be.wednet.edu/district-office/besd-school-board/district-road-map)

partners are and how they support learners to achieve this definition of success, guides the development of 18-month action plans and speaks to the district's commitment to

- creating a culture of learning;
- developing key learning competencies, such as communication, collaboration, creativity, and critical thinking;
- ensuring equity through high-quality practice;
- valuing the cultures and identities of each student and family; and
- engaging families and the wider community in students' learning and success.

In an effort to make this picture of success a reality, the district identified P–3rd, 4th–8th, and 9th–12th grade progress measures to demonstrate whether learners are ready to move on to the next phase of schooling and beyond. Learning partners recognized that although these progress measures worked, to some extent, in determining whether the district fulfilled its promise to its students, they didn't have an authentic way of supporting, tracking, and measuring students' development of the full range of outcomes that truly compose success. They needed a deeper approach to designing, assessing, and measuring learning, and they needed to implement it within the system's existing expectations and demands—not least of which were those relating to the Common Core State Standards (CCSS) and the Every Student Succeeds Act (ESSA).

> With the implementation of CCSS, we saw it as an opportunity to really rethink what we could and should be doing for our kids as a school system. Part of that was recognizing that the standards were attempting to speak at a higher level and have kids do more complex things. That led us then to study some of the research about forecasting for employment and the skills that were going to be necessary for kids in the future economy and then to the [realization] that these are not standards that you disaggregate and create a checklist with—the key is to find the big ideas. We realized that we needed a significant transformation in what we were doing. We needed a broader set of outcomes than just what the academic outcomes were going to provide in order for our kids to be successful. We recognized that this was going to be equity work, and that we needed to develop a system that was going to help each and every child reach their highest potential, including our highly capable and gifted students.
>
> —**K. C. Knudson**, Executive Director of Teaching and Learning, Burlington-Edison School District, United States

A lot of our measures are really binary measures: you can read or you can't read; you can do math or you can't do math; you can perform on this assessment or you can't. Trying to turn that tide is really difficult, because it's really entrenched in our federal and state accountability systems. They changed through ESSA what our accountability measures are going to be, and [although] it gets to some things that haven't traditionally been prioritized in our system, there are still wide variances in individuality and how children learn that we're not taking into account and can do a better job of. It's a matter of, for ourselves, determining what success looks like and what we want success to be locally.

For a long time, we've been labeled as "successful" or "not successful," and we're trying to figure out how to change that narrative through a more whole-child perspective and [through] learning what it looks like to communicate to our community what we value in our children. We've long had a strategic plan that values relationships, that values respect and diversity, and [that] values our community as a whole and how we want people to feel in our system, but we haven't had measures that accurately reflect those things. We need to find those other measures and [figure out] how to integrate them and communicate [those outcomes] to parents. [And while] we have to change that narrative, we [also] have to show results in traditional metrics because they're still a part of how we determine whether a school is successful. . . . I don't see those metrics going away any time soon. And looking at [other outcomes] is not saying that we don't want children to be able to read, write, do math, and be scientists. Our theory of action is that by looking through a whole-child lens, we're going to be able to shift the traditional metrics—[that] through focusing on these other things, we will be able to influence what the state is looking at in terms of being accountable.

—**Bryan Jones, EdD**, Director of Equity and Assessment,
Burlington-Edison School District, United States

It started with having conversations, reading articles, and then thinking about how we want our teachers to collaborate with one another to build strong, meaningful lessons. We started working around inquiry, transferable ideas, and concept-based units, all built on our state standards, but [we] were also trying to figure out other ways to show how our kids are progressing. Tied together around our Road Map and mission of wanting kids to aspire to learn, be thoughtful citizens, and be equipped to pursue whatever it is they want, it was really important that we capture how kids are thinking and creating and communicating, and we were struggling to find a good way to communicate that and build that into our lesson. We [also] needed to figure out ways to show multiple assessment points and create a wide system tracking past just state exams. That's when we started to look around the deeper learning work and went, "Wow, this is really aligned with what really matters to our district."

—**Laurel Browning**, Superintendent,
Burlington-Edison School District, United States

At BESD's Bay View Elementary, a K–8 school with some 530 students, a desire to focus on a deeper set of outcomes in line with the district's mission and strategic plan led to the creation of ten "Learner Attributes":

balanced

compassionate

reflective

resilient

principled

growth minded

inquirers

thinkers

communicators

risk takers

(See Figure 2.3.) The school's journey has mirrored that of the district as a whole in its recognition of the importance of deeper teaching and learning, as well as the challenges it presents up front, namely, the measurement of the outcomes that matter.

For the last three or four years, we've been really trying to transform our school from more of a standards-based, testing-driven environment to more of an International Baccalaureate model, where we teach through units of inquiry. We don't have measures for [the] attributes we have, [and] we've always been looking for something to [respond to] our need for assessing the whole child.

—**Amy Reisner**, Principal, Bay View Elementary School,
Burlington-Edison School District, United States

BESD's deeper learning journey began with learning partners' understanding that they weren't doing enough to attend to their community's complete picture of lifelong success. The journey continued through BESD's commitment to measuring the outcomes which that picture encompassed.

Figure 2.3 • **Bay View Elementary School's Ten Learner Attributes**

Learner Attributes		
WE ARE		**WE SHOW**
Balanced	We balance the physical, emotional, and intellectual parts of ourselves and promote healthy choices.	Well-roundedness, strength of body, mind, emotions, connections, health
Compassionate	We are caring, empathetic, and respectful. We are committed to service and making our world a better place.	Caring, empathy, respect, focus on service, global mindfulness
Reflective	We are aware of our own thoughts, strengths, feelings, actions, and learning strategies. We reflect to develop ourselves and to make a difference in the world around us. We understand our effect on others and the global community.	Thinking, acting, changing, impacting, analyzing
Resilient	We persevere. We stick to it and remain focused. With an open mind, we look for ways to reach our goal. We never give up.	Perseverance, focus, determination, learning from mistakes and misunderstandings
Principled	We always do our best. We value honesty, integrity, and fairness. We understand the consequences of our actions and look for opportunities to act on others' behalves.	Honesty, integrity, fairness, discipline, determination
Growth Minded	We embrace a growth mindset. There is no limit to what we can achieve. We empower each other to learn from our experiences and others' perspectives, valuing all cultures, languages, traditions, and ideas as we continue on a journey of discovery.	Empowerment, valuing differences, limitless potential, ongoing growth
Inquirers	We are curious and continually learning about the world around us. Through inquiry and research, we use critical thinking to understand and question for the purpose of learning, service, and action.	Curiosity, questioning, researching, thinking critically, wondering, analyzing
Thinkers	We are knowledgeable. We use this knowledge to think critically and creatively across disciplines to solve complex problems. We take responsible action to engage with issues locally and globally.	Knowledge, creativity, problem-solving

Learner Attributes		
WE ARE		**WE SHOW**
Communicators	We are valued human beings who collaborate for the purpose of developing ideas within our global community. We listen and share with understanding and empathy, celebrating that we communicate in different ways.	Communicating, collaborating, listening, speaking, presenting, sharing
Risk Takers	We are brave. We try new things, working independently and cooperatively. We are innovative and resourceful, and we embrace challenge and change.	Bravery, independence, cooperation, innovation, resourcefulness, trust, thinking for ourselves

Source: Bay View Elementary School, Burlington-Edison School District, 2018; attributes created collaboratively by Bay View Staff, 2015; attribution to the International Baccalaureate Organization; Habits of Mind, Costa & Kallick, 2000; Partnership for 21st Century Learning, 2014

When introducing something new into a system, it's important to remember that *the system was there first*. We're all working within a system, with our own combination of standards, strategic plans, desired outcomes, outside consultants, and bodies of research informing what we're doing and how we're doing it, and, likely, missions that resemble BESD's in its focus on a more complete picture of success than traditional school systems report out on and measure. No matter the level of the system at which you're working, the key is to establish alignment between what your system demands and what your learners do.

As demonstrated by BESD, measurement is at the root of that alignment. You may think that you or your systems aren't ready to use measures of deeper learning, but *you'll be using them throughout this chapter*. To help you work through the challenge, we've included a **rubric** for each capability in Appendix A. The measurement activities embedded throughout this chapter ask you to use these rubrics to assess and measure your system's capabilities. Once you have a sense of how your system rates on each rubric, we'll help you make a plan for developing each capability. Keep in mind that you're beginning from a position of trying to understand where you are and what you need. If you have enough evidence to form a complete understanding of where you currently are, measurement will show you the capability gaps you need to fill. If you don't have enough evidence, measurement will show you the *assessment gaps* you need to fill. The two are equally important for determining ways forward.

These capabilities apply in all systems and at all levels. What people are *doing* at various levels and in various roles within your system may look different, but what you're working toward is shared. *That's powerful*, and it holds true across all elements of deeper learning. If you're a teacher, you may want to measure your own capabilities, your school's, your district's—all will be valuable for you to understand. They'll inform what you need from—better yet, *what you can share with*—other levels of your system. Determine what to focus on throughout this chapter, whether it's at a personal level, a school level, a district level, a state level, or any other level, and remember that these **ratings** are the first of many—your capability will only improve over the course of your reading as your own deeper learning brings the pieces together. Throughout your collective work with deeper learning, look to these and other measures to track your and your system's progress, to celebrate successes and identify opportunities for growth, and to watch your learners grow as you do.

Putting Depth Into Practice

Activity 2.1: Measure Your Capability—Understanding Your System

Use the descriptions at each level of the Understanding Your System Capability Rubric (Figure 2.4) in Appendix A.1 to determine whether your system is *substantially off track*, *getting started*, *looking promising*, *well on track*, or *geared for success* in relation to each of the four dimensions. Record the evidence you used to make your decisions. Then synthesize the evidence that informs these **dimension ratings** to determine an **overall rating** for this capability, using the same five-point scale. What evidence are you using to determine your ratings? Are there aspects of the descriptions (a level, a line, or even a single word) for which more evidence is needed? What do your ratings tell you about where you are and how you can progress?

For Your Consideration . . .

There's a common and very human reaction to considering where we are in relation to where we want to be: *stressing out*. Deeper learning and the shifts it requires can seem daunting at first, and they *are* challenging. But they're nothing to stress over. Working through the prompts and activities throughout this book will help you put depth into practice slowly and surely and with greater and greater effect. With each step or progression, instead of thinking only about how much further you and your learning partners still want to go, reflect on and celebrate the fact that you're closer to your goals. Learning partners (including those whose stories in this book illuminate what depth looks like in practice) will be there to provide support along the way. Celebrate with them, and remember that every movement in the direction of depth takes your learners—*and humanity*—in the direction of success.

Figure 2.4 • Understanding Your System

Developing a deeper, evidence-based understanding of your system, its learners, and the capabilities and conditions that enable valued outcomes

Dimension	Substantially off Track	Getting Started	Looking Promising	Well on Track	Geared for Success
Establishing clarity around the real causes of underachievement	There's a widespread lack of clarity around the conditions that are fostering and hindering deeper learning, respectively. This often leads to a misplaced emphasis on perceptions of learners' abilities and backgrounds, as opposed to the system's inability to meet learners' needs.	Learning partners are beginning to understand that their own capabilities and the conditions they create have a lot to do with learners' capacity for success. What those conditions are and how they're linked to the needs of individual learners remain unclear.	Learning partners are developing a clear picture of their learners and their needs. There's a widespread shift in thinking, from "What's wrong with these learners?" to "What can we do to better meet their needs?" and "What can the school and wider school system do to help us meet those needs together?"	Most learning partners are clear about which learners are struggling the most and what conditions are limiting their potential. Partners are beginning to make links among learners' needs, their own capabilities, and the conditions at the school and wider school-system levels.	Learning partners know who their learners are, which ones are struggling the most, and what they and their learners need to be successful. They've established school- or system-wide clarity around the capabilities and conditions at play, and they look in all cases to self- and collective improvement in supporting all learners to learn deeply and succeed.
Developing a systemic professional learning strategy that addresses the real causes of underachievement	There's no clear emphasis on forming direct links between professional learning and student learning, resulting in a clear disconnect between what learners actually need and the professional learning opportunities offered by the school or wider system.	Professional learning opportunities are beginning to reflect an understanding of why learners are struggling and how those needs might be addressed. Learning partners are working to connect those opportunities with the causes they're intended to address and the outcomes they're intended to develop.	The professional learning strategy is intentionally designed to fill the gaps in capability at all levels of the system that are directly linked to the underlying causes of underachievement. Its impact is felt in pockets, but measured outcomes continue to expose a system whose strategy doesn't fully account for identified needs.	The professional learning strategy reflects widespread understanding of the system, its learners, and how the combined effects of learning partners' actions and decisions at all levels of the system impact learners' outcomes. Partners understand both what learners need and how those needs can be addressed systemically.	All professional learning is determined by current measures of learning outcomes and their enablers, and it reflects a clear understanding of root causes and how to address them. The effectiveness of specific opportunities is fully evidenced and directly linked to its impact on learning outcomes, and their success is both felt and measured school- or system-wide.

(Continued)

Figure 2.4 • (Continued)

Dimension	Substantially off Track	Getting Started	Looking Promising	Well on Track	Geared for Success
Understanding what works best, for whom, and why	Programs, initiatives, and approaches are implemented loosely, without an understanding of which learners will be impacted, how, and why. The focus is on what worked and what didn't, as opposed to whether this approach is working, why, and how it can be improved in real time to further develop learners' outcomes.	Learners' needs and learning styles are considered in light of approaches that have or haven't worked in the past, what is or isn't working now, and what needs to change. There's a lack of clarity around why certain approaches work for certain learners and how to gather the evidence required to inform that understanding in real time.	Learning partners are beginning to take a more active role in relation to school or wider system implementation efforts. This involves deliberate attention to and measurement of approaches' effects on individuals' outcomes, and reflection on what changes can be made mid-implementation to improve them.	There's a school- or system-wide understanding of the importance of linking initiatives and approaches to individuals' outcomes, and of the assessment evidence required in making those connections a reality. All implementation efforts in the school or wider system answer for, and adapt in light of, their measured impact.	Learning partners are gathering focused assessment evidence that provides not just a general understanding of which approaches are working but also a complete picture of whom they're working for and why. "What works" is known, understood, shared, added to, and continuously deepened throughout the school or wider system.
Gathering meaningful, collective evidence in the system and in the community	Learning partners' understanding of their system and its learners isn't rooted in the necessary evidence. Collected evidence fails to get at the heart of what really matters for learners, and learning partners aren't supported to provide or gather meaningful and authentic evidence of learning.	There's an emerging understanding of the importance of collecting assessment evidence to inform measurement and, in turn, change. Additional support is needed to create, monitor, and measure performance on assessments that demonstrate whether specific approaches, learning experiences, and professional learning opportunities effectively develop intended outcomes.	Learning partners are beginning to adopt a structured and consistent approach to assessment design and implementation that ensures healthy and informed measurement practice. Common challenges involve gathering the range of necessary evidence, synthesizing it, and engaging learners, parents, and others as active partners throughout the assessment process.	Learning partners at all levels of the school or school system inform their measurement, actions, and decisions with assessment evidence gathered throughout the system and in the wider community. Evidenced learning is fed back into improvement efforts, and learning partners play a prominent role in informing and enacting changes that improve learners' outcomes.	All actions and decisions in the school or wider school system reflect an evidence-based culture that puts learners and their outcomes first. Learning partners recognize that evidence is everywhere, and, therefore, assessment is natural and continuous. The evidence they gather collectively informs measurement *and* deepens outcomes.

Source: The Learner First, 2018

System Capability 2: Engaging Learners, Parents, and Communities as Real Partners

It's one thing to acknowledge that learners, their families, and their communities should be active partners in education; it's another thing entirely to achieve the cultural and behavioral shifts necessary for making it happen. So, what are the components of truly engaging these learning partners in their own, their children's, and your students' learning?

Dimensions of Engaging Learners, Parents, and Communities as Real Partners

- ✓ Partnering in every aspect of the inquiry process
- ✓ Working with parents to jointly discover, understand, and realize learners' interests, needs, and goals
- ✓ Supporting, valuing, and utilizing partner insights and engagement
- ✓ Providing opportunities for technology-enhanced, connected learning anytime and anywhere

In our own work with schools, the engagement of learning partners is often initially perceived as a strength. Most schools communicate with parents and invite them and other community members to participate in school activities. But when you drill down into what real *engagement* and *partnership* require, the depth and breadth of practice aren't always where they could be. A real partnership not only involves transfer of knowledge, ideas, and information; it also has to leverage the knowledge and abilities of all parties in an equitable way that leads to learning for everyone involved.

To deepen learning, students should partner—with their peers, their teachers, their families, and other members of their communities—in all aspects of their learning. Supporting students to identify and engage in opportunities to connect locally and globally, often through the use of technology, will support their development as citizens of the world, committed to positive relationships that push thinking and create real change.

A Recipe for Return: Models of Practice From BESD

Deeper Learning Is a Partnership

The following stories illustrate the power of partnerships to engage students, parents, and community members around learning and its outcomes. You'll know what success looks like and how to make it a reality if you explore the full range of learning partnerships.

[With deeper learning,] students are more empowered to not feel like school is being *done to* them and [to feel] that they're a partner with their teachers and their families. . . . I just had two kindergarteners teach me how to scan a QR code with a Chromebook, and I thought, "What a wonderful place this is, where they can be delighted to show an adult that this is how I do this." They were so matter-of-fact [about] using technology to learn. [Our school is] a place of questions—it's this calm, happy, engaged, meaningful place for kids. All our disciplinary referrals have gone down. We have teachers and staff members really talking with students, asking them about how they're feeling [and] why this happened. Taking a stance of inquiry and asking questions rather than making prejudgments or assumptions on our part has really shifted the culture.

—**Amy Reisner**, Principal, Bay View Elementary School, Burlington-Edison School District, United States

Last spring, I was walking through Bay View Elementary and stopped by [the second-grade teacher's] classroom. [I asked her:] "So, how are you doing? You holding it together?" She said: "I feel fantastic. I've never had this much energy at this time of the year as a teacher." I walked into the classroom, and the kids had developed the capacity to take ownership of their learning. There was a really strong sense of community in the room. By that time of the year, she would have been wiped out [if] she was doing all the talking and all the heavy lifting, [but] the students were collaborating and communicating with each other and helping each other move forward. The role of the teacher had certainly shifted. That was an interesting piece of evidence—for me to have a teacher explain it that way.

—**K. C. Knudson**, Executive Director of Teaching and Learning, Burlington-Edison School District, United States

In order to form a deeper connection between the district, the schools, and the community, BESD hosts an annual "Citizens Day," on which parents, business leaders, clergy, and other members of the community engage in a day of learning and celebration. Learning partners begin with an overview of the district's vision and discussion around various data points and learning focuses; they then tour the high school and interact with learners, on the lookout for the outcomes and focuses discussed. Following their experience at the high school, partners continue their learning at a K–8 school, where they meet with the principal and go over what's being done to improve practice and outcomes. Students share projects they want to highlight, providing a valuable opportunity for parents and community members to see what learners find engaging. As explained by Superintendent Laurel Browning, "[At] all my business roundtables, they want students [who] can communicate and think critically and work with one another, [who] are creative and can solve a problem. When we bring them in for Citizens Day, we're trying to capture that for them to see in real time in the classroom, coupled with when they're in buildings they can see it on the walls. It's helped break down those barriers and traditional ways of seeing schools, and [it's] helped folks understand why our systems are shifting."

Bringing the community into BESD schools has also opened the door for powerful "field experiences" that take students outside school walls *and* deeper into the curriculum.

We were thinking, you have the traditional field trips, [which] are more like, "Oh, it's fun to go to the zoo or to the pumpkin patch." So by saying "field experiences," it's more, "How are these experiences linking to the units, either as a front-loading to the unit to give a common experience to the students before diving deeper, or as a way of the students being agents of change and doing something in their local community?"

—**Brenda Booth**, Instructional Design Team, Burlington-Edison School District, United States

We recently met with a community partner to explore how we can systematically include science field experiences throughout all our units. We want our students to have the opportunity to actually be scientists in our community, to go take water quality samples, to restore wetlands, or to observe wildlife in a natural habitat. The person we met with had pages of other potential community partners. Our next step is to start linking the conceptual understanding or big ideas outlined in our curriculum with those community partners so that learning moves beyond the walls of our classroom.

—**Tiffanee Brown**, Instructional Design Team, Burlington-Edison School District, United States

Similar partnerships are forming and making a difference in other US school districts and globally. In 2016, in Australia, with a federal election approaching, last-year secondary (high school) students wanted to prepare themselves for their experience as first-time voters (Pickles, 2016). Over the course of a month, they researched party policies, interviewed their mayor, met with local political candidates, and engaged with important community groups and organizations. They invited the Bendigo Islam Association for an open discussion about culture, beliefs, and religious practices. Afterward, they said about the experience, "We learned a lot we didn't know and unlearned a lot we thought we knew that wasn't correct." They designed a mock political protest and ballot papers and capped the experience with an event at which they joined in discussion with a panel of political candidates and other community experts to hear multiple viewpoints, fill gaps in their learning, and better prepare themselves for an election that would have an impact on their own futures and their communities'.

In Oklahoma City Public Schools (OKCPS), educators' desire to learn more about their students led to the strengthening of learning partnerships with parents and the community.

When we started this process . . . we thought this was about behavior. We focused on students and *their* behavior for a while, until we realized it was about the learner and how we, the adults, should connect with the student and the student's parents. We truly had to remove layers of hurt and fear, and [we had to] really come and connect as a staff that could bond together and then reach out to our parents. We refocused and re-centered ourselves to identify that the parents are real partners. . . . We decided to make connections with our kids and to know who they are.

—**Cherron Ukpaka, MEd**, Former Principal, Martin Luther King Jr. Elementary, Oklahoma City Public Schools, United States

There is a mom this year . . . who has been really involved in her son's well-being. We met at the beginning of the year, and I had some assessments to let her know about. He is in third grade right now, and the assessment shows that he is reading at about a second-grade level. . . . All year she was working with him at home. I have been working with him at school. We have been communicating clearly. And he brought his reading grade up. . . . He is now reading at a fourth-grade level. And she is very grateful to *me* for that. I'm like, "No, I'm so grateful to *you*! Everything you have done at home has helped." She brought the support at home. I brought the support at school. It feels like a true partnership. I don't know . . . that's kind of amazing.

—**Molly Jaynes**, Teacher, Cesar Chavez Elementary School, Oklahoma City Public Schools, United States

A pastor in one OKCPS school community, drawn to and hoping to become involved in the change process, reached out to the school to ask how to align his church's outreach efforts with what was happening there. After brainstorming with change team members, he was able to work out action steps for his congregation that were aligned with the five system capabilities and designed to strengthen community and parent involvement. Another OKCPS school, Southern Hills Elementary, hosted a dinner for learners and their families, which some two hundred people attended to learn about the concepts behind their school's new approach and what it meant for their children. Parents learned that teachers and leaders at the school wanted to better understand their children, their goals, and anything else that could help make learning more relevant and meaningful to their lives. Parents and teachers began having conversations with their kids about their dreams and what they were interested in learning. By demonstrating to parents their level of interest in the children and what actually mattered to them, the teachers were able to change parents' perceptions of the learning process and the importance of their role in it.

These cases demonstrate the value of partnerships at all stages of the learning process to support a range of learning and practice. Consider the case from Australia, discussed earlier, in which students prepared to be first-time voters. Each of the partnerships formed throughout that learning experience provided opportunities for furthering, evidencing, and measuring students' learning while also serving as important evidence points to inform understanding of the system's partnership capability. The journey to system-wide deeper learning is collaborative—everyone is learning and growing together, engaging others around a common commitment to students and their learning.

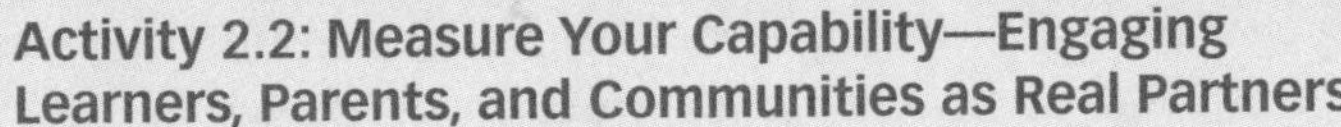

Putting Depth Into Practice

Activity 2.2: Measure Your Capability—Engaging Learners, Parents, and Communities as Real Partners

Use the descriptions at each level of the Engaging Learners, Parents, and Communities as Real Partners Capability Rubric in Appendix A.2 to determine whether your system is *substantially off track*, *getting started*, *looking promising*, *well on track*, or *geared for success* in relation to each of the four dimensions. Record the evidence you used to make your decisions. Then synthesize the evidence to determine an overall rating for this capability, using the same five-point scale. What evidence are you using to determine your ratings? Are there aspects of the descriptions (a level, a line, or even a single word) for which more evidence is needed? What do your ratings tell you about where you are and how you can progress?

System Capability 3: Identifying and Measuring What's Important

> If you ask parents and teachers what they want for their students and their children, they'll talk about things like, "I want them to be happy, well adjusted, good communicators, collaborative, critical thinkers," and then what do we measure? What do we celebrate? It's not the same. So it's a gap between what we say we value and then what we measure. We all know that what we measure is what gets done, so there's a bit of a disconnect there that we're still struggling with.
>
> —**Patrick Miller**, Principal, Ontario, Canada

Measurement. It's a driver of individual and system change centered on everything that makes our learners who they are. It's all about the learner, all the time. Measurement relies on knowing and capturing what's important for students, so that what they learn will contribute to their lives and communities. Enter *assessment*—what evidence will allow us to measure learning in a valid and reliable way, and how can we go about gathering it? This is truly important—from our experience, one educational leader identified the assessment of key outcomes and capabilities as "the priority for our government," while another referred to assessment that gets at the heart of deeper learning as the "holy grail" of engagement with a deeper set of learning outcomes. Authentic assessment practice involves establishing the evidence-based culture necessary for accurately and fully informing the measurement of student and professional learning.

If an outcome matters for your learners, you have to find a way to bring it to life—you have to measure it. You *start* the process by engaging learning partners in identifying and understanding what you and your learners value, and you continue it by developing and building clarity around deeper learning measures and then using them within the ongoing inquiry process toward greater and greater depth. It's the process of developing and sustaining a *comprehensive measurement framework*, and it's an important one. So important, in fact, that its five frames are deserving of seven full chapters of this book (Parts II and III), and a conclusion, to boot ("How Deep Are You?"). Again, at this early stage, when it comes to measurement or any other of the five system capabilities, remember that relative incapability is okay. Use the measures and other learning in these pages to find out what you need and how to get it, and celebrate that you'll always be "incapable" relative to where you're going.

Dimensions of Identifying and Measuring What's Important

- ✓ Collaboratively identifying what success looks like for your learners
- ✓ Establishing clarity using deeper learning tools
- ✓ Engaging in authentic assessment that fully informs the measurement of learning
- ✓ Moderating exemplars to ensure inter-rater reliability and to identify and spread best practices

If you truly understand your system and its learners, and you engage students and others as real partners, what's important to and for them will be abundantly clear. You'll know who your learners are and what they value, and you'll have the foundations in place for making *learners* the central component of learning. You have to uncover the gap between what you value and what you measure and then figure out a way to bridge it.

A Recipe for Return: Models of Practice From BESD

Identifying What's Important

A deeper understanding of assessment led learning partners at Bay View Elementary to pose the following question at a staff meeting: *What do you want to know and be able to assess about your students*? Teachers wanted to know their students' traditional learning levels, but they also wanted to know their students' learning styles, goals, and interests. They wanted to know other elements of their students' personal and family identities and stories. They wanted to know about their students' connections with others and their environments, their strengths and weaknesses, and their understanding of themselves both as students in school and as learners for life. It's a question all systems should pose to bring us face to face with our learners and their humanity and with what it really takes to assess and develop "the whole child."

At Burlington-Edison High School (home of the Tigers), in 2014 Athletic Director Don Beazizo and his coaching staff engaged more than three hundred student athletes, cheerleaders, and dance team, ROTC, and band members in a discussion of core values. From a long list of values, each student chose the eight that he or she felt were the most important. In groups, students discussed their selections and narrowed their lists until each group had decided on a single core value. After defining their group's value, writing the definition on poster paper, and displaying their posters on the walls, each student distributed eight to ten stickers among one or any number of posters, depending on how strongly she or he felt about each value. From this activity, four "Core Covenants"—*character*, *leadership*, *commitment,* and *integrity*—emerged as the values to instill in every athletics program. Building on students' definitions of each of these Core Covenants, learning partners defined what each value would look like in the classroom, in the community, during practices, and within games—not only for students, but also for coaches, the athletic director, and parents (Figure 2.5). Since then, the Core Covenants have been used to determine athletes of the month; as a powerful accountability tool between and among students, coaches, and others; and to define the "Tiger Way" at Burlington-Edison High School.

> This [tool] is what defines us. If a student starts to go off on the wrong path—for instance, if they choose to make a decision off the field or off the court, I, as well as the coaches, can refer back to these four Covenants, because if you look at any one of them you can tie them into kids making choices, [their] commitment to the team, their commitment to the community, and what it looks like in school. You can fall back on this tool for anything. If there's any area in athletics—whether it's talking back to officials or not communicating with your coach or parents, [or] talking about playing time—we can refer right

Figure 2.5 • Burlington-Edison High School's Core Covenants

	Character	Leadership	Commitment	Integrity
Definition	Doing what's right when no one is watching and in life's hardest moments.	Taking responsibility and having motivation to inspire and unite the group.	Being dedicated to bettering those around you through hard work and discipline.	Being accountable to those around you by keeping to the highest standards, expectations, and morals.
What Covenant Looks like in School				
AD	Role model the appropriate behaviors for athletes as well as support them to open up to other students.	Create culture for leadership training, sharing positive experiences and addressing concerns.	Get to know athletes personally.	Recognize athletes making good academic choices; help athletes struggling with academics.
Coach	Modeling appropriate behavior; setting a good example for your team and the rest of the student body. Holding players accountable and to a high standard regarding team and school rules.	Educating athletes about the importance of good leadership by providing them with outside resources, i.e., clinics, books, speakers. Providing and demonstrating real-life examples of excellent leadership.	Emphasizing the importance of being committed and having high expectations about it. Showing commitment as a coach and modeling this in and out of season. Sharing the knowledge gained to be successful and always being prepared.	Always stressing and never accepting anything less than the highest possible standards. Hold athletes accountable and follow through with behavior expectations set forward at the beginning of the season.
Athlete	Being thoughtful to those around you.	Be the person to do things the right way; refocus those that are not.	Getting to class every day and on time; keeping up in classes.	Being a role model, not being compromised, following rules and expectations.
Parent	Monitor and support needs for son/daughter's academic success. Stay current with school progress through Family Access.	Ensure athlete is in attendance for all classes and hold him or her accountable for grades.	Maintain high academic standards for athlete and hold him or her accountable for those standards.	Ensure athlete honors athletic code and exceeds classroom expectations.

	Character	Leadership	Commitment	Integrity
What Covenant Looks like In Community				
AD	Hire coaches that will work within the Covenants.	Participate in the public relations and promoting our commitment to the Covenants.	Connect with community for opportunities to help support B-E programs.	Provide students a feedback mechanism on how Covenants are going within programs.
Coach	Have a positive talk and share with all stakeholders in the athletic world about expectations.	Make Covenants available to public through appropriate program channels (i.e., Boosters).	Be dedicated to implementing and promoting the Covenants. Recognize those committed. Follow through with those individuals who are not.	Supporting all programs and attend to show support for one another.
Athlete	Reaching out and helping others.	Be positive about school programs.	Get involved to help others (i.e. help neighbors) show support for B-E.	Setting a good image of self; gaining respect from those around you.
Parent	Accept role as parent in program; work team events & participate in fundraising.	Be a role model; be positive and advocate for coach and team.	Attend and support other athletic events and encourage community support.	Promote and support athletic family and celebrate successes.
What Covenant Looks like In Practice				
AD	Provide environment that is conducive to learning and fun and that is open and welcoming.	Working with captain council to help programs build a championship culture.	Communicate with coaches/athletes and support them in their daily needs.	Show attention to detail in making sure all athletes are properly cleared, and make sure coaches have met requirements.
Coach	Rewarding examples of athletes showing good character on a daily basis.	Athletes demonstrating good leadership in practice by encouraging each other and never accepting any behavior below standard.	Creating practice plans that help the team and individual players develop training habits to improve individually and as a team with accountability.	Treating athletes who are demonstrating the Core Covenants with the utmost respect to get across to those who are not.
Athlete	Supporting and encouraging each other.	Motivate others; teach others; support others; lead by example.	Practice hard at all times; every practice do your best; do off-season work.	Teammates can count on you at all times because you are doing what is right.

(Continued)

Figure 2.5 • (Continued)

	Character	Leadership	Commitment	Integrity
Parent	Converse with athletes on their expectations, goal and how to achieve them.	Hold athlete accountable to attend all practices, persevere through adversity and complete the season in good standing.	Provide means to get to and from all practices; communicate with coach when issues arise that may inhibit best practices performance.	Hold athlete accountable for team rules. Accept coaching decisions.
What Covenant Looks like in Game				
AD	Congratulate all efforts and recognize Covenants in action.	Attends events across all sports and strive to make all District and State events.	Be visible and available at competitions to represent importance of all sports.	Ensure all competitors are eligible. Support all stakeholders during event regardless of contest outcome.
Coach	Being respectful of other team's school; winning and losing with class. Being respectful to officials and other coaches.	Lead by example with a positive and encouraging attitude; taking control in tense, stressful situations, keeping team in control and setting a good example.	Commit to holding your team to the highest possible standards and setting the bar at the highest level.	Represent the school with class and hold your team and coaching staff accountable.
Athlete	Treating each team with respect. Winning or losing while being classy.	Lead by example; never get down; always keep your head up and be supportive no matter the outcome.	Leave everything you have on the field/court/pool/course.	Setting an example of good sportsmanship.
Parent	Support athlete in leading a meeting with coach in a safe, private environment and wait 36 hours after a contest to initiate a discussion on any concerns.	Be positive and cheer for all athletes in all situations. Refrain from negative comments/dialogue that could hurt team morale.	Ensure athlete knows you love watching him or her compete. Celebrate progress, make sports fun, and relieve competitive pressure. Evaluate athlete only when asked by athlete.	Accept and support decisions made by coaches and officials regardless of contest outcome.

Source: Burlington-Edison High School

back to this sheet and say, "This is what we're about. This is the foundation that we expect all of our kids to have when they leave [school]."

—**Don Beazizo**, Athletic Director, Burlington-Edison School District, United States

Think about the power of engaging your students around identifying the outcomes that matter to them. When given the opportunity to reflect on, discuss, and determine what they value and how they'd like to be held accountable, students identify outcomes that are meaningful not only in academic settings, but all throughout their lives.

In our efforts alongside learning partners in systems throughout the world to collaboratively identify the outcomes that matter, what emerged were the deeper learning outcomes. When you think or talk about what matters for your learners, you're identifying the individual components of these overarching outcomes. For example, saying that students need to develop "knowledge" isn't enough. What you actually want them to know can be broken down into math, science, literacy, and other content areas encompassing the specific knowledge points important for carrying out tasks and processes, forming connections, and interacting with others and the world. Most standards and curriculums likely have a lesser handle on self-understanding, competency, and connection than they do on knowledge. But self-understanding, competency, and connection are equally important and valued in life, and so they're deserving of the same "knowledge treatment" in your school or wider system. We ask that you now carefully consider each of these deeper learning outcomes—looking for what it is, what it's made of, and what it looks like when developed. With this depth of understanding, you can then use the **Learning Development Rubric** to measure where you are as a system in relation to the development of each outcome.

CHAPTER 2

Putting Depth Into Practice

Activity 2.3: Break Down Deeper Learning

Reflect on and write down the specific outcomes you want for your learners, grouping them under each respective deeper learning outcome. When and wherever possible, fill in the gaps in your lists and descriptions in partnership with others. What *are* self-understanding, knowledge, competency, and connection? What makes up each of these outcomes, and what do they look like when learners have developed them?

Once you have an understanding of the specific elements of each outcome, use your lists alongside Figure 2.6, the Learning Development Rubric (Appendix B), to measure your system's level of progress in relation to each deeper learning outcome. What are your system's current levels of progress? What evidence are you using to determine your ratings? How and in what ways can your system evolve?

Figure 2.6 • Learning Development Rubric

Embedding a cultural commitment to learners and to reflecting learners' deeper learning outcomes in what, how, and where they learn

Dimension	Substantially off Track	Getting Started	Looking Promising	Well on Track	Geared for Success
Self-Understanding	Who learners *are* culturally and as individuals is widely unrepresented in what and how they *learn*, as well as in the culture and makeup of the school or school system at large. School does little to develop learners' understanding of who they are, what they're capable of, and how they can contribute back.	The school or school system has embraced a commitment to facilitating and accelerating learners' self-understanding. Leaders and other learning partners are getting to know their learners' cultures and identities by encouraging sharing by students and parents, and learners are starting to feel that they don't have to "leave their *selves* at the door."	An understanding of learners' interests and identities is reflected in key elements of the school or school system. Learning environments, the curriculum, professional learning, and learning experiences are adapting to account for who learners are and what matters for them. "Where do you see yourself in this learning?" is a focus in all experiences.	All changes are developed out of knowledge of, and considered in light of, learners' interests, cultures, and identities. Self-understanding is as integral to learning as the most basic content knowledge, and the school or school system is measuring learners' progress in developing it.	Everything about the school or school system reflects and celebrates both who its learners are and how they can make a difference in the world, now and throughout their lives. Learners' cultures and identities are fully represented in their knowledge, actions, and relationships. They understand and express who they are and how they can contribute back.
Knowledge	Through its words, actions, curriculum, and overall operations, the school or school system has embedded the understanding that what learners know is more important than who they are, what they can do, and their connections with others and the world. There's a system-wide emphasis on *content* knowledge rather than other types of knowledge *(cultural, new,* and *self-)* and their application.	Learning partners recognize that knowledge alone is not fulfillment. They're adopting a more comprehensive, culturally based view of their learners and the outcomes that matter, engaging parents, community members, and learners in the process. There's a shift from a sole focus on knowledge to its connection with the range of deeper learning outcomes.	Knowledge development isn't the "be-all and end-all" but is aimed instead at the simultaneous development of other deeper learning outcomes. This is reflected in learning experiences, where what's learned is closely tied to identity, competency, and connection and to the relationships between new and existing knowledge and their application.	Curriculum embeds a focus on and explicit connection between knowledge and the other deeper learning outcomes. Content knowledge is developed along with and in support of cultural and self-knowledge and self-understanding, and learners are creating new knowledge about the world and their place within it.	Students' knowledge is deepened and further embedded through the direct development of self-understanding, competencies, and connections. Teaching seamlessly integrates all four, attuning all learning to how it can be used to make a difference in lives and communities. Learners use what they know to contribute back.

Dimension	Substantially off Track	Getting Started	Looking Promising	Well on Track	Geared for Success
Competency	There's no or little emphasis on what students can do with what they learn—*aside from perform well on tests*. The skills and competencies they need to succeed now and throughout their lives may develop despite the school or school system, but there's no intentional focus on developing or measuring them. Learning begins and ends with knowledge—or with *acquisition*.	The world is constantly changing, and students' learning has to support them to succeed amid any and all changes throughout their lives, and to take action to change the world for the better. With this school- or system-wide understanding, learning partners are working to identify and emphasize the competencies that ensure lifelong learning, contribution, and success.	Learning partners have identified the competencies that are important for their learners in relation to cultural emphases and identities. They're embedding them in the curriculum, focusing on them in all professional learning, and creating tools to support their development and measurement. There's a noticeable, systemic shift in emphasis from *acquisition* to *action*.	Learning partners are measuring students' development of deeper learning competencies and applying those skills toward sustainable contribution. Students understand their capacity to use what they learn to make their own and others' lives better and that they can make a difference *now*. They're supported to do so throughout the learning process.	"Learning" is always accompanied by "doing"—there's a palpable "culture of competency." Student development of the competencies that matter is measured in school and felt in their relationships and communities. They're using their competencies, in conjunction with knowledge and self- and cultural understanding, to connect with others and contribute back.
Connection	Connections "happen as they may." School provides space for connections to form, but there's no or little intentional focus on making connections between one outcome and another, learning and doing, school and world, or self and others. Relationships are *transactional*, with an emphasis on "getting" as opposed to "giving" in return.	Real learning partnerships are forming between students, teachers, parents, school and school-system leaders, community members, and others. They're *relational*, reflecting deep connection around a common commitment to students and their learning and are breaking down the walls dividing learning and learners.	Learning partners are deliberately facilitating and strengthening learners' connections with peers and others, as well as between what they're learning and why it's important. Students and their learning partners have connected around deeper learning outcomes, contribution, and a human commitment to finding meaning and fulfillment.	The school or school system is developing citizens who connect for collective change. Learning partnerships are monitored and measured on their development of deeper learning outcomes, and learners see the entirety of the learning process as connected and reliant on their connections with others.	Connections form naturally on the depth of learners and the culture of their school or school system. These connections are built on giving back to others and the world—*human return*—and on celebrating the humanity we share. Along with who they are and what they know and can do, learners see how it all fits together—they know what it all *means*, and they use it to contribute back.

Source: The Learner First, 2018

Once you identify important outcomes, you'll start to look for them. Once you start to look for them, you'll start to implement solutions that reveal and develop them. In other words, you'll start to *assess* them. Whenever you learn about your learners and their levels of learning, about your own or other learning partners' professional learning, or about your system and its levels of development, you're assessing. When you talk to parents or learners themselves about their interests and needs, you're assessing. When you watch your learners interact with one another or other learning partners, you're assessing. Broadening your understanding of the outcomes that matter requires that you broaden your understanding of assessment. You have to set up your system and everyday learning experiences in ways that expose you to and support you to collect valuable assessment evidence every day, no matter the learning at hand. This doesn't mean you should test students every day. *Teach* them every day, embracing your responsibility as an educator to know and develop learners' self-understanding, knowledge, competency, and connection. Whether there's a learner who developed an especially creative solution to a problem or a learner who met academic standards on a team project but struggled to collaborate with peers, deeper learning will provide a measurable application for the information you've always known is important but that you may not have been able to track, interact with, or develop in a meaningful way. Shifting your thinking about assessment will support you to match a wealth of collected evidence to rich measures of deeper learning.

Understanding the importance of measurement won't do you any good if you fail to measure what's important. What good is it to

- develop a narrow understanding of your system and your learners that ignores who they are and what they really need;
- engage learning partners around outcomes that *don't* matter, or at least not in full;
- lead in a direction inconsistent with real success; or
- develop a culture more committed to standards than to learners?

When a system serves restrictive measures of progress and success, all its other capabilities are wasted.

Hold on to your lists and descriptions of what each deeper learning outcome means to you and your learners, building on them whenever necessary. For now, measure your capacity to identify and measure what's important, reflecting on initial successes and challenges in your use of the rubrics so far, as well as on what you might need to improve your measurement practice.

Putting Depth Into Practice

Activity 2.4: Measure Your Capability—Identifying and Measuring What's Important

Use the descriptions at each level of the Identifying and Measuring What's Important Capability Rubric in Appendix A.3 to determine whether your system is *substantially off track*, *getting started*, *looking promising*, *well on track*, or *geared for success* in relation to each of the four dimensions. Record the evidence you used to make your decisions. Then synthesize the evidence to determine an overall rating for this capability, using the same five-point scale. What evidence are you using to determine your ratings? Are there aspects of the descriptions (a level, a line, or even a single word) for which more evidence is needed? What do your ratings tell you about where you are and how you can progress?

For Your Consideration . . .

You won't be able to *measure* what's important if you haven't *identified* what's important. That identification requires a deeper and more authentic understanding of your system and your learners; the engagement of students, teachers, and school, community, and other leaders; and a culture of learning and belonging in which people care about what's important for every student. In short, it requires a focus on all the other system capabilities. Our focus in this chapter is on assessing and measuring system capabilities, identifying areas of strength and areas for improvement, and gathering the evidence needed to identify the outcomes that matter for learners. Soon enough, we'll help you measure those outcomes, too.

System Capability 4: Leading for Deep and Sustainable Change

Effective leaders have a clear understanding of what they're doing and why they're doing it, and they're able to *live* and *communicate* both of these things in a way that supports others to do the same. They know and deeply understand the people they lead, as well as what each group and each individual needs to be successful. Effective leaders aren't alone—they're surrounded by other leaders at all levels of the system who are working collectively to embed and sustain deep cultural change. As leaders in education, we have to challenge everything we do in light of its effect on the learner and how it supports learners to support themselves, their families, their communities, and the world.

Effective leaders encourage, foster, and support leadership from everyone in their systems. Don't stop at supporting learners to *grow up to be* leaders in their communities—support them to be leaders *now* and over the course of their lives. Teachers, principals, and administrators, parents, and members of the community can be leaders, too, granted they're provided with the opportunities to take active and prominent roles in the education process. In our school systems, we need leaders capable of doing what it takes to develop the full range of important learning outcomes—leaders who not only know what's important but also are committed to intentionally developing and, therefore, measuring it.

CHAPTER 2

Dimensions of Leading for Deep and Sustainable Change

- ✓ Focusing every action and decision through the lens of the least-served learners
- ✓ Prioritizing what needs to change and collaboratively designing solutions
- ✓ Leading change all the way through to measured, sustainable outcomes
- ✓ Fostering and supporting student, teacher, system, parent, and community leaders

From day one, effective leaders in education ensure that deeper learning isn't just another add-on but an embedded and authentic mindset that enables and enhances daily practice. They evidence the capacity to leverage deeper learning measures and other tools to develop a shared language and understanding around deeper learning, they align current planning documents with the language of the tools, and they focus and frame implementation efforts within the wider inquiry process. Leaders identify other leaders, embrace a continuous focus on deepening learning outcomes, and enable the conditions that foster them. Those conditions support learning partners to "play"—to develop new ideas or practices, run with them, learn and build from their outcomes, and celebrate successes, as long as these actions are aimed at developing deeper learning outcomes. Students are prepared to lead and take action to solve questions of profound local and global importance—they need leaders at all levels of the system who are prepared to let them.

A Recipe for Return: Models of Practice From BESD

Leadership at Every Level

The importance and interdependence of leadership at all levels of a school system is best demonstrated by its combined effect on student (and educator) outcomes. Let's follow the thread of effective leadership practice from wider system levels to individual school principals all the way through to the teachers and students leading deeper learning in their schools and beyond. It never hurts to have a leader at the top.

As a superintendent, you better not have a big ego when you're trying to lead this work, because it is a little of the unknown. You have to have the heart and the belief in the moral imperative to do something . . . other than look at standardized test scores. [Students] still have to have the fundamental knowledge to be able to leave us and be successful, but it's more than that. What do we want for our kids? You really have to be able to ask yourself what really matters for our students, because that's why we're doing this work, and it's bigger than a test score. I ask myself every day, "What do I really want for my own child in the real world? What's relevant? How will we help them succeed?" That's what's motivated me to take a look at a deeper set of frameworks.

[We've] redesigned what it means to lead, [because it takes] more people than just the administrator. We have lead teachers, consulting teachers—it's really at the building level that we've gotten the traction. I just step back and figure out how [to] support everybody in a whole-systems approach to change outcomes. You really need the teachers to begin to understand why this work's so important, and it's what they went into the business for in the first place. It's about championing the work, staying the course, telling the story, and supporting our teachers as lead learners. It takes everybody in the system. It starts with support at the top, but [it's] the support in the classrooms with the teachers that makes all the difference.

—**Laurel Browning**, Superintendent,
Burlington-Edison School District, United States

In individual schools across BESD, leaders embed the understanding that anyone can lead this work—anyone, from students and teachers to parents and any other staff members, can discover what makes a difference for learners and share their learning with others.

> [With] just one person leading it, I just don't see it being successful. It really needs to be the work of everyone. [It takes] collaborative structures, small groups that meet, and being careful when people are trying things. [You] have [to demonstrate] a collective efficacy for teachers: that I know they can do it and I know it's worth it.
>
> —**Amy Reisner**, Principal, Bay View Elementary School, Burlington-Edison School District, United States

A commitment to developing teacher and student leaders has translated to weekly, student-led assemblies centered on the sharing of students' learning and framed around Bay View Elementary School's Ten Learner Attributes (Figure 2.3). The general idea: If students have engaged in learning worth sharing, they should have an opportunity and the platform to share it. Around the attribute of compassion, for example, third-grade students talked about what it means to be kind and compassionate, and they demonstrated the idea of "paying it forward" by writing cards for the local sheriff's department, leaving the school with one parting question: "How can *you* pay it forward with kindness?" In another assembly, the kindergarten class shared their learning about Martin Luther King Jr. and talked about what it takes to change rules we don't agree with, concluding with one of King's quotes: "The time is always right to do what is right." A group of fifth graders recognized a problem in the school and used an assembly as a platform to engage others in solving it together. After teaching their learning partners about landfills and associated environmental concerns, they shared their plans for collective action:

> Did you know that Bay View only has a plastic bottle recycling bin in the teacher's lounge? Well, we want to add several around our school, so be on the lookout! Another thing we will do is, every week, we will get parents or anybody who has the time to sign up and take some recycling from our school to the recycling plant.
>
> —**Fifth-Grade Students**, Bay View Elementary School, Burlington-Edison School District, United States

They sustained their call to action and kept other students engaged in the cause by organizing a monthly challenge "to help remind you about saving our earth one water bottle at a time." These individual cases demonstrate students' development of deeper learning outcomes and their efforts to develop those same outcomes in others—in other words, *using learning to contribute back*.

So, what's leadership got to do with measuring deeper learning? Leaders want what's best for others, and they know how to make it a reality. They recognize what's important, accept responsibility when they aren't doing enough to develop those outcomes, and figure out what they need to do better. If you're serious about developing the type of outcomes embedded in BESD's district-level Road Map (Figure 2.2), Burlington-Edison High's athletic program's Core Covenants (Figure 2.5), or Bay View Elementary's set of Learner Attributes (Figure 2.3), you need measures and other tools that are up to the task. Leadership leads to deeper learning—it leads to the outcomes that matter and, in turn, the measures that help you achieve them.

Putting Depth Into Practice

Activity 2.5: Measure Your Capability—Leading for Deep and Sustainable Change

Use the descriptions at each level of the Leading for Deep and Sustainable Change Capability Rubric in Appendix A.4 to determine whether your system is *substantially off track, getting started, looking promising, well on track*, or *geared for success* in relation to each of the four dimensions. Record the evidence you used to make your decision. Then synthesize the evidence to determine an overall rating for this capability, using the same five-point scale. What evidence are you using to determine your ratings? Are there aspects of the descriptions (a level, a line, or even a single word) for which more evidence is needed? What do your ratings tell you about where you are and how you can progress?

System Capability 5: Creating a Culture of Learning, Belonging, and High Expectations for All

No matter what we say or even what we think we believe, it will never make a real difference for learners unless it's deeply embedded in the cultures of our systems and the practice of those within it. Deeper learning can be fostered only within a *culture of learning* characterized by innovation, reflection, and a willingness to allow learning partners to try new things and learn from mistakes, as long as their new practices and approaches are aimed at deepening outcomes for learners. Everybody has to be learning—otherwise, it isn't *deeper* learning. The other key characteristics of deeper learning cultures are *belonging* and *high expectations* for every learner. It's easy to think that our schools or systems are welcoming and accepting of all learners and that, regardless of background, race, culture, or identity, everyone is expected to succeed. But *belonging* runs deeper than words or policy. It requires genuine, equitable relationships in which learners truly feel they're expected to—and believe they can—succeed, on both the strength of their own capabilities and the strength of their connections with others. Our expectations are *truly high* only if they're *deeply felt* and reflected in our relationships with every learner and in the systems-level actions that affect them.

Such a culture is possible only in systems in which *learners'* cultures, identities, and goals are known, celebrated, and supported to take center stage in their learning. It's commonly said (and very true) that culture eats strategy for breakfast. Know your system, allow the space to understand and engage your learners for who they are, and develop a culture that celebrates and serves them all. Otherwise, your culture will eat your learners for breakfast, too.

Dimensions of Creating a Culture of Learning, Belonging, and High Expectations for All

- ✓ Providing the freedom to learn, share, celebrate, and improve
- ✓ Engaging in deeper learning experiences and teaching for 100 percent success
- ✓ Embedding a deep commitment to and expectation of success for all learners
- ✓ Cultivating genuine personal relationships
- ✓ Celebrating students' learning and identities everywhere and in all things

One of the most important conditions for developing deeper learning outcomes is, fittingly, *deeper learning*—or a system-wide *commitment to learning deeply* instilled in every learning partner, as well as the freedom to engage in it. When this condition is in place, everyone has the opportunity to form powerful learning partnerships built on trust and shared ownership of learning and shaped by individual identities and interests.

> Our classroom culture has been built in a way that embeds the learning [outcomes] into our daily classroom life. Children have the opportunity to explore, develop, and build upon these lifelong skills through explorations, provocations, classroom learning spaces, and learning opportunities. Creating a culture like this provides us with the opportunity to feel comfortable with mistakes, the determination to work through challenges, and the collaboration skills to work together to problem solve, think critically, and celebrate!
>
> —**Lisa Michaluk**, Teacher, Sigurbjorg Stefansson Early School, Canada

It's devastating to know how many learners experience challenges at school on a daily basis that could be alleviated if others had more personal knowledge of and connection with their lives. Whether it's a young boy whose learning is disrupted by the fact that he couldn't find his shin guards and socks and thus couldn't play soccer (Morris, 2016), or a young girl who felt out of place both because she'd been forbidden to speak her native language in the classroom and because, although the flags of students' home countries were displayed in the halls, hers was hidden behind a soda machine, there are solvable problems that learners hide when they don't feel acceptance and belonging. It's our responsibility to develop cultures that instill a sense of belonging in all learners so that they never have to—and never want to—hide who they are, what engages or troubles them, and how they can contribute within their classrooms, their schools, and beyond.

Celebrating and reflecting learners' cultural identities has received exemplary emphasis in New Zealand, where the Ministry of Education identified Māori and Pasifika students, those for whom achievement was "disproportionately lower than other ethnic groups," as "priority learners." As department head Gwyneth Cooper explained, the system endeavored to connect learning and success to who these learners actually are by shifting its focus to "Māori achievement as Māori."

Whakawhanaungatanga—who we are, our location, our relationships, and the time and place that they're built.

"Māori achievement as Māori" [is] essentially saying that our Māori students should not have to stop being Māori when they come in the school gates in order to be successful in education, that their ways of knowing and understanding are important and valid and should be valued by schools. We have several government initiatives specifically about Māori achievement as Māori . . . and [we] work on recognizing Māori success, the ways that Māori are successful, saying that every Māori student can be successful and still express their cultural identity, whatever that is, whatever part of the country they're from. If we're effective teachers of Māori students, what things will we be doing? What attributes will we have?

[We used to hear,] "Those Māori parents, they just don't really care about education. . . ." And teachers would trot that out as a reason why these Māori parents didn't come to school meetings. They were hard to get a hold of on the phone. And now we've shifted our talking and our thinking. . . . You're more likely to hear, "These parents have different ideas about what school's about . . . how are we going to bridge that gap?" or "These parents maybe had a negative idea of school from their own experience; how are we going to make school more welcoming?" . . . "Maybe they have a different idea than mine; how can I understand what that idea is?"

A question for all of us: "To what extent are you differentiating the delivery of deep learning to meet the social and cultural needs of your context?"

—**Gwyneth Cooper**, Head of Science, Bream Bay College, New Zealand

New Zealand offers a powerful example of a system that recognized its failure to meet the needs of its least-served learners and took a meaningful, culturally relevant approach to addressing them. Who are *your* least-served learners, and what role might their identities play in making learning more relevant to their lives and more achievable as a result?

Working with The Learner First, a group of schools in Hawaii arrived at a similar understanding through a focused, collaborative lens (The Learner First, 2016). In 2014, a network of early childhood schools in Hawaii established a model for a collaborative approach to learning. One of its primary objectives was to increase school-readiness skills in order to positively impact school engagement and future academic success. Through a culturally and partnership-based evaluation of the model, learning partners discovered that school readiness required three interdependent elements:

1. Competencies and knowledge that *keiki* (children) need in order to succeed in school
2. Parent and *'ohana* (extended family) readiness to support and advocate for their *keiki*
3. Readiness of schools themselves to help *keiki* thrive and succeed

Learning partners identified competencies relating to social and emotional readiness, independence, perseverance, problem solving, leadership, and confidence as those that they wanted their *keiki* to develop in school alongside more traditional, knowledge-related outcomes. The other major aspect of readiness was identified as *'ike Hawaii*: "The blessing and the challenge—what is that Native Hawaiian way of thinking?" In addition to traditional knowledge and key learning competencies, confidence and pride in their own culture and language help prepare *keiki* for school. At the same time, celebrating and teaching Hawaiian language and culture empowers parents and *'ohana* to support their children's education—it connects them to their *keiki*'s school and connects generations as well. Knowledge that their culture is an integral part of their children's or grandchildren's education (and hearing them speak Hawaiian) revitalizes families' sense of pride and belonging, strengthening relationships that benefit everyone—*keiki*, parents, and *'ohana*. Families can't be expected to fully support their children's education unless (1) they're informed about and have opportunities to engage in what's happening at school and (2) what's happening at school is invariably connected to their own and their children's lives, forming a transformative link between school, home, and community.

Educators aren't involved in every stage of a child's life. Students pass between any number of schools before, during, and after their experience in the K–12 educational system before transitioning to the rest of their lives, shedding the title of *student* and baring themselves as *human being*. The more our educational systems are concerned with and connected to our learners' humanity, the more our learners will be prepared to leave them, using their self-understanding, knowledge, competencies, and connections to find and take on new roles, titles, and responsibilities (both personal and professional) through which their humanity can shine and their communities can thrive. Families, communities, and our *selves* are lifelong—the extent to which education nourishes each of these determines the degree to which our children will do the same for the rest of their lives. How can you mold your school or wider system into one that will make others, and the world, better?

> [We set *keiki*] up to become leaders at their [new] school—they make it a better place.
>
> —**Teacher**

In Hawaii, educators, parents, ʻ*ohana*, and community members spoke about preparing their *keiki* to "walk in both worlds" as (a) culturally confident Native Hawaiians and (b) members of a diverse global community. No matter what educational system you're in, and no matter the cultures and identities of your learners, you should believe in and support every one of them to walk and succeed in any number of worlds, whose qualities—and quality—they'll play a lead role in determining.

A Recipe for Return: Models of Practice From BESD

Accelerating Students

Whereas New Zealand's school system recognized Māori learners as those for whom achievement was disproportionately low, learning partners in BESD identified impoverished and minority students and English-language learners as those they had traditionally underserved.

> When we're identifying the kids that are going to help inform our system and inform our learning design and delivery, we're identifying students from those sub-populations [and] using our data to make decisions about next steps. When you discover the strengths and assets of your students, of your students' families, this opens the door for really understanding your families and your students and then incorporating that into the learning design.
>
> —**K. C. Knudson**, Executive Director of Teaching and Learning, Burlington-Edison School District, United States

> I tell people my job is to ask questions of our district. When we talk about "all students," I ask the questions, "Well, what does that mean by 'all'?" and

"Do we really mean 'all' when we say that?" When there are traditionally marginalized populations in our system that [lack] the same access to quality education programs or outcomes that we see of our other students, my question is "Why? How are we digging into that, and what are we doing from a systems perspective for many of our students that have been marginalized for years and years in our system?" From an equity perspective, we have a moral imperative to serve our students. If we aren't asking ourselves how to do a better job of reaching our students and including their perspectives on what is meaningful to them, then we're going to continue to miss [the] mark.

So what we've asked a lot of our teachers to do is to step outside of their classroom and have conversations with parents we've failed to communicate appropriately with. Not from a communications standpoint of telling them what to do, but from a communications standpoint that's more reciprocal—listening to them and learning about their children and what they want us to know about our children as we start to educate them in our system. It reinforces that notion that there really are high expectations for all our children and [also that] all our parents really care about their kids and have high expectations for their children. When you come to BESD [as an educator], one of the things we prioritize is that you know who your students are.

—**Bryan Jones, EdD**, Director of Equity and Assessment, Burlington-Edison School District, United States

BESD learning partners recognized that embedding a deeper commitment to and expectation of success for all learners was going to require personal relationships not only with students but with students' families as well. In BESD, as in many districts, one of the main challenges in engaging the families of English-language learners (ELLs) is the communication barrier. In order to overcome that barrier, each teacher across the district is paired with an ELL specialist, who has intimate knowledge of his or her students. Teachers start by identifying two or three students they want to learn more about and want to engage more deeply in their learning, and they reach out to those learners' parents, enlisting the ELL specialist's help as necessary. The first conversations center on who they and who their learners are as a family and as individuals. From there, with relationships and communication lines in place, it's an open dialogue.

Embedding students' interests and wider identities in their everyday experience of school is a sure path to belonging, and it opens the door to a wealth of opportunities for learning. At West View Elementary, one of those opportunities takes the form of a dual-language newspaper (Wanielista, 2017a). Sixth-graders Iliana Lopez and Erykah Livingston-Haggard founded the *Bobcat Gazette* to inform their classmates, families, and other learning partners about what was happening at West View, and they wanted the newspaper to be in both English and Spanish "so people learning English could read the Spanish side." The result is a monthly publication for which fourth-, fifth-, and sixth-grade students interview classmates and other learning partners, write and edit articles, draw pictures, and take photos. For one of their features, the newspaper team attended a school board meeting and interviewed the board president. Here's what some BESD learning partners had to say about the *Gazette*:

One of the things they're trying to do with deeper learning is get kids involved with things they're excited about. All those kids were excited, and that's what I like to see.

—**Rich Wesen**, President,
Burlington-Edison School Board, United States

I love that it was student-driven. They had the idea; they advocated for it. This is what we want at school—kids with ideas.

—**Tamara Skeen**, Principal, West View Elementary,
Burlington-Edison School District, United States

I like sharing stories with people, and I thought it would be even cooler to share with the school.

We decided we needed to do something special that could carry on.

I think I have special talents, and I wanted to bring news to West View.

—**Iliana Lopez, Erykah Livingston-Haggard, and Jose Lopez**, Students,
West View Elementary, Burlington-Edison School District, United States

---

What are *your* students' special talents, and how can you support them to let those talents shine? Students shouldn't have to put their talents "on hold" inside school walls. Try to develop a culture in which all learners know they are encouraged and supported to pursue their passions and interests in an academic setting and well beyond it. Your school or school district may not have Māori or Native Hawaiian students or English-language learners, but you do have learners who are struggling. Find out and celebrate who they are and what they're passionate about so that their experience of school will be one of success, belonging, and contribution.

Putting Depth Into Practice

Activity 2.6: Measure Your Capability—Creating a Culture of Learning, Belonging, and High Expectations for All

Use the descriptions at each level of the Creating a Culture of Learning, Belonging, and High Expectations for All Capability Rubric in Appendix A.5 to determine whether your system is *substantially off track*, *getting started*, *looking promising*, *well on track*, or *geared for success* in relation to each of the five dimensions. Record the evidence you used to make your decisions. Then synthesize the evidence to determine an overall rating for this capability, using the same five-point scale. What evidence are you using to determine your ratings? Are there aspects of the descriptions (a level, a line, or even a single word) for which more evidence is needed? What do your ratings tell you about where you are and how you can progress?

Reflect

Analyzing your current ratings as a whole across each completed Capability Rubric, where are the greatest opportunities for progress, and how will you begin? Are these capabilities you want yourself, others, and your school system to develop? How might these capabilities transform your system into one that supports students to use their learning to contribute back—every day, both during and outside of school? Look back through this chapter and reflect on what's been presented, with special attention to the examples of learning partners evidencing and working to develop these capabilities in their school systems. What did you learn from these cases, and how can you apply those lessons? Who are your learners, what's important for them, and what can you do to make your school or wider system a place where their passions are celebrated, shared, and allowed to shine?

In this chapter, we've discussed the capabilities of healthy, deeper learning systems built for and centered on learners. You've explored what it means and what it takes to understand a system and its learners, to engage learning partners around outcomes that matter, to identify and measure those outcomes, to lead for deep and sustainable change, and to develop a culture with a continuous, central focus on learners, their needs, and their humanity. You've also—maybe for the first time—measured your system's development of these capabilities, identified what constitutes self-understanding, competency, and connection to you and to your learning partners, and used your descriptions alongside the Learning Development Rubric to measure where your system is in relation to the deeper learning outcomes. In the next chapter, we'll look at what it takes to commit to a collaborative, student-centered, and partner-based approach to embedding and spreading deeper learning throughout your system and beyond.

Access the appendices at **resources.corwin.com/MeasuringHumanReturn**

Chapter 3

THE CHANGE TEAM PROCESS

Collective Cognition for Collaborative Change

The journey to system-wide deeper learning is collaborative. This is one of the assumption-shatterers introduced in Chapter 1, and it's not an easy one to embrace in practice. The depth and breadth of the required collaboration often represent significant shifts in "the way we do things around here." Deep, lasting change doesn't happen within isolated levels or pockets of a system, and it certainly can't be achieved as a result of individual action. It requires collective commitment to the vision and process for change, to involving learning partners at all levels of the system, and, ultimately, to the learner. Unless we make these commitments, we'll never achieve the outcomes our learners really need.

The vehicles for system change take the form of connected, multilevel change teams designed to ensure that ideas and practices that have a positive impact on learners are fostered, spread, supported, and developed at all levels of the system. Change teams track and measure progress at individual system levels, identify areas of success and areas for improvement, and drive necessary changes from, within, and to any level of the school system at large. The **Capability Rubrics** (Appendix A), because of their focus on developing the capabilities that enable deeper learning for students, take on a major role in the operation of change teams all throughout the process.

In a traditional school system, change teams are formed at three levels:

- School
- District
- School system

The change team process, loosely based on Kotter's eight-step process for leading change (Kotter, 2012), occurs within and between each of these three levels, with members of each team serving on a team at another level as well. This connected, collaborative approach aligns the system vertically, from the learner to the top leadership, and horizontally, between schools and districts, while building *coherence* in ways of thinking, knowing, and doing throughout the system at large (Fullan & Quinn, 2015). Echoing earlier discussions of deeper learning in relation to our school systems, *initial* engagement doesn't have to start with or even involve the state or district level. We'll describe the change team process as a school-system-wide endeavor, since that's the ultimate goal. But any school taking on deeper learning and its framework can form a successful change team with the resources and learning partners already in reach. Let's take a look at who makes up each change team and how they operate together.

Figure 3.1 • The Whole-System Change Team Process

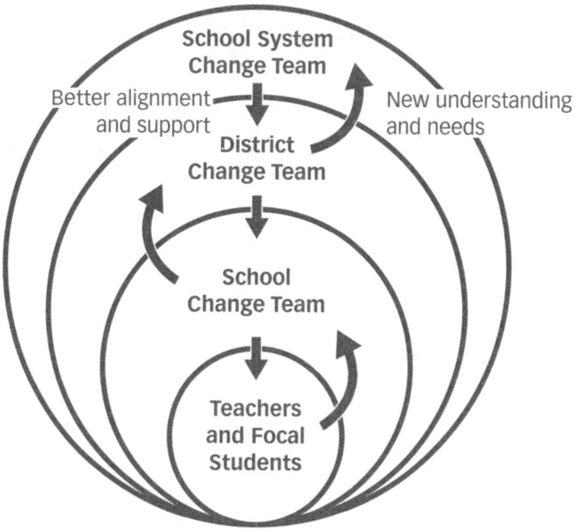

School System Change Team
Better alignment and support
New understanding and needs
District Change Team
School Change Team
Teachers and Focal Students

Source: The Learner First, 2018

School change teams are formed within each school and consist of the following:

> *Students.* As the central focus of the change, students have to be supported to play a central role in driving it. Their engagement can take on any number of forms, and they might attend every change team meeting or certain meetings throughout the year, depending on the circumstances and on the focus of individual meetings. Schools might also form student-led change teams that engage students and other members of the school change team, along with additional learners who would benefit from, and benefit others through, the opportunity to share and lead. Student change teams offer exciting possibilities for gathering insights from and spreading influence to a greater number of learners and for forming a strong link between the student population and the work of change teams at other levels of the system. Student engagement in the change team process isn't only a method for keeping students informed of the changes that are or will be taking place; even more, it's also an opportunity for learners' voices, opinions, and actions to have a real impact on what goes on in their own and other schools.

Teachers. Change team teachers should include teachers of the change team students, as well as other teachers with the capacity for—better still, a history of—leading change.

School leaders. The principal will always be on the school change team and will likely play a lead role in selecting its other members. Other school leaders could include administrators, academic deans and coaches, or anyone capable of adding valuable insight and leading others.

Parents and family members. Students' parents or other family members have an important role to play as the leading experts on their children and what matters to them. At least some members of the change team should be related to the most-struggling learners, and they should be welcomed to offer insight into why the system hasn't worked for their children and how it can be improved.

Community members. Representatives capable of voicing the needs, concerns, and values of the broader community (such as local business leaders, health or social service providers, tribal or spiritual leaders, and philanthropists) can offer expertise on what students need in order to be successful, and they form an essential link between school and community. Such members of the change team should have strong cultural and community ties and expertise relevant to the change process and plan.

A district representative. To ensure that learning and best practices identified at the school level can reach other districts, schools, and learners and to remove barriers between schools and the wider system, each school change team should include one or more members of the district-level team. Sitting on multiple change teams is a big commitment, but it's the only way to stay truly connected to the change processes happening in schools.

When I informed our leadership team, consisting of twelve people representing all aspects of the organization, that they were assigned to a school change team, they were less than enthused. They were already stretched thin working long hours and weren't happy about committing two hours every other week to a meeting in a school. What happened over the course of the next three months was nothing short of a miracle. In our weekly leadership team meetings, they would report out with great passion, to the point of tears, what was happening in "their" schools. Our chief operations officer indicated that, for the first time [and] after fifteen years, he now understood what he did for a living. The building principals reported feeling connected to the Central Office for the first time, because we were able to quickly support their needs through this open system of communication.

—**Rob Neu**, Former Superintendent,
Oklahoma City Public Schools, United States

The district change team consists of

- the district superintendent,
- the associate superintendent,
- district cabinet leaders or members (who may be in charge of areas such as professional development, curriculum, student services, student discipline, PK–12 schools, human resources, capital projects, legal, finance, research, evaluation, measurement, and assessment), and
- a school-system change team representative.

Similarly, the *school-system change team* includes leaders at the wider system level, along with the superintendents of all districts. At the school level or any other, you can form a change team with representatives from each of the groups of learning partners listed above, with only those you're initially able to engage, or with whoever can best kick-start the process. For example, school change teams may form with teachers and school leaders before other learning partners are engaged. What's important is that each change team work to eventually engage the full range of learning partners, adding members as it's able and as makes sense in the circumstances, ensuring that all voices are heard and everyone has a valuable role to play in leading change.

With a line of sight between each level of the system and, most important, all the way through to learners, connected change teams throughout the system can collectively refocus the system's efforts through the lens of the learners who are struggling the most. Which brings us back to another assumption-shatterer: focusing on the least-served learners creates shifts that benefit everyone. When beginning the process of change with their learners, teachers use assessment evidence to identify the handful of learners most in need of support in developing their learning outcomes. This process of rethinking practice through the eyes of the least-served students, and of collectively determining what they really need in order to be successful, frames the formation and operation of change teams at each level:

The school level. At the classroom level, teachers gather evidence about students and their levels of learning to identify those students who are struggling the most. Work with those learners begins with getting to know them as individuals: Who are they, what interests and excites them, how do they learn best, and what can be done to make learning more engaging for them? As we have discussed, engaging the learner *and* the learner's parents is key to uncovering the answers. Once teachers begin to design learning that meets their needs, work within a school change team provides the opportunity for sharing experiences and learning with the rest of the team. Based on learning from direct work with students, and from the students' own input and experiences, the school works collaboratively to create a welcoming and nurturing environment for all learners, building teachers' capacity to design deeper learning in the process. Each school change team focuses on building clarity around what needs to change and why, removing barriers and creating the conditions that'll best enable deeper learning, and fostering a welcoming and inclusive environment for all learners, families, and the community.

The district level. Members of district change teams, having learned from their experiences on school change teams, work to develop district capabilities that enable the design of learning experiences that address learners' identified needs. They strive to build learning partners' capacity at the district and school levels, align district focuses and expectations with deeper learning, and identify and remove each school's obstacles to the implementation of deeper learning.

The school-system level. The sharing of learning by districts and schools helps wider-system leaders examine their own capabilities, policies, resourcing, service provision, and measurement and assessment systems for students, teachers, schools, and districts. Similar to its district change teams, the school-system change team works to create the shifts and alignment necessary for implementing and sustaining deeper learning at the district and, in turn, school levels. School-system-level learning partners ensure that each district is working collaboratively and in partnership, sharing learning and best practices across districts and schools.

All decisions, at every level, are considered in light of their impact on the full range of deeper learning outcomes. The change teams maintain this focus and bring the necessary capabilities to life at each level of the school system by using (1) the Capability Rubrics and (2) an inquiry process that embeds a deeper and more authentic approach to measurement and assessment.

An Inquiry Approach

In each change team, and in all individual and collective work throughout the system, the process for knowing, understanding, and responding to learners and their needs is **inquiry**, which describes the fluid and continuous process of learning *assessment*, *design*, *implementation*, *measurement*, and *reflection and change* shaping work with deeper learning at all levels of the system (Figure 3.2).

We've delved into each element of this process in our discussion of the five system capabilities (Chapter 2), and we'll go into inquiry and its components further in the pages to come. To connect what you've learned so far, let's examine the inquiry process in light of change teams' efforts to develop the five system capabilities. Asking the questions associated with each capability and gathering evidence from throughout the system will help your change team *assess* the extent to which you (1) know your system and its learners, (2) engage all stakeholders as active partners, (3) identify and measure what's important, (4) lead change within and beyond your level of the system, and (5) have developed a culture in which all learners can succeed. Synthesizing the assessment evidence they have collected, change teams *measure* and *reflect* on current levels of development and then *change* practice and processes to address identified needs. Solutions are collaboratively *designed* and *implemented* throughout the system, providing opportunities to assess

Figure 3.2 • The Inquiry Process

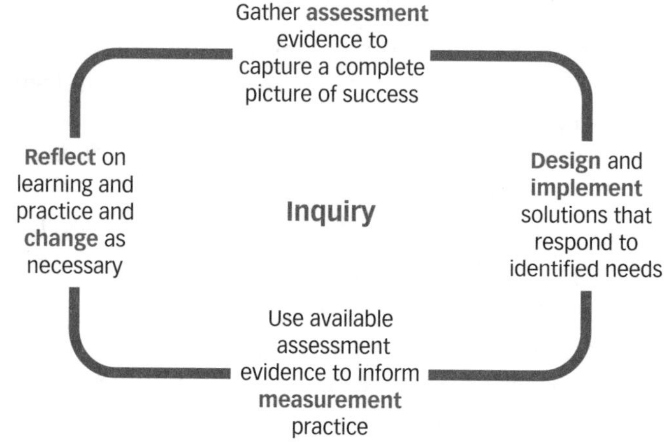
Gather **assessment** evidence to capture a complete picture of success
Design and **implement** solutions that respond to identified needs
Use available assessment evidence to inform **measurement** practice
Reflect on learning and practice and **change** as necessary
Inquiry

Source: The Learner First, 2018

and measure progress, identify new learning and needs, and design and implement additional solutions as necessary to respond to the needs of the change team members, their learners, and others, in real time.

As you can see, inquiry, as well as the change team process itself, is ongoing. They're designed to help you gather and then act on the evidence you need, and that evidence is constantly changing as your practices and your learners' outcomes change. As you've seen in your use of the Capability Rubrics so far, you simply can't measure deeper learning using just one or two performance indicators. To measure deeper learning, you need authentic mixed-method assessment (AMMA). AMMA takes into account not only tests and other structured performance indicators but rather *all* indicators and evidence of deeper learning outcomes *and* what enables them as well. We're not only talking about *student* learning, either. In relation to system or professional learning, AMMA will provide the evidence you need to measure the depth of your own practice and capabilities. When wrapping your head around what "evidence" really means, it helps to remember that it's all around you. What you see, hear, and feel as a professional educator every day in your school system evidences where you are and tells you where you can improve. The process of gathering evidence is inquiry: designing and implementing assessments that evidence and support the measurement of learning, reflecting at all times and changing practice as necessary. Whether you're using a project, a conversation, an observation, a test, an in- or out-of-class assignment, or any other way of gathering relevant data (any other *assessment*), what's important is that you think about the best way to capture the specific evidence you need at that point in time to develop and evidence intended outcomes. From there, what remains will be measurement—synthesizing the range of assessment evidence to inform an overall understanding of performance in relation to deeper learning outcomes.

Think about the evidence you used to measure your system's capabilities (in Chapter 2) in light of this new discussion on AMMA. Now, think about whether you used the *right* evidence. Did you have everything you needed to make a fully evidence-based judgment of your system's current capabilities? If this was your first time measuring these capabilities, it's likely the answer is no. Because without measures to identify and demonstrate the importance of a given outcome or capability, no one had looked for, or designed solutions to gather, the necessary evidence in a way that was intentional, meaningful, and deliberate. Now that you know the importance of these capabilities and their underlying dimensions, you'll perceive that evidence more readily. The vehicles for capturing, sharing, and then developing *change plans* built on that evidence are change teams.

Putting Depth Into Practice

Reflect

Reflect on your understanding of AMMA, measurement, and the wider inquiry process, as well as their roles in relation to change teams. Do you understand the relationship between evidence and assessment, between assessment and measurement, and between each individual element of the inquiry process? How might AMMA give you a deeper understanding of your students, your systems, and their learning? What would a change team look like in your own school or at other levels of your school system, and what might it take to put the process in place?

Activity 3.1: Gather Actionable Evidence

Look back to your recorded evidence used to inform the measurement of your system's capabilities, and add or make any changes to your evidence and ratings as necessary based on our exploration of AMMA earlier. Select a single capability, or even a single dimension of that capability, for which your evidence demonstrates the greatest need for improvement. Using the template in Figure 3.3 (also included in the Change Plan in Appendix C.2), come up with an action plan that responds to that need. If helpful, repeat with additional dimensions or capabilities.

Figure 3.3 • Change Plan

A template for use at any level of the school system to design an action plan framed around particular capabilities or dimensions

Capability/Dimension: **Description of desired outcome:** (This description should reflect the language of the rubric.)	
Description of action/s	
What evidence will you use to measure progress and success?	
Action tracking (record notes, evidence, and progress)	
Resulting changes in outcomes, practices, beliefs, behaviors, policies, etc.:	

Source: The Learner First, 2018

CHAPTER 3

If you completed the preceding activity on your own, *imagine the value of completing it with others*. Identifying, discussing, and working through evidence with a range of learning partners, measuring your system's capabilities together, and using your new knowledge to determine ways forward—that's the level of **collective cognition** we need in our school systems, and it's the level that change teams provide. Different learning partners bring different evidence to the table, and the conversations that result from that intersection of evidence result in deeper outcomes for students. The Capability Rubrics are designed to demonstrate and describe what's important, in order to facilitate conversation among learning partners around what must be done to improve student outcomes. As individuals, we each see a small piece of what happens in our systems. Collectively, we see it all. When considering the formation of change teams, it comes down to the evidence base you'd rather be working with.

> The change teams have been a powerful part of changing mindsets, changing ownership, and changing the way we work. . . . It's powerful, because you're all working in that same direction, [and] you're leveraging your school community assets and the assets of your teachers and your students and families, and that's a big shift. It's moving us from this idea of dependent leadership, where there's one person in a space who makes all the decisions, to everybody having leadership responsibility and wanting it. It's the teachers taking collective responsibility and wanting to engage in the collective cognition around [this] work. So, as a result of the change team, it's become really school-driven work.
>
> —**K. C. Knudson**, Executive Director of Teaching and Learning, Burlington-Edison School District, United States

Change teams driven by the inquiry process are powerful levers for mobilizing and sustaining change, developing shared and collective purpose, and focusing everyone's actions and decisions on learners' outcomes. Learning about and measuring your system's capabilities has already taken you deep into your system, but there's a lot more to learn about change teams, AMMA, the use and development of deeper learning measures and other tools, and how they all come together in the overall inquiry process to measure and develop deeper learning outcomes. We'll dive deeper and deeper as we go, continuing to draw on examples from BESD and other school systems to inform practice in your own system and relating ensuing discussions to the change team process.

Putting Depth Into Practice

Reflect

Here at the end of Part I, take some time to reflect on what you've read so far. What have you learned, and in what ways have you shifted your thinking? How have you changed, or how will you change your own and others' practice? Are you committed to continuous learning, both during your reading and all throughout your engagement with students and other learning partners? In what ways and with whom can you partner for deeper change? Do you have a new way of thinking about evidence and a different perception of your learners?

For Your Consideration . . .

You've come a long way. You've engaged in authentic assessment practice to inform your use of the five Capability Rubrics and the Learning Development Rubric, reflecting on your own, your systems', and your learners' levels of development. You may have already changed your thinking and your practice; you may even have designed and implemented ways of meeting identified needs. In short, *you've engaged in the inquiry process*. Whether or not it's collaborative at this stage, you're already using the ongoing process for enabling, sustaining, and deepening learning. Your inquiry practice may not yet be as advanced as you want it to be, but the chapters to come will help you get there. Think about the questions you have at this stage, and use the upcoming activities to answer them—to take yourself, your learners, and your systems *deeper*.

Access the appendices at
resources.corwin.com/MeasuringHumanReturn

Final Reflections on Part I

Hopefully, reading through these first three chapters and engaging with each measure and activity has connected you to your students and your systems more deeply than ever. You've developed an understanding of the relationship between learners, other learning partners, and school systems, and you've come to see your own classes, schools, and districts as complex and interconnected "systems within systems," in which your thinking and practice can *shift* to develop and measure all the outcomes that matter for learners, and from which your practice can *spread* to deepen learning for everyone. You've also identified the outcomes that matter for learners, and so you know the outcomes you need to focus on. No matter where or who you are, developing the five system capabilities will foster the conditions required to bring deeper learning to life. No matter where or who you are, the spreading of deeper learning and practice within and outside your level of the school system can begin with you. Partner with your learners and others in and outside of your change teams; connect with them and their development of deeper learning outcomes; and measure and celebrate their, your own, and your system's progress every step of the way. You've already kicked off your measurement journey, meaning you're already closer to the outcomes your learners need. Now that you've laid a solid *foundation*, you're ready to put together the *framework*, which is the topic of Part II.

Part II

FIVE FRAMES OF MEASUREMENT

Chapter 4

ENGAGING PARTNERS AROUND WHAT MATTERS

Engage, Empower, and Transform

Because of its deep and inseparable connection to learners and their success, identifying and measuring what's important has emerged as a *driving capability*. It acts as a lever for helping systems develop each of the other capabilities and for leading sustainable system-wide shifts centered on students. Embedding a comprehensive *system of measurement* built for the development of deeper learning outcomes will engage and empower your learning partners and transform your system into a place of learning, action, meaning, and fulfillment. The following five frames of measurement, examined throughout the ensuing pages in light of leading examples in school systems globally, will help you set up, sustain, and continually deepen a comprehensive system of measurement.

Five Frames of Measurement

1. *Engagement.* Engage learning partners to identify and describe what's actually important for learners and what contributes to their success.
2. *Development.* Use your descriptions to fill existing measurement gaps—developing rubrics, learning progressions, guides, or other measures and tools that, collectively, measure and develop deeper learning outcomes and enablers.
3. *Clarity.* With your new toolkit, take time to develop a shared language and understanding of deeper learning among all learning partners, as well as to align the deeper learning framework with your school or wider system.
4. *Inquiry.* Embed the inquiry process in your daily, strategic, and overall practice, designing, implementing, and moderating assessments and making authentic, evidence-based decisions through the lens of their impact on learners.
5. *Depth.* Leverage your new learning to continuously deepen your measurement—and educational—system, ensuring that your students are at the center of it all.

When setting up a system of measurement, it helps to follow these frames like steps on the journey of implementing deeper learning in your system and schools. But the deeper learning journey is continuous, and it's far from linear. You have to be prepared to move into and out of each frame at will, simultaneously

- engaging new learning partners as they enter your school system or your community and constantly deepening your engagement with existing partners,
- developing new measures and other tools alongside ever-changing descriptions of what matters for learners,
- building your capacity to use those tools to inform practice and improve learning outcomes, and
- engaging in inquiry as the process for continual monitoring, response, measurement, and improvement.

The ultimate outcome is depth—for yourself and your learners, your system, and your community—and a true deeper learning mindset requires the unshakable knowledge and belief that you can always go deeper. These next chapters focus on the processes of building *engagement* and *development* capacity, as well as embedding the *clarity* consistent with deepening outcomes for individual learners and achieving system-wide deeper learning for all. In Part III, we'll dive into the fourth frame, *inquiry*, before one final exploration of *depth*. You'll find that, with deeper learning, *the depths just keep on coming.*

Composing an Evaluative Snapshot

You're a teacher—your own, your school's, or another person's interest in deeper learning, measurement, assessment, general instructional practice, or more general personal or collective advancement led you to this book and a desire to engage learning partners around the outcomes that matter. Or, you're a principal or other educational leader hoping to engage learners, teachers, and other leaders around a deeper set of learning outcomes. Or, you're a student, parent, or community member looking to identify the outcomes that actually matter and then bring them to life for yourself, your kids, or others. Whether your initial engagement is personally driven, facilitated by a small group of learning partners, or part of a whole-school, community-, district-, state-, or national-level change process, if you want to be successful you won't be working alone.

All you really need to get going, in addition to yourself, are *your* individual learners—who are they, what's important for them to know and to be able to do, and in what ways is it important for them to connect with others and within the world? It's likely that your existing knowledge of and connections with learners go a long way, and that may be what you used to complete Activity 2.3, "Break Down Deeper Learning." If so, your list provides a solid building block with which you can already do a great deal for your learners and from which you can build up to a great deal more. If you want to get this right, you'll need more than what you already have or is available in your classroom or even your school walls. "Getting this right" will require deeper engagement of and partnerships with your learners, their parents, your peers, others within your school system, and community members capable of offering understandings and perspectives that differ from or constructively widen your own. Engagement is about enabling the full range of learning partners to make deeper learning outcomes a reality, now and at every stage of the learning process.

It helps to think of the initial engagement process as an instrument for composing an **evaluative snapshot**. Collective work within schools and districts, or at any other level of a school system, should begin with just that—forming a complete, overall picture of the system, its learners, and what's important in individual contexts, identifying the strengths and needs that lay the foundation for change plans. Evaluative snapshots are driven by engagement and may involve

- interviews with, surveys of, and system-organized events that engage students, parents, teachers, leaders, community members, and any other learning partners around who learners are, where you are as a system, and where you need to be;
- formal reviews in areas including system environments; policies; curriculum; standards, measures, and other tools; professional learning opportunities; technological infrastructure; parent and community engagement; unit or lesson design; and learning experiences; and
- analysis of achievement, behavioral, attendance, and other relevant data.

Why is this information important? While necessarily incomplete, this list should give you an idea of what types of assessment evidence can inform the measurement of system capabilities (Figure 4.1). The Capability Rubrics will drive your ongoing evaluation of where you are in relation to where you want to be. Think about this evaluative snapshot in relation to inquiry. The process of gathering the necessary assessment evidence is the process of designing and implementing assessments that give you the information you need to measure system capabilities, reflect on where you are, and change as a result. Some of the most important pieces of evidence collected during this initial evaluative process, given measurement's role as a change lever in our school systems, will be those that inform whether and to what extent you've identified and are measuring what's important. Using the process of engagement to develop an initial evaluative understanding of where you are and where you need to be will set the stage for measuring and developing the range of successes you value.

Figure 4.1 • **Synthesizing Assessment Evidence to Make Capability Ratings and Determine Ways Forward**

Source: The Learner First, 2018

A Recipe for Return: Models of Practice From BESD

From Picture to Practice

So far, you've learned a lot about what it took for Burlington-Edison School District (BESD) to create an evaluative snapshot of where learning partners were and what they would have to do to get deeper learning going. BESD's journey started with the introduction of CCSS and continued with ESSA, which had learning partners looking to identify and develop the "bigger ideas" with a deeper set of outcomes and the shifts in practice they would require. Learning partners created a Road Map with district-wide outcome and foundational focuses, but it didn't take them long to realize that identifying what matters wasn't the be-all and end-all—they had to design assessments to help them measure what matters, too, which would require a range of additional capabilities and cultural conditions. The change would have to be connected and led from every level of the system. Enter the change team process.

> In terms of our overall equity and assessment goals, having functioning change teams at each of our sites is critical.
>
> —**Bryan Jones, EdD**, Director of Equity and Assessment, Burlington-Edison School District, United States

Prior to engaging with the deeper learning framework, each of BESD's schools had an Instructional Leadership Team (ILT), which consisted of teachers and other school leaders at different grade levels and with complementary focuses, acting as the decision-making body for school-improvement planning. These existing leadership teams provided a foundation for transitioning to change teams, in which the collective focus shifted to deeper learning and each change team member took responsibility for building capacity among learning partners in their schools. At the district level, change teams consisting of the superintendent, other district-level leaders, and members of each school change team met once a month to discuss targeted actions from previous meetings and their impact on learners' outcomes. At Bay View Elementary, ILT members who demonstrated exceptional leadership in relation to focuses including equity and deeper unit planning joined with the school principal, two consulting teachers, and a district representative to form a change team that operated in conjunction with the continuing ILT team, meeting multiple times a month, planning professional learning, and sharing their learning more widely in monthly ILT meetings. What helped drive the work in the change teams were measures and other deeper learning tools.

> [Deeper learning tools are] referenced quite often and give guidance for change teams to have conversations about "What are we really seeing right now; where do we find ourselves?" And it does give a nice idea of what those next steps could possibly be.
>
> —**Grant Burwash**, Instructional Design Team,
> Burlington-Edison School District, United States

> To go back to the adage about culture eating strategy for breakfast, establishing that culture that values risk-taking has been incredibly important. There was a perception before that the ILT was a rubber-stamp committee, [that] it was all about technical work. And so the change team part of that shift is big picture and taking ownership for what success looks like for our kids in our school. Our change teams understand that they're driving this work, [they're] not rubber-stamp committees that are operating at the behest of the district. They really do have authentic governance at the school level for trying to figure this work out. . . . It's been empowering for . . . teachers to come together as professionals and talk about their craft through this lens of deeper learning and use the tools that [focus] their craft toward this desired end of supporting all students.
>
> At Bay View Elementary, the parent [and] teacher group [has] ongoing conversations about how to support deeper learning. They ask the change team what [they] need to have this kind of learning enhanced. Now [they're] specifically fundraising to figure out how to support the work during the school day.
>
> —**K. C. Knudson**, Executive Director of Teaching and Learning,
> Burlington-Edison School District, United States

In the last couple months, parents have been [in the change team meetings], and it's been really powerful to have that communication. Where the educators may think they're being really clear about their vision and goals, the parents are saying, "Well, I'm not really sure what the vision and goals are," so that communication piece [has] been a nice layer to have.

—**Brenda Booth**, Instructional Design Team, Burlington-Edison School District, United States

Evaluative snapshots paint a vivid picture of what's going on and what needs to change in our schools and school systems. Change teams move us from the picture of where we are now to our picture of real success.

In order to understand what's important, we have to understand what's happening *now*. Think back to the case from Chapter 2 that explored the network of early childhood schools in Hawaii and their journey to discovering and measuring what mattered for their learners when they entered a new school. A culturally based evaluation provided actionable evidence of what learning partners valued and how to develop it for later application in measurement tools that captured the complete picture of success, not just the traditional academic side. Ideally led by change teams, the same approach should kick off the change process in all schools, districts, and wider systems working toward greater depth, so they can then use their collective insights and descriptions to work with or develop the tools required by a deeper commitment to their learners.

Guided by the inquiry process, change teams work to understand their systems, their learners, and what's important; engage learning partners around deeper learning; leverage tools to measure progress and success; lead throughout the district and its schools; create a culture that fosters deeper learning outcomes; and support others to do the same. It's a critical process that requires deeper learning and intentional planning from everyone involved up front. Look to the learning from Chapter 3, along with BESD's process for setting up change teams throughout the district, to inform your own change team formation and development. From there, look to the change team tools (listed and described in Figure 4.2) in Appendix C to help you visualize and plan your own inaugural and other change team meetings and strategies. You already kicked off your change plan in Chapter 3, and while this and other tools are always valuable at an individual level, remember that one of their primary objectives is to facilitate conversation and collaboration—in other words, *sharing*.

Figure 4.2 • Change Team Tools in Appendix C

Appendix C.1	*Capability Discussion Starters*	questions to kick off your discussion and measurement of the five system capabilities both inside and outside of your change team
Appendix C.2	*Change Plan*	a template for use at any level of the school system to design an action plan framed around particular capabilities or dimensions
Appendix C.3	*Your First Change Team Meeting*	a suggested schedule for your first change team meeting
Appendix C.4	*Baseline Capability Snapshot*	a guide for determining your first collective Capability Rubric and Learning Development Rubric ratings within your change team
Appendix C.5	*Individual Action Plan*	a template for an action plan centered on who your learners are as individuals and what they need to be successful
Appendix C.6	*Individual Profile*	a tool for teachers who wish to develop a deeper understanding of their learners as individuals, laying the foundation for the design of action plans centered on the learners' interests and needs
Appendix C.7	*The CORE Approach*	a description of the process of synthesizing evidence to determine valid and consistent ratings using measures of deeper learning
Appendix C.8	*Exemplar Moderation*	a guide for use in conducting change team, whole-school, and inter-school moderation processes

Source: The Learner First, 2018

Putting Depth Into Practice

Reflect

Think back through all the cases that have described learning partner engagement in school systems globally, and reflect on your own system's engagement of learning partners around what's important for students. Do students, parents, teachers, school leaders, and community members all play a critical role in determining what success is and how to achieve it? What would it take to compose an evaluative snapshot of your own system, and what pieces of evidence are important to consider? How can the Capability Rubrics help you evaluate where you are now, where you want to be, and how to get there?

Identifying and Describing What Matters

Our "buckets" for identifying and describing what matters are the deeper learning outcomes, system capabilities, and elements of authentic practice. All schools, districts, and wider systems can use these **outcomes** and **enablers**, embedded within the five frames of measurement, to identify, describe, and subsequently measure what matters for their learners. Beginning with the deeper learning outcomes, let's take a look at how engaging learning partners around identifying and describing what matters lays the foundation for measuring and developing it.

At an overarching level, success is embodied by the deeper learning outcomes. They're the components of a meaningful and fulfilling life no matter where you are in the world, and we hope you've felt them seeping through these pages and reflected in all that's been described. Figure 4.3 presents the reasoning for their importance in yet another way.

Figure 4.3 • Reasoning for the Development of Deeper Learning Outcomes

1. Humanity demands that everyone have the opportunity to lead a successful life marked by meaning and fulfillment.
2. Therefore, education has to support learners in this process of personal, collective, and global development—it's our moral, progressive, and evolutionary imperative.
3. In order to fully support this growth, everything we do as educators and learning partners working within and in partnership with educational systems has to be tuned to developing the outcomes consistent with how we as humans find and sustain success.

Source: The Learner First, 2018

Let's dive deeper into the deeper learning outcomes and the role they play on a local level in your own classroom, school, or wider system.

Self-understanding. Who are you, really? Self-understanding is about who we are, who we will be, and why. Who learners really *are* as individuals is tragically underrepresented in what traditional school systems set them up to *learn*. In your own school or school system, does your students' learning—the way they learn, what they learn, and how they demonstrate their learning *in and for school*—say enough about who they are, what they're interested in and capable of, how they can make a difference in the world, and whether they've found meaning and fulfillment? Further still, does it do enough to support them to develop that understanding of themselves? It's possible to find meaning and fulfillment independent of education, but saying that education can contribute to that process is a massive understatement. It can *enable* and *accelerate* it, for every learner. No school system is the same, because no student is the same. On a local level, we need to celebrate our students' differences and ensure that what we learn about them informs what and how we teach them. It starts with knowing who our learners really are—it starts with engagement.

Knowledge. We're not trying to give knowledge a bad rap. It's incredibly important in the makeup of who we are, what we're capable of doing, and the connections we form on academic, professional, and personal levels. What's important to realize, and to reflect in students' learning, is that *knowledge alone is not fulfillment*. The acquisition of knowledge has to be aimed at the simultaneous development of other important outcomes, so that knowledge isn't only *acquired* but also *enhanced*, *leveraged*, and *created* as a direct result of the way it's developed. Consider this: If you ask learners to memorize subject-related content as it's presented to them by a teacher or in a textbook, perhaps they'll succeed on a multiple-choice and short-answer test. But if you support them to partner in designing, implementing, assessing, measuring, reflecting on, and improving learning that incorporates that content in a way that connects to their lives and interests, then existing and new knowledge will be *embedded* along with other learning outcomes, supporting them to succeed throughout school and beyond.

Competency. What can you *do* with your learning? Deeper learning competencies are those that allow who we are, what we know, and how we connect with others to make a real and lasting difference in our communities. What good are our individual differences and our identities, knowledge, and connections if what we do with them doesn't improve our own and others' lives? No matter the learning experience, think about how it can be deepened through the development of competencies that support the meaningful application of knowledge both within and beyond the walls of the classroom. Learning is exceedingly more appealing—and more likely to "stick"—when the focus is shifted from the learning acquired to its application; specifically, the role of its application in deepening learners' self-understanding, relationships, and lives. Not surprisingly, the competencies identified as important in individual contexts are highly similar to one another. In Chapter 1, we introduced NPDL's 6Cs—character, citizenship, collaboration, communication, creativity, and critical thinking—which neatly encompass the skills that are critical for learners today. Early implementation efforts have made it clear that engagement with these competencies and any other deeper learning outcome can't stop at identification—it has to extend into measurement.

Connection. As humans, we think about our lives in relation to the connections we share with others and the world. The strength and nature of those connections in large part determines how we feel about the world and our place within it. In turn, place is at least as much a function of our relationships as it is a function of our physical location. Nobody enters the world on the strength of their own merit, and what we do in the world is invariably connected to what others have done and are doing. Human lives are more meaningful and fulfilling when they're shared with others and when they contribute to the general wholeness of humanity. The connections we make within school systems are lifelong. Rather than merely providing a space for them to form, education should do everything it can to facilitate and strengthen learners' connections with their peers, other learning partners, their learning environments and communities, and the world. It should do everything it can to develop citizens capable of connecting for collective change. The answers to the possibilities for connection in our educational systems are learning partnerships. Such partnerships are not *transactional* but also *relational*, reflecting the deeper relationships formed around a common commitment to students and their learning. Positive, sustainable change comes as a result of feeling deeply connected to and working deeply with others. Education has to provide the opportunities and develop the outcomes required for both.

The culture of our educational systems should be such that every action or decision is made in light of these desired deeper learning outcomes (self-understanding, knowledge, competency, and connection). The deeper learning outcomes are highly interconnected—they all contribute to learning that develops students' capacity to contribute back, and they lead to the unique, meaningful, and fulfilling lives we want for each of our learners (Figure 4.4). What will these outcomes look like for *your* learners? What will it look like when *you* develop them? Collectively, you and your learning partners have the answers you're looking for.

Figure 4.4 • The Deeper Learning Outcomes

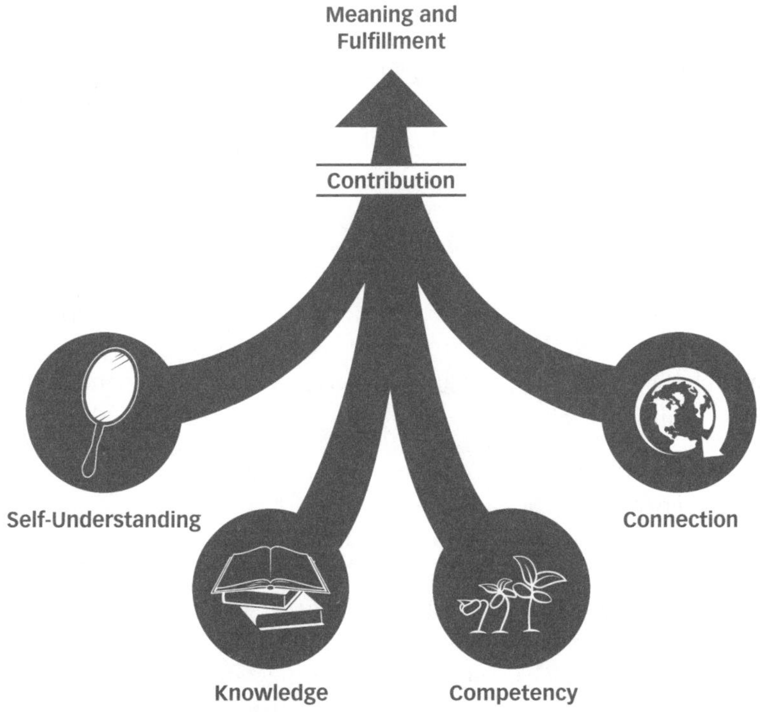

Source: The Learner First, 2018

Breaking Down Deeper Learning

The deeper learning outcomes not traditionally focused on in school systems in the United States and globally are those focused on here: self-understanding, competency, and connection. Knowledge is just as important—but it differs from the other outcomes in that its importance is already recognized, not simply in principle, but also in practice. As we'll continue to explore, measuring and intentionally developing self-understanding, competency, and connection enables us to develop that knowledge more deeply and meaningfully than ever. It's a win–win situation—our learners develop the necessary knowledge *better* while also developing the full range of complementary outcomes they need to succeed now and all throughout their lives. In the past, we haven't developed and adequately focused on this full range of outcomes because we (1) hadn't explicitly identified them and their importance and (2) didn't know how to measure them. So now that we've identified the deeper learning outcomes and their importance, *how can we measure them*?

First, *describe* them in your context and for your learners. You've already broken down self-understanding, competency, and connection in your descriptive lists (Activity 2.3, "Break Down Deeper Learning"). As we'll demonstrate shortly, that description is foundational to the process of measurement. If you completed that activity only once and on your own, think of it as a single assessment—it provides valuable information that serves as one piece of a picture, but it must be synthesized with a wider range of evidence if you want to most effectively measure and develop what matters. Of course, that's *exactly* what you want to do, and it's exactly why measurement depends on engagement.

What you've already accomplished in describing these outcomes has been accomplished by learning partners in school systems throughout the world—through similar activities, formal and informal descriptions, discussions, and learning experiences. It was that very partnership that resulted in the identification and description of the deeper learning outcomes. Globally, learning partners have shared and illuminated what matters for their learners, the components of those outcomes, and what it looks like when learners develop them. You have to capture that evidence, synthesize it, and use it to measure the learning that helps people contribute back to the world in meaningful and fulfilling ways. Here's what that looks like for self-understanding and connection.

No matter where we are or what we do, *who we are* is important. Understanding who we are is important, too—if we don't understand who we are, we won't understand how to *use* who we are to make a difference in the world. Refer back to the cases from BESD and their school-wide and district-wide efforts to identify and describe what matters. Whether your initial evaluative snapshot and ongoing evidence gathering involves interviews or surveys, whether it involves formal reviews of standards, learning experiences, and lesson designs or whether it involves the analysis of whatever range of existing data, if those pieces of evidence are framed around what matters for learners they'll support you to identify and describe self-understanding. The evidence we've gathered and continue to gather with learning partners in BESD and a diverse range of other school districts not only reveals the importance of self-understanding; it fully describes self-understanding, in the depth and richness required for the measurement and development of deeper learning. Learning partners have identified the following outcomes and components of self-understanding as important (see Figure 4.5).

Figure 4.5 • Components of Self-Understanding

Interests	History	Dreams	Potential
Strengths	Passions	Strivings	Actions
Weaknesses	Emotions	Biases	Sharing
Needs	Feelings	Perspectives	Motivations
Personality	Attitudes	Perception	Drive
Preferences	Beliefs	Viewpoints	Knowledge
Traits	Struggles	Respect	Competency
Attributes	Challenges	Awareness	Connection
Qualities	Frustrations	Belonging	Humanity
Characteristics	Stressors	Relationships	Contribution
Values	Wants	Growth	Meaning
Culture	Goals	Progress	Fulfillment
Family	Hopes		

Source: The Learner First, 2018

In addition, learning partners describe learners who are developing self-understanding as individuals who understand

- what's important to them;
- their knowledge, competencies, and connections (i.e., personal learning levels);
- how to reflect who they are in what and how they learn;
- how to deal with challenges and frustrations;
- what personal success looks like;
- how their experiences, history, and heritage shape their perspectives, their values, and the ways they view themselves and others;

CHAPTER 4

- the purpose of learning; and
- how they can contribute back in a range of contexts and situations.

Learners who are developing self-understanding engage in and demonstrate continuous learning; meaningfully interact with and grow alongside others and the world; feel confidence, pride, and belonging; celebrate what makes them and others who they are; understand the potential of their learning for supporting them to achieve their hopes and goals; and connect, teach, and share as means of achieving both personal and collective meaning and fulfillment—all these are only some of the outcomes and indicators that demonstrate individual learners' understanding of who they are.

Refer back to your own descriptive list for self-understanding (from Activity 2.3). It's likely that you included some of the same items as in Figure 4.5, as well as some that weren't mentioned. The items above reflect an abbreviated synthesis of the learning shared and collected in lists like your own and with learning partners in a range of contexts and formats. Taking our synthesis further, it's important to form *connections* between individual outcomes and descriptions, placing them in buckets that speak to common threads and themes. For example, it makes sense to group (1) interests, strengths, needs, values, learning levels and styles, traits, passions, beliefs, and challenges; (2) viewpoints, perception, perspectives, awareness, belonging, respect, culture, family, and history; (3) growth, progress, and potential; and (4) sharing, motivation, and drive. When fully formed, these buckets become the *dimensions* of each outcome—in this case, the dimensions of self-understanding.

Dimensions of Self-Understanding

- ✓ *Identity:* understanding who we are and how we learn as individuals
- ✓ *Place:* understanding how we impact and "fit into" others' lives and the world
- ✓ *Capacity:* understanding our potential for learning, progress, and success
- ✓ *Purpose:* understanding why we learn and how we can make a difference

Overarching each of these dimensions and the outcome as a whole are themes including the other deeper learning outcomes—knowledge, competency, and connection—along with humanity, contribution, meaning, and fulfillment. Through the process of engagement, these overarching themes and the deeper learning outcomes themselves, their dimensions, and the components of those dimensions all come together to inform a fully evidenced understanding of what each outcome really *is* and what it really *means*. Engagement ensures that everyone's voice is heard. "Listening" (and, later, *development*) ensures that what's said comes to life.

Overlapping with, and in addition to, the components that combine to identify and describe self-understanding as a deeper learning outcome, when talking about what really matters, learning partners identify specific outcomes relating to individuals' interactions and relationships with others, their environments, their learning, and the world. In a word, they talk about *connection*. From there, the process mirrors the one earlier, for self-understanding. Words and descriptions such as *partnership, respect, admiration, equality, empathy, symbiosis, sustainability, impact, necessity, safety, community, processing, analyzing, interest, balance*, and *collective cognition* combine to give life to individual dimensions of connection.

Dimensions of Connection

- ✓ *Interpersonal*: connecting with the people we know and interact with
- ✓ *Environmental*: connecting with natural and built environments
- ✓ *Conceptual*: connecting what we learn and with our learning
- ✓ *Universal*: connecting with all of humanity and the world

In our schools and every other local and global community, we think, talk about, strive for, and experience self-understanding and connection on a regular basis. Based on our experiences, we all bring our own insights into what self-understanding and connection are and feel like. And in the same way that our experiences are limited, our understanding of these and other outcomes are necessarily limited to what we've experienced—in other words, our personal understanding is important, but it's incomplete. In partnership with students, teachers, parents, and others throughout and outside of your school system, you can apply this same process to gain a deeper, collective understanding of any idea, item, or outcome at hand. Whether it's self-understanding, connection, an individual competency or knowledge pursuit, or any other specific, contextually important indicator underlying these overarching outcomes, if it matters for your learners you have to understand what it is and what it means before you and your learning partners can work together to bring it to life.

Putting Depth Into Practice

Reflect

Reflect on how far you've come in your understanding of self-understanding and connection, and add to or alter your descriptions as necessary, placing each individual descriptor within the dimensions of each outcome listed earlier. How will your deeper understanding of these outcomes impact the way you see your learners, and how will it improve your daily, strategic, and overall practice?

Activity 4.1: Describe "Progress"

Using your bucketed descriptions, for one, some, or all of the individual dimensions of self-understanding and connection, write a brief paragraph that paints a picture of learners at one end of the spectrum, those who demonstrate little to no evidence of development. Then do the same to create a picture of learners who have reached the highest level of development. What does each type of learner know, understand, and feel, and what can these learners do well? On the flip side, what do they struggle with? Then discuss or write down what it might take for the first type of learner to *progress* to the other end of the spectrum—in other words, *to progress from surface to deep*.

We've described self-understanding and connection—so what about competency? Ask learning partners what skills or abilities they want their learners to develop, and they'll describe a range of outcomes related to who we are, what we know, how we're connected, and how these all come together in the form of meaningful and fulfilling *action*. As with each of the other outcomes, some competencies are important for any learner to develop regardless of country, system, or culture. Naturally, these competencies speak to the development of self-understanding and knowledge, the process of connecting with others, and the skills required to make those connections work in the world. In the same way that each outcome is interconnected, the competencies that matter for our own, others', and global progress and advancement work together toward sustainable contribution, meaning, and fulfillment.

Recently, the New Pedagogies for Deep Learning (NPDL) global partnership, introduced in Chapter 1 and which has a led to a wealth of global learning and progress, engaged learning partners to identify six *deeper learning competencies* (the 6Cs) on which educators globally should focus their efforts (Fullan et al., 2017):

> **Character:** possessing the traits of grit, tenacity, perseverance, and resilience and the ability to make learning an integral part of living (learning to "deep learn")

Citizenship: thinking like a global citizen, considering global issues based on a deep understanding of diverse values and worldviews, and demonstrating a genuine interest in and ability to solve ambiguous and complex problems that impact human and environmental sustainability

Collaboration: working interdependently and synergistically in teams with strong interpersonal and team-related skills, including effective management of team dynamics and challenges, making substantive decisions together, and learning from and contributing to the learning of others

Communication: communicating effectively using a variety of styles, modes, and digital and other tools tailored for a range of audiences

Creativity: having an "entrepreneurial eye" for economic and social opportunities, asking the right questions to generate novel ideas, and possessing the leadership skills to pursue those ideas and turn them into action

Critical thinking: evaluating information and arguments, seeing patterns and connections, constructing meaningful knowledge, and applying it in the world

Take some time to think about your descriptions in relation to each of these competencies—where do your competency descriptors fit in with the 6Cs? Giving shape to the individual dimensions of each competency will further your understanding of what it really means, for instance, to communicate, to think critically or creatively, or to collaborate with learning partners. Let's take that last one, *collaboration*, as an example. As collaboratively identified by learning partners throughout NPDL, collaboration is embodied by the following five dimensions (NPDL, 2016).

Dimensions of Collaboration

- ✓ Working interdependently as a team
- ✓ Interpersonal and team-related skills
- ✓ Social, emotional, and intercultural skills
- ✓ Leveraging digital
- ✓ Managing team dynamics and challenges

Proficient collaboration isn't evidenced simply by the quality of a joint work product. It encompasses learners' ability to make substantive group decisions, learn from and contribute to the learning of others, and develop the understanding necessary for forming connections, exploring important issues and content, and creating new knowledge together (NPDL, 2016). These represent qualities and capabilities we all want for our children and for our learners. Engaging learning partners in this identification process provides the actual *language* with which to describe the competencies all learners need to develop.

Just as change doesn't happen in isolation, none of these competencies (or other outcomes) can be developed in isolation either. They're all connected and interdependent—supporting, relying on, and building on one another in the direction of one coherent outcome: meaning and fulfillment marked by positive contribution. Taking the example of *communication*, we can't be effective communicators if we don't understand

- who we are and what's important to us (*character*),
- what's going on in our communities and what needs to change (*citizenship*),
- how to work with others and share our knowledge and opinions to solve interpersonal or global challenges (*collaboration*),
- how to ask creative questions that spark our own and others' thinking (*creativity*), and
- how to share difficult ideas in ways that are clear, concise, and persuasive (*critical thinking*).

You can apply this same exercise to the other competencies and outcomes as well, which you have to understand in relation to every other if you're going to successfully develop and measure them. You've come a long way in engaging with self-understanding, competency, and connection. There's more to each of the deeper learning outcomes than any of us could ever identify and describe alone. Their depth demonstrates the depth of humanity, as well as the depths we have to reach together to support our learners in all the ways that foster and sustain success. Before we begin to explore the same depth of understanding in relation to system capabilities and the elements of inquiry, take some time to think about each of the deeper learning outcomes, how they're connected, and where you and your learners are in the process of developing them.

Putting Depth Into Practice

Activity 4.2: Form Connections

After reflecting on your understanding of each of the individual deeper learning outcomes, refer to the exercise above, in which we examined communication in light of each of the other deeper learning competencies, and do the same for one, some, or all of the other competencies. How does the development of each competency inform and enable the development of the others? Using the same process, explore how the development of each deeper learning outcome informs and enables the development of the others. Think about how they all come together around sharing and contribution to provide meaning and fulfillment.

For Your Consideration . . .

Although the process of identifying, describing, understanding, and breaking down a deeper learning outcome may seem new, it's not so far removed from the process that governs the design of traditional curriculums. School systems have broken knowledge (and, in best cases, other learning) into a number of subjects—or *dimensions*—that collectively embody what's expected to be taught and learned. Within those dimensions, we find descriptions of the specific learning we want students to know or develop. By developing a deeper understanding of and commitment to self-understanding, competency, and connection as outcomes in addition and connected to those represented in your school's or your school system's curriculum, you're already deepening, if not yet the wider curriculum, then at least your own "personal curriculum," in your intentional efforts to develop the full range of outcomes that matter. That's no small step in the direction of real success for you, your learners, your system, and the world.

In addition to outcomes, the elements of deeper learning are *capabilities* and *practice*. No matter your school, your school district, or your role in relation to them, a major part of the change process will be your work at each level of the system to develop the system capabilities required to foster deeper learning (with which you're already well familiar). There's a lot that goes into engaging learners, parents, and communities as real partners, for example, and breaking it all down into smaller dimensions is an important lever for deepening your understanding (refer back to Chapter 2 or the Capability Discussion Starters in Appendix C.1 for a refresher on each capability's dimensions). Like the deeper learning outcomes, the capabilities are deeply connected and intertwined, and none of them can be developed in isolation. Just as engaging learners, parents, and communities as real partners is critical to the development of every capability, so are understanding your system, measuring what's important, leading for deeper learning, and creating deeper learning cultures. They're all geared toward the same outcomes, and they can all be developed using the same elements of authentic practice, described in the following.

Elements of Authentic Practice

- *Partnerships*

  Leveraging student, teacher, parent, community member, and other learning partner engagement to enable and deepen learning

- *Environments*

  Leveraging where, why, and how we learn in a range of natural and built environments to enable and deepen learning

- *Technology*

  Leveraging digital tools and other technologies to connect learners, expand learning environments, and otherwise enable and deepen learning

- *Inquiry*

  Leveraging the continuous process of assessment, design, implementation, measurement, and reflection and change in partnership with learners to enable and deepen learning

At school, district, or wider levels, these practices show up in the development of system capabilities. At the level of individual learners (or groups of learners), they show up in deeper learning experiences. We noted that change teams are guided by the inquiry process, and they're guided by the other practices as well—how can environments and the use of digital and other technologies more directly enhance and enable learning, and how can you partner with students, parents, community members, and one another in the ways that will best identify, develop, and support you to measure what's important? Look back at the language used to describe each element of authentic practice. Your focus has to remain at all times on *leveraging* these elements' underlying practices to *enable and deepen learning*. For example, it's not enough to merely *use* technology or the environments you happen to find yourself in; rather, you have to *leverage* them, intentionally and purposefully, toward greater depth for yourself and every learner. When you leverage partnerships, environments, and technology within the inquiry process to develop system capabilities, you'll be enabling learners' development of deeper learning outcomes.

Putting Depth Into Practice

Reflect

How do you envision the deeper learning outcomes, system capabilities, and elements of authentic practice coming to life for yourself, your system, and your learners? In what ways do your own or your system's partnerships, environments, and technologies directly enable or deepen intended learning, and where might there be additional opportunities? Now think about these outcomes and enablers in relation to engagement. How can you leverage them within and outside of your change teams to more deeply engage the full range of learning partners in every aspect of learning?

Engagement brings us closer than ever to our learning partners, our own practice, and our learners' outcomes. As educators, we don't have all the answers. As students, parents, teachers, leaders, and community members—*all learning partners*—we do. Of course, deeper learning and measurement don't stop at engagement. A deeper understanding of what matters for us and our learners is a great thing to have, but we aren't truly acting on that understanding until we're measuring what matters. Every bit of evidence and knowledge about our learners must go into developing the measures that will bring deeper learning outcomes to life—not just in pockets but also for everyone.

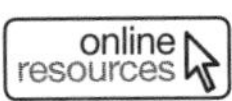

Access the appendices at
resources.corwin.com/MeasuringHumanReturn

CHAPTER 4

Chapter 5

DEVELOPING MEASURES OF DEEPER LEARNING

Authentic Measures and a System of Tools

It's learning for life, but how do we measure the learning for life? We don't have students coming back to us five years, ten years, twenty years down the road and checking in with us to find out how did they do, are they still learning? . . . We're trying to move from engaging kids to empowering kids to generating learning momentum . . . so that when they leave our classrooms at the end of the day or [leave] our schools at the end of the year, or graduate and leave us altogether, do they carry on learning? That's one of the things that we focus on, and it's really difficult to measure.

—**Patrick Miller**, Principal, Ontario, Canada

Deeper learning outcomes extend outside the confines of education, beyond graduation at any level and throughout the course of our lives, but their measurement is well within those confines—it's very possible, *and it's already happening*. It requires that we shift the focus of measurement from a static representation of current learning to a dynamic understanding of present success and its sustainability. Presented differently, traditional measurement asks of learners, "What do you know *now*?" Authentic measurement asks,

- Who are you—*and who will you be*?
- What do you know—*and what will you know*?
- What can you do—*and what will you do*?
- How are you connected—*and how will you connect*?

- How do you contribute to the lives of others and the world—*and how will you contribute back*?
- Have you found meaning and fulfillment?

And, ultimately, "*Will you lead a meaningful and fulfilling life*?" In addition to whether they're succeeding now, we need to know and respond to whether—throughout the rest of their education, after graduation, and throughout the course of their lives—everything our students are and have learned will lead to a lifetime of learning, progress, and success. Think deeply about the nature of this shift, and think about the differences between where you are now with your measurement practice and where you need to be. In order to demand more from measurement, all of us have to first demand more from ourselves.

If you've successfully engaged your learning partners to find out who your learners are and what's important for them, then you're already well on your way to measuring deeper learning. The definitions, descriptions, and very language gathered throughout the process of engagement tell you not only what success is but also what it looks like when your learners both progress toward and achieve it. The language of deeper learning reflects *progression* and *formation*—where learners are now, where they're going, and how their outcomes can be continuously deepened. In other words, it reflects *humanity* and our capacity for continuous growth and progress. Contrast this with the static, unmoving language of traditional measurement, and you'll see how authentic measures of deeper learning, written using the "language of depth," can create the shifts necessary to celebrate your learners and their outcomes.

Comprehensive systems of measurement have to include **measures** and other **tools** that

- embody a central focus on learners and their outcomes;
- describe each important outcome, capability, or practice using the language of depth (progression, formation, and humanity);
- shift the focus from the *here and now* to the *present and future*;
- develop a common language and understanding around deeper learning—its mindset, practice, indicators, and outcomes;
- build, in and of themselves, learning partners' capacity to assess, design, implement, measure, reflect on, and deepen learning; and
- enable opportunities that inform their use.

Collectively, the measures and other tools required for deeper learning address each of its elements and their dimensions. Through the process of engagement, you've *identified* the outcomes, capabilities, and elements of teaching and wider-systems-level practice that are important for you, your learners, and all your learning partners. Better still, you've *described* them. With this learning in place, you now have what you need to figure out how to *measure* them.

Measuring Self-Understanding, Connection, and Competency

You've gathered the breadth of evidence required to determine the outcomes that matter for your learners, along with their dimensions. Their descriptions reflect the *progression* that characterizes the deepening of student and systems-level learning. Refer back to Activity 4.1, "Describe 'Progress,'" which involved writing descriptions of learning at the lowest and highest levels of advancement for each outcome's dimensions, along with descriptions of what it might look like and what it might take for learners to progress from one level to the other. If you completed the activity for the *place* dimension of self-understanding, you may have written descriptions similar to the following:

> *No or limited progress.* Learners struggle to understand who they are in relation to others and the world. They have limited awareness of and are disconnected from the external effects of their actions. They don't see how experience shapes their perception, viewpoints, perspectives, and ways of being with others and living in the world. They undervalue themselves, others, and their own relationships, culture, family history, and environments.
>
> *Advanced progress.* Learners have a nuanced and complete understanding of the "big picture" of who and where they are, how they got there, and how they're connected with others and the world. They know their story and why they matter, they feel pride and belonging, and they celebrate what makes them and others who they are. They interact with and grow alongside others and the world in meaningful and fulfilling ways.

When describing how learners might move or progress from one level to the other, you may have focused on learners' deepening sense of and appreciation for their relationships and the impact of others on who they are and what they believe; their developing cultural identity and pride in who and where they are and where they came from; and their growing respect for and celebration of themselves, others, their natural and built environments, and their capacity for meaningful contribution.

Learning partners' *language*, collected throughout the process of engagement and including concepts and ideas such as awareness, perception, viewpoints, perspectives, culture, family, history, belonging, and respect, exist explicitly and implicitly all throughout these descriptions—they're products of engagement and the partnerships it fosters. When we engage learning partners around what matters for learners now and throughout their lives, they describe important outcomes, what it looks like when those outcomes are developed, and what exactly happens throughout that process of development. What results is the identification of *outcomes*, descriptions of those outcomes' *dimensions* at varying levels of progress, and, ultimately, *Learning Progressions* for measuring students' development of deeper learning outcomes (Figures 5.1, 5.2, and 5.3 and Appendix D).

These **learning progressions** demonstrate how all we collectively know and understand about our learners and their needs comes together to support both the measurement and the development of deeper learning outcomes. As evidenced by the descriptions included above and the *place* dimension of the Self-Understanding progression, the language used by learning partners to describe each of the outcomes and its dimensions is the same language used in the progressions. We call these measures "Learning Progressions" ("progressions" for short) because of the learning continuum they describe—students' movement along the continuum reflects their levels of development at varying points in time. What will tell us where individual learners are along the deeper learning path? The answer is *assessment evidence*, and it's what we use to track and measure learners' progress all throughout their learning journeys. In order to build your capacity for assessment, each of the other elements of inquiry and authentic practice, and each of the system capabilities, let's explore the tools that will help you measure, embed, and develop your capacity to leverage them.

Putting Depth Into Practice

Reflect

Record your initial thoughts about the Self-Understanding, Connection, and Collaboration Learning Progressions in Appendix D. What do you *see*, and how do they make you *feel*? What's the potential of measures like these to enable students' deeper learning outcomes? How would you assess your initial confidence in using these measures to measure your learners' progress?

Activity 5.1: What's in a Measure?

Drawing on your reflections, design a comparative model or diagram (e.g., Venn diagram) depicting the Learning Progressions in relation to your system's current measures of performance. How are they similar, how do they differ, and what do you perceive as their respective or comparative strengths and weaknesses? Reflect on what those strengths and weaknesses say, indicate, or imply about your own practice, your current levels of understanding, and your confidence in

(Continued)

(Continued)

relation to using each of the measures. Then, jot down some ways you might go about gathering the *assessment evidence* that matches these progressions' descriptions. Whether it's a conversation with a student or a parent, an observation, a survey, a group project, a worksheet, or an assignment—how can you learn what you need to learn? It's worth noting that what you're starting to design here are *assessments*.

For Your Consideration . . .

One of the readiest concerns about the introduction of deeper learning measures and other tools may be one of your own—*accessibility*. One glance at the Learning Progressions and rubrics may be enough to tell you they're different from and deeper than what you're used to. You have to approach this work with an open mind and with open eyes—try to *see* your learners in light of the deeper learning outcomes and the progressions' descriptions; these are the outcomes your learners need. From there, go slow, and engage in collaborative learning conversations using the language of the measures and the "dialect" of your individual context. It takes time, but anyone can master the language of deeper learning and the practices that will bring it to life. It's only a matter of committing to seeing yourself as a learner and your students for all that they are. Try it—*you'll see.*

Capability and Practice Tools

Like deeper learning outcomes, and seeing as they're another element of deeper learning, capabilities are best measured along a progression. Describe the capabilities of a healthy system as it achieves greater and greater depth, and what results is a *Capability Rubric* to measure your system's development of them (Appendix A). (Note that while both describe levels of progress, we use the term *rubrics* to differentiate measures of *professional* learning from "progressions," which are measures of *student* learning.) At the very least, simply engaging with the Capability Rubrics in Chapter 2 helped you develop your capacity to use them, and it's likely you were able to make valuable judgments about your system's strengths and needs. Now, with new learning in tow, your engagement with these measures will only be deeper.

You now have a greater understanding of what you need to uncover to make reliable, evidence-based judgments. Referring to the language and intent of the Engaging Learners, Parents, and Communities as Real Partners Capability Rubric (Appendix A.2), a system that successfully engaged all its learning partners would foster a culture of learning, belonging, and collaboration. Everyone's insights would be sought, valued, and examined collectively, supporting a continuous commitment to improvement and innovation. Digital and other

Figure 5.1 • Learning Progression: Self-Understanding

Understanding who we are, what we're capable of, how we impact and fit into others' lives and the world, and how we can make a difference

Dimension	Substantially off Track	Getting Started	Looking Promising	Well on Track	Geared for Success
Identity (understanding who we are and how we learn as individuals)	Learners struggle to identify and evaluate who they are in relation to individual interests, strengths, needs, goals, hopes, values, learning levels and styles, traits, passions, beliefs, and challenges. Their personal experiences and identity are largely unknown and unexplored. They have a limited understanding of what matters to them, who they want to be, and how they grow.	Learners are beginning to recognize the value and meaning of their individuality. They are beginning to explore their interests and experiences, identify their values and needs, and consider how learning relates to their life. They may still have a narrow view of the "self" and of its state, formation, progress, and multitudes.	Who the learner is and wants to be are formulated self-interests. Learners understand the significance of and differences between individual components of their identity. They actively engage in self-discovery centered on who they are, what matters to them, what challenges them, and how they develop as individuals in relation to identified outcomes and goals.	Learners have a well-developed understanding of what's important to them, their current and desired learning levels, and how they can most effectively bring their learning to life. They know what they want, and they evidence the ability to connect desired future states to present actions, mindsets, and behaviors.	Learners deftly balance who they are with who they want to be, communicate both, evaluate their identity in light of their values and life experiences, and learn in ways that reflect who they are and make their goals a reality. They assess and measure their progress toward clearly identified outcomes, and they demonstrate continuous growth.
Place (understanding how we impact and "fit into" others' lives and the world)	Learners struggle to understand who they are in relation to others and the world. They have limited awareness of and are disconnected from the external effects of their actions. They don't see how their experience shapes their perception, viewpoints, perspectives, and ways of being with others and living in the world. They undervalue themselves, others, their relationships, their culture, their family history, and their environments.	Learners have an emerging sense of and appreciation for the importance of others' experiences, and their relations with others, in the formation of self. They recognize that where and who they are as individuals are functions of internal *and* external factors and forces, but they struggle to understand and accept differing views and perspectives and to figure out what they "mean" to and for others and the world.	By developing their understanding of their cultural identity and personal and family backgrounds, learners are starting to take pride in and make connections between who they are, who others are, and their combined experiences. They're mindful of the environments and people they interact with, and of the influence they have on them.	Learners form connections between and among personal, family, and outside experiences; actions and effects; and the *self* as a derivative ("shaped"), unique, unified, and connected whole. They respect themselves, others, and their natural and built environments. They know where they stand in relation to diverse and wide-ranging viewpoints and perspectives.	Learners have a nuanced and complete understanding of the "big picture" of who and where they are, how they got there, and how they're connected to others and the world. They know their "story" and why they matter, they feel pride and belonging, and they celebrate what makes them and others who they are. They interact with and grow alongside others and the world in meaningful and fulfilling ways.

(Continued)

Figure 5.1 • (Continued)

Dimension	Substantially off Track	Getting Started	Looking Promising	Well on Track	Geared for Success
Capacity (understanding our potential for learning, progress, and success)	Learners don't know or understand (1) their hopes, goals, and opportunities for personal growth, (2) how to develop and grow as an individual, (3) that they (like everyone) always can and need to improve, or (4) their extraordinary, human capacity for innovation, progress, and advancement. They don't think they have what it takes to succeed.	Learners are starting to reflect on what they're capable of and to pay closer attention to what they learn and achieve on a daily basis, celebrating their successes and points of progress no matter how small. They may still feel discouraged, behind in their learning, and as if the level or amount of progress required is unachievable.	Based on identified interests, strengths, values, and other key identity components, learners are beginning to look beyond immediate, non-self-identified learning goals to focus on "what's possible" and where they can take their learning. They know and value their need for progress, and they are beginning to realize the scope of their capacity for growth and improvement.	Equipped with the understanding that there will always be further opportunities to deepen their learning and grow as an individual, learners have developed a mindset of progress, characterized by curiosity, liveliness, and continuous learning. They truly believe they can be who they want to be and achieve what they want to achieve if they put all of their "self" to it.	Learners have a deep understanding of their capacity to grow as an individual and collectively, as well as of the potential of their learning to support them to achieve any, and any number of, personal and collective goals. They celebrate and exemplify the human capacity for progress and advancement, knowing that they can and will succeed.
Purpose (understanding why we learn and how we can make a difference)	The purpose of learning, and learners' purpose in relation to their own life, others' lives, and the world, remain unclear to them. They're unaware of what they have to offer to or share with others and their community, and they lack the drive and motivation to deepen their learning. They don't know how they can make a difference in the world.	Learners are beginning to understand the importance of who they are, what they know and can do, and how they connect (i.e., their learning) in determining their success now and in the future. While they may have a developing sense of identity, place, and capacity, they don't know what success will look like for *them* as individuals or what they need to learn to achieve it.	As who they are, how they fit into others' lives and the world, and their potential for growth and change take on a more substantive or realized form, learners are discovering what makes them "tick," what excites them in their learning, and what they can't help sharing with others. The effects of what's shared motivate them to progress in ways that deepen its impact.	Learners understand that meaning and fulfillment occur at the intersection of self-understanding, knowledge, competency, and connection. They focus their learning on personal, collective, environmental, and global progress and advancement. They learn in order to contribute back.	Learners have a fully developed and ever-deepening understanding of how they *are making* and *can make* a real difference in the world. Learning and living are one and the same to them, and they give back even more than they're given. They connect, teach, and share as means of achieving both personal and collective meaning and fulfillment—they know how to find and sustain success.

Source: The Learner First, 2018

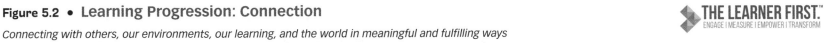

Figure 5.2 • Learning Progression: Connection

Connecting with others, our environments, our learning, and the world in meaningful and fulfilling ways

Dimension	Substantially off Track	Getting Started	Looking Promising	Well on Track	Geared for Success
Interpersonal (connecting with the people we know and interact with)	Learners are disconnected from the lives, feelings, and actions of their peers, their family members, and other potential learning partners in their local and global communities. They struggle to collaborate, listen to, and trust others, to share who they are, and to open themselves to what others have to share. They don't understand others; they see others as less than or distant from them.	Learners show emerging admiration, trust, empathy, and compassion in relation to others through their interactions and reflections. They're drawn and open to people and experiences that reach out to or resonate with them, but they still have a narrow sense of where others are "coming from," their reciprocal effects on one another, and the importance of connection in relation to *every* other.	In comfortable or familiar settings and environments, learners demonstrate the desire and ability to engage with others, listen to and take in what they say and do, and share their own and support others' learning. They're deepening their understanding of others and the power of close, human relationships, using this understanding to solve problems and work through conflicts.	Learners connect with others with a wide range of interests, personalities, and ways of life in a variety of familiar and unfamiliar environments. They explore partnerships with people inside and outside their local communities, reflect on and communicate their sense of and capacity for connection, seek out and form relationships, and open themselves to all.	Learners feel necessary to others and the necessity of others in finding personal and collective meaning and fulfillment. They feel deeply connected to the lives of the people they interact with, and they embody and inspire mutual sharing, admiration, empathy, success, and understanding of reciprocal impact. They grow with and for others, progressing or *"moving"* with them easily.
Environmental (connecting with natural and built environments)	Learners' actions and ways of living and being in the world have a destructive or otherwise negative impact on natural, built, or digital environments. They don't respect, benefit, or show any interest in their environments or plant and animal life; they struggle to balance actions with their environmental impact; and they feel unsafe, unwelcome, or antagonistic in relation to their environments.	Learners are mindful of the differences between varying environments. They're starting to recognize their own importance in giving, fostering, supporting, and sustaining various forms of life. They may not interact with life-forms in purposefully destructive or harmful ways, but they have a narrow view of their impact on and a limited desire to sustain a range of environments.	Learners are developing a real interest in and knowledge of natural and built environments centered on what they can share with one another. They understand the nature of their symbiotic relationships, and they think deeply about ways to improve their environments from sustainability, health and safety, practical, and creative perspectives.	In wide-ranging natural, indoor, outdoor, and digital environments, learners assess and understand the impact of their actions. They take a constructive approach, identifying and acting on opportunities to improve their environments for themselves and others.	Interest in and respect for their environments has translated into a deeply felt and realized connection between "learner" and "learning space" (i.e., any and all environments). They make these spaces safer, more suited to intended or previously unrecognized purposes, and more welcoming and sustainable for varying forms of life. They and their environments truly depend on one another.

(Continued)

Figure 5.2 • (Continued)

Dimension	Substantially off Track	Getting Started	Looking Promising	Well on Track	Geared for Success
Conceptual (connecting what we learn and with our learning)	Learners struggle to process, analyze, and make connections between and among the elements, outcomes, and objectives of their learning, as well as between "learning" and "life." They don't see their interests or who they are reflected in their learning, and they either struggle or don't try to form those links. As a result, they feel disconnected from learning and have trouble developing it.	Learners form basic connections between certain elements of their learning and outcome or content areas. They understand that learning can't be crammed into isolated boxes, or "silos." They approach learning with energy and excitement when it easily connects to their interests, but they remain disengaged from "un-relatable" learning.	As their understanding of learning develops to account for more of what makes them who they are, learners are starting to more regularly form connections between what they "have to" and what they want to learn and do. They analyze certain learning outcomes in light of others, and they look to bring what they learn in certain subjects or spaces to what they're learning in others.	Learners connect important learning in a rational and meaningful manner to solve problems and deepen their learning. They're open to and engaged in what and how they learn, have highly developed analytical abilities, and leverage the learning and teaching practices that connect them and others to, and consequently deepen, desired learning outcomes.	Learners see their learning as necessary to and indistinguishable from their life, their actions, and their contributions. They feel a deep connection to their learning and its collective impact on their own and others' lives, easily connect what they learn, and integrate digital and other tools in their learning. They leverage partnerships, environments, and inquiry to create new learning and relevant assessments.
Universal (connecting with all of humanity and the world)	Learners evidence acute disinterest in or intolerance of the diverse people, cultures, environments, communities, and contexts of the world. They feel no or little connection with the wholeness of life and humanity, lack appreciation for varying perspectives, and promote or turn an "indifferent eye" toward injustice and inequality.	Learners pay attention to and sincerely reflect on what they see and hear from unfamiliar people and places. They demonstrate interest in learning about other worldviews and ways of life. Still, they tend to think of their own cultural, family, or personal ideas and beliefs as "right" and of others' as either wrong, misguided, or unimportant, without meaningfully weighing them against their own.	Learners are developing respect for and understanding of situations and beliefs that are different from their own and those of the people they regularly interact with. They see things happening to others and the world that they want to prevent, further, or change, and they feel and evidence a growing connection between their life and what happens outside its immediate reach.	Learners have a genuine interest in and respect and appreciation for humanity and the world. They think and are starting to act globally, focusing not only on their own communities but also others in which they can share themselves, make an impact, and grow. They see purpose in deepening and widening their sense of place.	Learners' fully developed global connection drives and supports them to deepen the general good and wholeness of humanity and the world in meaningful and fulfilling ways. They have a balanced and truly global understanding and perspective, striving to eliminate inequalities and better the complex and interconnected workings of life and the world.

Source: The Learner First, 2018

Figure 5.3 • Learning Progression: Collaboration

Working interdependently and synergistically in teams with strong interpersonal and team-related skills, including effective management of team dynamics and challenges, making substantive decisions together, and learning from and contributing to the learning of others

Dimension	Limited Evidence	Emerging	Developing	Accelerating	Proficient
Working interdependently as a team	Learners either work individually on learning tasks or collaborate informally in pairs or groups but do not really work together as a team. Learners may discuss some issues or content together but skip over important substantive decisions (such as how the process will be managed), which has significant adverse impacts on how well the collaboration works.	Learners work together in pairs or groups and are responsible for completing a task in order for the group to achieve its work. At this level, tasks may not be well matched to each individual's strengths and expertise, and group members' contributions may not be equitable. Learners are starting to make some decisions together but may still be leaving the most important substantive decisions to one or two members.	Learners decide together how to match tasks to the individual strengths and expertise of team members and then work effectively together in pairs or groups. Learners involve all members in making joint decisions about an important issue, problem, or process and developing a team solution.	Learners can articulate how they work together in a way that is interdependent and uses each person's strengths in the best possible way to make sound substantive decisions and develop ideas and solutions. Interdependent teamwork is clearly evident in that learners' contributions are woven together to communicate an overarching idea and/or create a product.	Learners demonstrate a highly effective and synergistic approach to working interdependently in a way that not only leverages each member's strengths but also provides opportunities for each to build on those strengths and learn new skills. This includes ensuring that substantive decisions are discussed at a deep level that draws on each team member's strengths and perspectives are infused to come to the best possible decision that benefits all.
Interpersonal and team-related skills	Although learners may help each other on tasks that contribute to a joint work product or outcome, interpersonal and team-related skills are not yet evident. Learners do not yet demonstrate a genuine sense of empathy or a shared purpose for working together.	Learners report and demonstrate a sense of collective ownership of the work and show some interpersonal and team-related skills. The focus is on achieving a common or joint outcome, product, design, response, or decision, but the key decisions may be taken or dominated by one or two members.	Learners demonstrate not only good interpersonal skills and collective ownership of the work; an active sense of shared responsibility is also evident. From beginning to end, the team listens effectively, negotiates, and agrees on the goals, content, process, design, and conclusions of their work.	Learners can clearly articulate how joint responsibility for the work and its product or outcome pervades the entire task. Strong skills in listening, facilitation, and effective teamwork ensure that all voices are heard and reflected in the ways of working or work product.	Learners take an active responsibility, both individually and collectively, for ensuring that the collaborative process works as effectively as possible, that each person's ideas and expertise are used to maximum advantage, and that each work product or outcome is of the highest possible quality or value.

(Continued)

Figure 5.3 • (Continued)

Dimension	Limited Evidence	Emerging	Developing	Accelerating	Proficient
Social, emotional, and intercultural skills	Learners have a basic awareness about themselves and how their behavior affects others. They tend to see things only from their own perspective. In some cases, this may inhibit their ability to form positive relationships.	Learners have a growing awareness of who they are, where they fit in the world, and how their behavior affects other people. This self-awareness is starting to provide a base for better understanding of how other people's emotions and viewpoints differ from their own.	Learners have good awareness of who they are and where their own perspective comes from. Self-awareness and listening skills allow them to better understand and empathize with the emotions and viewpoints of others, moving beyond "tolerance" or "acceptance" to genuinely valuing perspectives quite different from their own.	Learners have a strong sense of self. They understand where their own perspective comes from and how it differs from others'. They listen carefully, empathize with the emotions and viewpoints of others, and use these to enrich their own learning. As a team member, they work effectively in ways that support, encourage, challenge, and grow not just themselves but others as well.	Learners have highly developed social and emotional skills, grounded in a clear sense of their individual and cultural identity. They communicate well across cultures and disciplines, work effectively in teams, and form positive relationships. The skills they have developed in perspective-taking and empathy, understanding someone else's perspective, and changing their behavior as a result clearly enhance team functioning.
Leveraging digital	Although learners use some digital elements for the task, these were very "surface level" and did not substantially contribute to the quality or output of the collaboration.	Learners used digital opportunities to facilitate shared ways of working, in ways that could not have been done otherwise, although they are unlikely to have significantly deepened the collaborative process.	Learners used digital aspects effectively to encourage interdependent work, speed up feedback, accelerate innovation cycles, and deepen the nature of the collaboration among members.	Learners can clearly articulate how infusing a digital element has facilitated interdependence, deepened the nature of the collaboration, built a better sense of shared responsibility, and improved the team's ability to make substantive decisions together.	Learners used digital elements ubiquitously throughout the task in powerful ways to deepen the quality of collaboration and encourage innovation. Learners can articulate in detail how each digital element has accelerated and enhanced the team's learning and can apply that understanding to new and different contexts.

Dimension	Limited Evidence	Emerging	Developing	Accelerating	Proficient
Managing team dynamics and challenges	Learners mishandle team challenges in one of two ways: (a) They get deeply invested in their own viewpoint, lack the empathy to hear or learn from others, and have difficulty suspending judgment to genuinely listen to others' views; or (b) They avoid conflict by deferring to others' views instead of sharing their own or will change their views quickly in the face of inappropriate peer pressure. As a result, the team gets "stuck" in conflict or may move forward in the wrong direction or one that the team does not share.	Learners still need guidance to forge and maintain positive working relationships and to resist inappropriate peer pressure. They are starting to take a more considered approach to dealing with disagreements, asking each member to share their perspective and discussing any differences. They are only just beginning to dig beneath those differences to identify what underpins them, which makes it difficult to resolve issues effectively and without unnecessary conflict.	Learners generally work quite effectively in a team, although they are likely to need help with conflict resolution, inappropriate peer pressure, and other challenging issues from time to time. They are developing the ability to identify what underpins their own and others' points of view. They are getting better at clearly and respectfully expressing their own viewpoints while listening to and learning from others. They still need to better "pick their battles" in order to ensure that in-depth discussion on relatively minor issues doesn't hold up team progress.	Learners are more skilled at identifying what underpins their own and others' points of view. They "pick their battles" in deciding what to debate. They are building both courage and clarity to express their own viewpoints while listening to and learning from others. They are becoming skilled at exploring different opinions in ways that contribute to the learning of others without holding up team progress.	Learners have a deep understanding of what underpins their own and others' points of view, the courage and clarity to effectively express their own viewpoints, and the empathy to hear and learn from others. They respectfully explore different opinions in ways that enrich both their own and others' learning and thinking and allow the team to move forward in the direction that the team identifies.

Source: McEachen, J., & Quinn, J. *Collaboration Deep Learning Progression*. Copyright © 2014 by New Pedagogies for Deep Learning™ (NPDL)

Note: Learning Progressions for each of NPDL's 6Cs (character, citizenship, collaboration, communication, creativity, and critical thinking) are in use throughout the global partnership, but all but the collaboration progression are currently unpublished.

Figure 5.4 • Learning Progressions in Appendix D

Appendix D.1	*Self-Understanding* (Figure 5.1)	measures students' understanding of who they are, what they're capable of, how they impact and fit into others' lives and the world, and how they can make a difference
Appendix D.2	*Connection* (Figure 5.2)	measures students' connections with others, their environments, their learning, and the world
Appendix D.3	*Collaboration* (Figure 5.3)	measures students' capacity to work interdependently and synergistically in teams with strong interpersonal and team-related skills (measure created by NPDL)

Source: The Learner First, 2018

technological tools would be seamlessly integrated into learning, and all partners would have (and want to take advantage of) the professional learning opportunities necessary for shifting practice around changing roles and learning environments. Learning would happen not just in schools but also within families and communities (at any time) so that the learning shared and developed between students and partners would reflect a range of perspectives. Students would be encouraged and supported to connect their learning to their lives and interests; to develop self-understanding, knowledge, competencies, and connections; and to share their learning with the world.

How can we evidence progress toward these desired outcomes and enablers? It's a process—and that process is *inquiry*. In order to gather the evidence we need to inform each measure's use, we have to develop additional tools to support learning partners through each individual inquiry process. Let's start with assessment. You've read this refrain throughout these pages: you have to design and implement *assessments* that inform the measurement of learning, reflecting on and changing your practice as necessary. Notice assessment's importance and place in the structure of the inquiry process. Assessment is the object of learning design and implementation, and then it's leveraged to measure that learning. So what would a tool designed to support the assessment of students' deeper learning outcomes look like?

Ours is the Student Inquiry Guide: Authentic Assessment (Figure 5.5) in Appendix E.1. It reflects every additional element of authentic practice, demonstrating the fluidity of the process and its elements' interdependency. It asks questions that

- enable the *design* of assessments that reflect who learners are and fully respond to evidenced needs and evidence gaps,
- embed the practices required for authentic assessment *implementation*, and
- facilitate *reflection* on and the *measurement* and *change* of outcomes and practices, in real time, using assessment evidence.

In this way, the framework for student assessment lends itself to the entire inquiry process, supporting us to identify what's needed and to track progress and performance, in real time, throughout implemented learning experiences. Of course, we're concerned with assessing not only *students'* learning (with the Learning Progressions) but also *system* or *professional* learning (with the Capability Rubrics). There's a tool for that, too—the Professional Inquiry Guide: Authentic Assessment (Appendix F.1). The guides are highly similar; they simply shift between the lenses of outcomes (student) and capabilities (professional). When assessing system or professional learning, remember that while the object of assessment is your own, other professionals', or your system's development, it should always be driven by student learning. *We assess our own and our systems' learning in order to better develop our students'.*

It's a similar story with measurement. The Authentic Measurement Guides will support you to use all the evidence gathered in the design and implementation of assessments in order to measure your own or your students' levels of learning. (See Figure 5.6 and Appendix E.2: Student Inquiry Guide: Authentic Measurement and Appendix F.2: Professional Inquiry Guide: Authentic Measurement.) In short, they'll support you to match assessment evidence to the language of the measure, providing an evidence-based understanding of where you or your learners are and where there's room for improvement. As we know, measurement is best supported by assessments that are purposefully *designed* to develop intended outcomes while also providing the learning evidence we're looking for. The Authentic Design Guides will enable assessments that do exactly that, focusing assessment design around the already-described elements of authentic practice: partnerships, environments, technology, and inquiry (Appendix E.3: Student Inquiry Guide: Authentic Design and Appendix F.3: Professional Inquiry Guide: Authentic Design).

As a complete set, these inquiry guides will support the development and measurement of the full range of learning outcomes, capabilities, and practices. Note that implementation, reflection, and change are deeply embedded within them all—they're meant to develop the practices required for assessment implementation, and reflection will help you understand what's working and what needs to change at every step of the way. Remember, the student guides are for use alongside the Learning Progressions, and the professional guides are for use alongside the Capability Rubrics.

There's one more piece of the development puzzle, complementing each of the other tools as they all do for one another. In addition to having tools for designing and implementing assessments, you have to be able to measure the effectiveness of those implemented learning experiences and their embedded practices in developing deeper learning outcomes. That process is integral to *collaborative moderation* (Chapter 10), which engages learning partners in the discussion, sharing, and subsequent measurement of teaching and learning using the **Learning Experience Rubric** (Figure 5.7) in Appendix G. As with the Student Inquiry Guide: Authentic Design (Appendix E.3), the dimensions of the Learning Experience Rubric are the four elements of authentic practice. By focusing on these elements, the rubric supports learning partners' measurement of the extent to which specific practices develop specific deeper learning outcomes. Through collaborative moderation, those practices can be illuminated, shared, and strengthened. If you examine the student design guide and Learning Experience Rubric together, you'll see that the language of the rubric closely mirrors that of the guide, and it has to—as educators, we have to design assessments based on the same criteria on which those assessments are measured. It wouldn't make sense to design an assessment around certain success criteria and then measure students' learning on different criteria entirely. That same logic holds for the design and subsequent measurement of the success of assessments and embedded practices themselves. Of course, their success is dependent on their development or demonstration of deeper learning outcomes.

While we'll engage more deeply with the Learning Progressions, the Authentic Inquiry Guides, and the Learning Experience Rubric in Part III, we ask you now to reflect on each Learning Progression and student inquiry guide to deepen your understanding of their meaning and intent. This chapter has already introduced a number of new measures and other tools, but their contents are far from new. You possess a wealth of prior knowledge about learning assessment, design, implementation, measurement, and reflection and change, as well as what makes up the contents of individual learning progressions and rubrics. It's that very sort of knowledge and language that goes into the development of deeper learning measures and inquiry guides.

Putting Depth Into Practice

Reflect

Reflect on the individual Learning Progressions and student inquiry guides, beginning with a single measure or guide. What's the specific *purpose* of the tool, and how might it bring learners' outcomes to life? Is it clear how the process of engagement and learning partners' collective insights come together in the development of this tool? What questions do you still have regarding its use? Are you committed to using it to deepen your own and others' learning? Repeat with other progressions or student inquiry guides as needed.

Developing Measures in Individual Contexts

Every tool included or described above has a common focus—developing students' deeper learning outcomes. While their emphases differ to account for everything that goes into that development, they never lose sight of what

Figure 5.5 • **Student Inquiry Guide: Authentic Assessment**

An inquiry guide that can be used alongside the Learning Progressions to support the assessment of student learning

Student:

Assessment Process/Questions	Your Notes, Reflections, and Evidence
Authentic Mixed-Method Assessment (AMMA) Aims Who is this student—what are his or her individual and family backgrounds, interests, and goals? What makes him or her who he or she is? What are the student's current levels of learning? Where is he or she in relation to curriculum content? Where is he or she on the Learning Progressions? What does the student need to learn next? **Depth and Diversity of Assessment** What assessment evidence (quantitative and qualitative) are you using to capture the above information? Is gathered assessment evidence enough to fully inform the measurement of student progress on the Learning Progressions? Where are there evidence gaps? **Implementation and Evidence Tracking** Working closely with the Learning Progressions, what is each individual assessment telling you about levels of learning? What assessments (e.g., conversations, tests, assignments, activities, observations) are providing what evidence of learning? What assessments are developing what outcomes? How are you ensuring real-time tracking of student progress and performance to inform the measurement and direction of learning mid-implementation? Are formative self-, peer-, and teacher-assessment processes embedded throughout the implementation process? How are you responding to *evidenced needs* and *evidence gaps* mid-implementation? **Assessment Partners** How are the student and other learning partners engaged as active partners throughout the assessment process? How does the student's engagement in each aspect of the inquiry inform and progress his or her levels of learning?	

Source: The Learner First, 2018

Figure 5.6 • Student Inquiry Guide: Authentic Measurement

An inquiry guide that can be used alongside the Learning Progressions to support the measurement of student learning

Student:		
Measurement Process/Questions	**Your Notes, Reflections, and Measurement**	
(Pre-Ratings) Measure and record the student's current levels of learning for the focus outcomes/dimensions. Drawing from gathered assessment evidence, what are this student's current levels of learning or progress? Which outcomes/ dimensions will be most important to develop, track, and measure for this student? What assessment evidence are you using to determine this student's ratings? Does the evidence provide a complete picture of the student and his or her learning? How are you synthesizing assessment evidence to come to your rating decisions? Would another teacher arrive at the same ratings based on collected evidence? **Throughout the learning experience, use the assessment guide to record evidence of learning as it occurs.** Reflect on the following throughout implementation, and change accordingly: Are implemented assessments enough to fully inform the measurement of intended learning? **(Post-Ratings) Measure and record the student's current levels of learning to determine levels of progress and further learning opportunities.** Refer to the Pre-Ratings questions above.		
Has the student progressed in relation to focus outcomes or dimensions? What does this student's level of progress indicate about the effectiveness of the given assessment or set of assessments as a whole, along with the effectiveness of embedded practices? What are some of the experience's strengths, and where are there opportunities for improvement? Are there specific changes that can be made in your measurement and assessment practice to further deepen student outcomes?	**Pre-Ratings**	**Post-Ratings**

Source: The Learner First, 2018

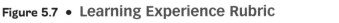

Figure 5.7 • Learning Experience Rubric

A rubric that can be used within the inquiry process to measure the depth and effectiveness of a learning experience's embedded practices

Dimension	Substantially off Track	Getting Started	Looking Promising	Well on Track	Geared for Success
Partnerships	The learning experience is delivered *by* the teacher, *for* the students. "Teaching" and "learning" are clearly divided, and the experience is marked by a lack of choice, equity, transparency, and engagement. Students, parents, community members, and other potential learning partners don't have a meaningful opportunity to connect, collaborate, and share in ways that directly enable and deepen learning.	Students are emerging partners in the learning—they understand the success criteria and purpose for learning, and it's driven by their interests and needs. Students partner with their teacher and one another in aspects of the learning but remain disengaged from important elements of the inquiry process. Parent, community, and other "outside" involvement lacks meaning and equity.	Partnerships between and among students, teachers, classes, grade levels, schools, families, or communities connect learners and deepen outcomes. While existing partnerships advance the learning at hand, they are limited in scope, largely teacher-driven, or predetermined, not adapting or expanding to pursue new learning opportunities as they arise. Certain elements of the inquiry process, however, reflect real partnership.	The experience evidences a collaborative culture in which learners are encouraged and supported to pursue partnerships that deepen their learning outcomes. Inquiry is a partnership, and students collectively drive their learning with peers and others. The experience is marked by clear communication, shared vision and goals, and equitable learning opportunities for all partners.	Students, parents, and all others involved are engaged and valued as real learning partners: Everyone contributes to the learning of others. Students partner for improvement—of ideas, solutions, and products, and of personal, peer, and community outcomes—and in the ways most suited to their own and others' development. Teaching and learning connect partners to one another and the world.
Environments	*Where*, *why*, and *how* we learn aren't integral to the learning. There's little evidence of student voice, agency, or engagement, or of a commitment to learning and success for all. The learning environments fail to enhance the experience, and little attention is paid to how alternative natural or "built" environments (and their "cultural" characteristics) might effectively deepen the learning at hand.	The learning experience embeds a commitment to and expectation of success for every learner. Mistakes are treated as valuable opportunities for learning, and the space and mode of learning are important design considerations. There are significant missed opportunities for expanding the learning environments, and students have little control over the direction of their learning.	Students have opportunities to take their learning in exciting directions, even when initially unintended. *Everyone* can and is expected to learn—the teacher doesn't always have to be the "expert." The leveraging of learning partnerships and technologies expand and enable environments that deepen outcomes.	All learners have a sense of belonging, are supported to succeed, and are connected to their learning, their learning environments, and their learning partners. They lead their learning and pursue learning goals in personally and culturally relevant ways and in varied natural and built environments most suited to the learning intentions. Student outcomes and identities drive the learning.	Learning environments are partners in learning—they directly contribute to deeper learning outcomes and support learners to contribute back. All learners and learning are celebrated, and every student succeeds in a range of interactive, varied environments that support deep connections between learners and learning partners, purposes, modes, and spaces.

(Continued)

Figure 5.7 • (Continued)

Dimension	Substantially off Track	Getting Started	Looking Promising	Well on Track	Geared for Success
Technology	Learning partners are concerned more with *what* and *that* technology is incorporated than with *how* it might directly deepen outcomes. Technology fails to enable, enhance, accelerate, connect, or share learning or to expand learning environments and opportunities. It's "fit into" the learning, not matched to learners' needs or leveraged to make a real difference.	Close consideration is paid to when, what, and why technology is incorporated, and it enables learning that otherwise wouldn't take place. However, it may not be seamlessly integrated into the experience or may fail to take learning and its application to new, deeper environments. Students *use* technology but aren't supported to *drive* its use in a meaningful, self-directed way.	There's evidence that the use of technology directly deepens learner outcomes. Digital learning environments connect learning partners and enable and enhance learning, and students display fluency in their use of the tools. There is, however, a heavier focus on incorporating technology than on identifying what's needed at what times and leveraging it to accelerate learning.	Learning partners know what specific tools are needed at what specific times to enable, enhance, or accelerate intended outcomes—and also when digital or other technologies *aren't* needed. Students are supported to be technology experts, to drive the identification and use of digital tools, and to use them to take their learning in meaningful, relevant directions and to greater depths.	Digital and other technologies are seamlessly integrated throughout the inquiry process in partnership with learners and in the direct development of deeper learning outcomes. They connect learners, provide access to learning locally and globally, communicate learning, and are used, improved, or developed to make a difference in the lives of others and the world.
Inquiry	The experience reflects limited, incomplete, or incoherent attention to the inquiry process. It doesn't connect to or build on prior learning, leverage timely and relevant instructional practices, or develop or provide the evidence required to measure learning. Learning is aimed at acquisition, not at co-inquiring in ways that directly deepen learning and that support students to *use* their learning to contribute back.	The experience isn't simply an *assessment* but a "full-blown," connected, and intentionally designed *inquiry*. While it connects to learners' needs and has a clearly identified intention, it is overly strict or structured, reflects a lack of understanding about what practices or assessments develop or evidence what outcomes, or fails to embed co-design, self-assessment, or clear curriculum links.	The inquiry is "purpose built" to develop and evidence intended outcomes. It connects to learners' interests and prior and future learning, reflecting a clear line of sight between practices and their effects. Ongoing reflection and flexible learning design and implementation support the identification and pursuit of new "wonderings" or goals, pointing to valuable opportunities for further assessment.	Learning partners' critical, creative, cross-curricular, reflective, and analytical thinking are deepened in a fluid, connected, and student-driven inquiry process. Clear curriculum links frame the learning, and each element of inquiry is leveraged as an opportunity to engage and assess students. Whether or not the inquiry embeds layered or "nested" assessment, it provides the evidence required to measure intended outcomes.	Students are partners in purposeful inquiry, collectively leveraging partnerships, environments, technologies, and each element of inquiry in the direct development, assessment, and measurement of meaningful and fulfilling learning. They direct the inquiry process toward greater self-understanding, knowledge, competency, and connection and then use it to contribute back.

Source: The Learner First, 2018

Figure 5.8 • **The Authentic Inquiry Guides and the Learning Experience Rubric**

Appendix E	*Student Inquiry Guides*	three inquiry guides that can be used alongside the Learning Progressions to support the assessment, measurement, and design (respectively) of student learning
Appendix F	*Professional Inquiry Guides*	three inquiry guides that can be used alongside the Capability Rubrics to support the assessment, measurement, and design (respectively) of professional learning
Appendix G	*Learning Experience Rubric*	a rubric that can be used within the inquiry process to measure the depth and effectiveness of a learning experience's embedded practices

Source: The Learner First, 2018

we're ultimately working toward—and they help ensure we never will, either. More important than any individual measure or other tool, you now know the characteristics of and process for developing them in your own school or your school system. *You have what you need to develop deeper learning tools.* To illustrate, let's turn to examples from Oakland Unified School District (OUSD) and Oklahoma City Public Schools (OKCPS) and their work to develop the measures their learning partners needed. (The first case comes from a personal interview with Young Whan Choi, Manager of Performance Assessments at OUSD. The other comes from The Learner First's implementation of the change team process in OKCPS.)

California's OUSD serves some 37,000 students, including 9,000 high school students across fourteen high schools. The district is 73 percent free and reduced-priced lunch, and some 90 percent of its students are students of color, with both numbers increasing at high school as compared to K–8 levels. Teachers came to Young Whan Choi (Manager of Performance Assessments, OUSD) and other district-level leaders with concerns about the equity of the senior project (now called the graduate capstone project). Teachers had varying expectations of and methods for measuring success, and learning partners wanted to create a more high-quality experience for their high school seniors. Drawing from the district's "graduate profile," learning partners selected three attributes to focus on—*civic engagement, academic proficiency*, and *essential communication*—and identified a core competency tied to each: field research (civic engagement), research writing (academic proficiency), and oral presentation (essential communication). Building on learning from throughout the district and from teachers who had worked with measurement rubrics in the past, the district broke each competency into a number of dimensions ("scoring domains"), described learning at four levels of a fluid progression, and used those descriptions to create measures for each competency (the oral presentation measure is included, in part, in Figure 5.9 and in full in Appendix H).

Figure 5.9 • **Oakland Unified School District's Oral Presentation Measure**

Scoring Domain	No Score	Emerging	E/D	Developing	D/P	Proficient	P/A	Advanced
MULTIPLE PERSPECTIVES *What is the evidence that the student considers other perspectives?*	Element not yet present	Mentions questions or alternative interpretations		Acknowledges and briefly responds to questions or alternative interpretations when appropriate		Acknowledges and responds to questions or alternative interpretations when appropriate		Acknowledges and responds to questions or alternative interpretations to explore the complexity of the topic when appropriate
EVIDENCE AND ANALYSIS *What is the evidence that the student can support an argument with relevant evidence?*	Element not yet present	Restates or refers to facts, experience, or research to support the argument		Summarizes relevant facts, experience, and/or research to support the argument		Elaborates on sufficient and relevant facts, experiences, and research to support the argument		Elaborates on extensive and relevant facts, experience, and research; synthesizes ideas from multiple sources to support the argument

Source: Oakland Unified School District, modified from the Stanford Center for Assessment, Learning & Equity (SCALE) © 2012

OUSD designed professional learning around developing a shared language and understanding of each measure, calibrating for quality, and revising the measures as necessary. The district is currently working to identify examples of student projects at each level of the measures' progressions, to generate discussion and improve inter-rater reliability. Although they were designed with the senior capstone project in mind, they have begun to be adopted at prerequisite high-school grade levels as well, in some cases with a focus on certain dimensions at each grade level to ensure that students are fully prepared for the project by the end of their senior year. OUSD continues to develop its measures, but they've already proved to be powerful tools for increasing communication and collaboration among learning partners and for deepening assessment practice.

In the beginning . . . we had a small number of teams, three or four, that took on the rubric, but then as we kept using it and kept designing our professional development around it, more and more teachers saw the value of adopting it. . . . It was very much on an opt-in basis, and I think over time there was enough momentum from the core group and people saw the value of the collaborative space. It's not about the compliance; . . . if you're using the rubrics, that means you can be in community and collaboration with others as opposed to working in isolation, and . . . really what I'm striving to do for our teachers and school sites is [to] get them into more collaborative practice. . . . [A]dopting the common rubrics . . . allowed us to really engage with one another in a more meaningful way.

I always try to caution our teachers into not thinking that the rubrics are the end goal; that just because you understand the rubric really well and then, therefore, are better able to communicate what's in the rubric to students, if you as a teacher aren't changing what's happening in the classroom so that students are more engaged, more motivated, [and] better supported, then you can talk all you want about "This is where we want you to be," but ultimately it's about changing the experience for students so they can get there. The professional development leads from a place of really understanding what we mean by "high quality," because once we're really clear about that goal, it's easier to support and understand what we're trying to support students to be able to do.

—**Young Whan Choi**, Manager of Performance Assessments,
Oakland Unified School District, United States

In OKCPS, district leadership introduced "The Four Pillars" as those which would help them reach a number of district-wide and community-wide goals:

1. Culturally responsive, rigorous teaching and learning
2. Strong relationships with families and communities

3. Effective teachers, leaders, and staff

4. Data-informed, needs-based resource allocation

Starting with these pillars, learning partners identified the overarching goal of *accelerated performance for underperforming groups* across one district-level and twelve school-level change teams. Using the change team process as a lever for understanding their system and identifying those learners who were least served and most in need of improvement ("focal students"), and with the goal of better developing and measuring students' learning outcomes, learning partners set the following three targets:

> *Target 1:* one hundred percent of our focal students enjoying reading and reading at grade level
>
> *Target 2:* one hundred percent of our focal students demonstrating competence in and application of grade-level math concepts
>
> *Target 3:* one hundred percent of our focal students thriving and succeeding in high school

Why 100 percent targets? Think back to Chapter 1's *assumption-shatterers*—the only acceptable mindset is 100 percent success. As we know, the best way to make any targets or outcomes a reality is to measure them. At OKCPS, learning progressions were designed to more meaningfully and intentionally track and measure students' progress toward *enjoying reading and reading at grade level, demonstrating competence in and application of grade-level math concepts*, and *thriving and succeeding in high school*, respectively (the measure for demonstrating competence in and application of grade-level math concepts is included, in part, in Figure 5.10, and all three measures are included in full in Appendix I).

Figure 5.10 • Demonstrating Competence in and Application of Grade-Level Math Concepts

Rating	Performance Picture (Description of Evidence)
Geared for Success	*All* of the following: Clearly achieving at or above standard in math for this point in the year (overall teacher judgment based on student coursework, in-class assessments, teacher observation, tests, conversations, interviews with students, and/or other relevant assessments). The learner is actively and usefully applying grade-level math concepts to everyday life, even outside the classroom (as reported or observed by parents, students, and others). The learner sees math as relevant and meaningful for his or her life, now and in the future (as evidenced by surveys, coursework, and/or other relevant assessments).

Source: The Learner First, 2018

CHAPTER 5

These measures are designed so that any student who remains at the same level of progress over the course of a rating period demonstrates the standard level of progress in relation to the specified target. Any movement "up" the progression indicates *acceleration*—above standard progress for the given period of learning. Over the course of one academic year, the number of focal students succeeding as measured using the progressions rose from 29 percent to 48 percent and from 29 percent to 41 percent in relation to Targets 1 and 2, respectively. Students who had never before succeeded in reading and math *accelerated* their progress in a single school year, with the support of teachers and other learning partners who cared about them as individuals and embraced a deeper picture of success. As we emphasized in Chapter 1, focusing on the least-served learners creates shifts that benefit everyone, and it was evident in this case. Teachers' capacity for understanding their learners and their needs extended outside their group of focal students to accelerate another 20 percent of learners further up the progressions as well.

Even when we frame success within traditional curriculum areas such as reading and math, *AMMA is just as important.* A test score alone won't tell us whether a student is truly succeeding in reading, math, or any other subject area—we have to develop an understanding of what success really looks like and then find a way to make sure all the evidence comes together to inform a complete picture of performance. It's only when we've informed an authentic understanding of a student's progress toward each deeper learning outcome that we've informed an authentic understanding of that student's success. As evident in the progression, when learning partners at OKCPS envisioned and described what it really means to be thriving and succeeding in high school, they weren't only looking at whether a student was on track for graduation. That's one important indicator of success, but students' self-understanding, competency, and connections with others are equally important as on-time graduation in developing their capacity to contribute back—in other words, in supporting students to thrive and succeed both in high school and beyond.

Putting Depth Into Practice

Reflect

Reflect on the cases from OUSD and OKCPS and those districts' approaches to measuring the outcomes they value. Have you or others in your school or your school system engaged in a similar process of development as described throughout this chapter? What would it look like for a student to be thriving and succeeding in your school or in your schools, or in any particular subject area? What are some specific ways that your schools or classes can better reflect a complete picture of success, both at the whole-school level and in any particular subject area?

(Continued)

(Continued)

For Your Consideration . . .

It's likely that at least some of the concepts behind the tools we're discussing and some of what they ask you to do aren't entirely familiar. However, you're an educator—*you deal with the unfamiliar every single day*. Think about your prior experiences learning new standards or curriculums or taking on new frameworks or processes. You've already learned a great deal to further your own and your learners' outcomes, and you're capable of learning a great deal more. And although it's true that change can be hard, we're confident that the changes we're asking you to make, *which you've already begun*, will be easier and feel more purposeful than any previous changes in your practice. The reason behind our faith is simple: while the standards or frameworks you're working with now may not be exceedingly energizing or aligned with what you want for your learners, *deeper learning is*.

Right now, you may not need to develop your own measures and other tools—the tools in this book (and any others that are available) may be enough for you to get deeper learning going. Use the tools presented here to bring deeper learning to life, measure your own and your learners' progress, and respond to—better yet, *anticipate* and *better*—whatever changes are in store for your learners and the world. Simply put, education is lagging behind human and global advancement. Measures of deeper learning will support us not only to catch up to these advancements but also to get ahead of and deepen them. That's the power of putting our learners at the center of everything we do, and it's the power of learning partners working collectively to accelerate students' journeys toward meaning and fulfillment.

We've been through the frames of engagement and development, and now we're ready to establish the clarity so essential to collective work with deeper learning and to use of its tools. Now that you have your comprehensive set of measures and tools, you're ready to develop a greater proficiency in their language, align their priorities and your system's, and increase your capacity to use them.

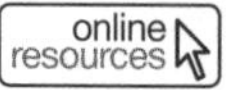

Access the appendices at
resources.corwin.com/MeasuringHumanReturn

Chapter 6

FINDING CLARITY IN DEPTH

Riding the Wave

We're not going to try to downplay the magnitude of the shift toward deeper learning. What we're describing, and what all educators will be charged with describing and embedding in our systems, represents a "sea change" that spans every corner of our systems and questions our very ways of doing and being. The idiom is an especially fitting one—everything we strive for in the name of deeper learning can be framed as a movement from surface to deep. For this journey to work for *all* learning partners, we have to take the time to slow down and dive deeply into what it is, why it's important, and how to bring it to life.

Think back to Chapter 2's discussion of the capability to lead for deep and sustainable change; and especially to the role of leaders in developing a shared understanding of deeper learning and its underlying concepts. We noted the importance of aligning deeper learning, the curriculum, and other frameworks and processes already in place within our schools and districts. Your initial engagement of learning partners has given you the foundational understanding required to move forward. Now, you're ready to establish the *clarity* that's needed to bring the deepest levels of learning to life.

Deeper learning takes patience. If you take the time to be deliberate, go deeper, and develop a shared understanding of your collective purpose and its importance, your work will be remarkably more meaningful—and less frustrating. You'll find that, despite the breadth of the transformation required, *deeper learning comes naturally*. It's what teachers and other leaders have always wanted to make possible for every learner. Going forward, you'll have the tools, language, and processes in place to enable it.

> [Deeper learning is] like a kind of relief—something [learning partners] have been waiting for for so long. Now their ideas have a name, a structure, and it's not very tight. It gives them space for their own development *and* is giving them direction.
>
> —**Marlou van Beek**, General Director of Turning Learning, Amsterdam, Netherlands

As we've discussed, establishing clarity in your school or your school system involves using measures and other tools to inform the breadth of professional and student learning. We'll focus on how clarity informs two additional processes here: *language development* and *system alignment.*

Language Development

Language is written all over depth. To "read" it, look no further than the deeper learning outcomes—language is closely tied to our cultures and identities, it facilitates the development and communication of knowledge, it works in partnership with competencies to add meaning to our actions, and it connects us in a variety of forms to people of all cultures and walks of life. Without it, we'd have no way of knowing what anybody *means.*

Imagine learning language to describe something you've felt and thought about deeply but been unable to quite put your finger on. That's the power of deeper learning measures—they give us the language we need to talk about the outcomes we want for our learners and how to develop them. As discussed, since we're talking about not only outcomes, but also the people who develop them and the ways they develop, the language of deeper learning—or the language of *depth*—is characterized by three primary features: *progression*, *formation*, and, ultimately, *humanity*, in that it moves beyond static and unchanging descriptions to capture our human capacity for continuous growth, improvement, and contribution—or *return*. These measures are professional learning tools in their own right and must always be considered in that light. They're intended not simply for measuring and *recording* growth but for *facilitating* your and your learners' progress as well. If a measure or other tool is truly designed for deeper learning, its language will make this readily visible.

We've already spent a significant amount of time going over the language of the tools. Within the engagement frame (Chapter 4), we broke down the language of learning partners' descriptions of what matters for learners, and we had you engage in a number of reflections and other formative activities to unpack this language for every measure and other tool. You won't be able to use the tools to their full potential until you understand what they're made of and what they mean. Fortunately, they're made up of the very concepts essential for deeper learning and practice, ensuring that you and your learning partners will develop not only a shared language but also a real, collective understanding of the elements of deeper learning and their components. When we talk about a comprehensive *system* of measurement, we're talking about a set of tools relating to the development and measurement of outcomes, capabilities, and practice. The very tools that allow you to measure what matters—whether that be deeper learning outcomes, system capabilities, or inquiry and other practice—are those that will build your learning partners' capacity to develop it. For this reason, if professional learning is truly centered on your learners, your professional learning processes will be built around your measures, as we've seen in the cases of OUSD and BESD, with a focus on understanding deeper learning tools and the opportunities they support us to reveal and respond to. In addition, having a shared language and understanding of depth is important not only for building professionals' capacity but for spreading clarity to other learning partners both inside and outside of our school systems as well.

A Recipe for Return: Models of Practice From BESD

Shared Language, Collective Purpose

> If a culture in which educators and students trust and respect one another and feel responsible for each other's success as learners is established, and teachers function as professionals in a collaborative community, then teachers can design or adapt learning experiences that are meaningful to students, which will lead students to regularly engage in acquiring and applying knowledge and skills through the deliberate practice of Deeper Learning outcomes. This will result in students leaving school with the knowledge of how, why, and when to apply content knowledge and a set of non-cognitive skills to answer questions and solve problems related to the challenges of college, career, and life.
>
> —**Burlington-Edison School District** Theory of Action

> If we don't change, we're kidding ourselves. [At the same time,] we have to be clear about what the change is that we're going to embark upon in order to expect a different outcome.
>
> —**Bryan Jones, EdD**, Director of Equity and Assessment, Burlington-Edison School District, United States

Every individual, school, district, or wider system has a unique road to deeper learning. Our paths are always intertwined and connected, but no two journeys are the same. When working toward collective outcomes, everyone involved is responsible for determining how deeper learning will look, feel, and *sound* in their own context. *Your* what, why, and how of deeper learning should be those that best speak to your unique set of learning partners, meaning that your theory of action, starting point, professional learning focuses, and even definition of deeper learning may not match up with those in other schools. What matters is that your actions, purpose, and meaning be consistent with self-understanding, knowledge, competency, connection, and the contribution that results. If they are, then you'll all be speaking the same language.

Figure 6.1 • BESD's "Deeper Learning" Community Flier

BURLINGTON-EDISON SCHOOL DISTRICT

Deeper Learning

Deeper Learning for Lifelong Success

Students need to be able to successfully navigate a rapidly changing world, participate in a complex and increasingly diverse democracy, and engage fully in the ever-evolving 21st century workplace. Students must be able to communicate their ideas effectively, think creatively, work collaboratively to solve problems, and manage their own learning. They need to develop dispositions—or mindsets—that empower them to confront new challenges, take initiative, and persevere through difficulties and setbacks.

This combination of (1) deep understanding of core academic content, (2) the development of core competencies, and (3) the ability to transfer that skill and understanding to novel problems and situations prepares each student to be a transforming influence in the world.

iStock/MachineHeadz

iStock/kali9

Shifting the Learning

When educators and students trust and respect one another and feel responsible for each other's success as learners, and when teachers function as professionals in a collaborative community, then they can design learning experiences that are meaningful to students. These experiences will lead students to regularly engage in acquiring and applying knowledge and skills through the deliberate practice of Deeper Learning outcomes. This will result in students leaving school with the knowledge of how, why, and when to apply content knowledge and a set of non-cognitive skills to answer questions and solve problems related to the challenges of college, career, and life.

Source: Burlington-Edison School District; photos updated from original publication

"All" means *all*. As you know, learners are at the center of deeper learning, and families and communities take on equally meaningful roles in the process. For that reason, you should look to engage them with deeper learning not only in practice but in name, too. In BESD, students know the outcomes they're working toward, display them on walls, assess their own progress, and share their learning with peers, parents, and the community. The home page of the district's

BURLINGTON-EDISON SCHOOL DISTRICT

Deeper Learning

iStock/PeopleImages

Each Student
A program of deeper learning seeks to provide each student with the skill set necessary to excel in a complex world. The deeper learning outcomes of collaboration, creativity, critical thinking, citizenship, character, and communication are equal to, and a catalyst for, mastering academic content.

Leveraging Teacher Capacity
Deeper learning supports teachers in being opportunistic in support of each child. The goal is to leverage the professional capacities of teachers working collaboratively to design and deliver deep, meaningful learning experiences to all students. Support for teachers is transformed by providing regular professional learning and collaboration, peer partnerships with consultant teachers who have developing expertise, and dynamic resources. Deep learning supports teachers as developing leaders and leaders as lifelong learners. Deeper learning must also leverage the knowledge, expertise, and resources of the entire community in order for staff and students to succeed.

"Our mission is to educate each student for life-long success."

iStock/skynesher

website describes "The Road to Deeper Learning" and invites visitors to scroll through the 6Cs and their definitions. Its theory of action comes to life in a community flier that describes deeper learning and the district's engagement (Figure 6.1). Remember that the deeper learning outcomes are global outcomes. They must extend beyond school walls.

Vesa Äyräs, a school principal and educational leader in Finland, described the country's "hype" around deeper learning, saying that the schools not yet engaged in deeper learning were excited by the prospect and noted that the schools that were actively engaged were "speaking [their] own language." The goal is to spread that language throughout school systems and globally so that the language of deeper learning becomes common language, and its outcomes common, too. Students, educators, and other learning partners all over the world already speak the student-centered, humanity-driven language of depth, and they're making a real difference in their school systems and communities. They're talking about the learning outcomes that actually matter and measuring them in a way that develops them. It's amazing what the capacity to *talk* about something can do to help bring it to life.

Putting Depth Into Practice

Activity 6.1: Learn the Language of Depth

Previous activities have taken you into the meaning of the tools and what they're designed to accomplish. Let's go deeper still, with an even sharper focus on language and its power to connect learning partners and build capacity. Within the measures and other tools, pick out and write down specific language that's new, challenging, or exciting or that you otherwise see as critically important to the use of the tool. As before, you may want to engage in this activity using a single tool or even a single dimension, with the knowledge that you can apply this same process at any time to deepen your understanding of the other tools. You can't learn a language overnight, after all.

Establishing System Alignment

Because what's important in your own system won't match exactly with that in any other system, wider school systems won't be able to explicitly cater to the particulars of your goals. For this reason, no matter your alignment with the wider system, you'll have to ensure some degree of alignment between what matters to you and how your system's expectations are written. Depending on how closely they're already aligned, this might require a good deal of your thought, as well as your time. The excitement around deeper learning makes it difficult to slow down in the early going, but trying to implement deeper learning without clarity is like trying to run a marathon at full sprint—and on an empty stomach. Mindful preparation and a steady jog off the starting block will ensure you won't have to slow to a walk later on.

Remember that alignment is possible—and critical—at whatever system level you're working. As an example, let's examine this process at the level of an individual school. Assume that the students, teachers, leaders, and other learning partners have collectively identified what matters, possess the tools to measure and develop it, have used those tools to form a shared language and understanding, and know how it all fits together systemically. But the school still operates within a wider school system, and there are national, state, and local curriculum goals and standards that need to be met. Where does deeper learning fit in with all that? At its best, deeper learning not only *fits in*; it *seeps into*, connects with, and deepens it all. It isn't an add-on but a lens over everything you do and stand for.

Curriculum and other standards serve as valuable examples when we consider the process of alignment. Schools are expected to follow the curriculum and ensure that students meet its standards, and there's not a lot of wiggle room in terms of *what* (the content) students are expected to learn. The "wiggle" is in the *how*—how can you support your students to learn what's required in ways that also support them to develop the other outcomes that matter? Just because there are elements of self-understanding, knowledge, competency, and connection that aren't well represented in the curriculum doesn't mean your learners can't develop them, and it doesn't mean your schools can't facilitate that development. If you want the curriculum to *work* for your learners, you have to align it with what you *want* for your learners.

A Recipe for Return: Models of Practice From BESD

Enhancing Everything You Do

While the broader focuses (those often present in mission statements and district road maps or goals) of school systems find a ready-made home within self-understanding, competency, and connection, knowledge may be trickier to fit into the deeper learning framework. When it comes to the other outcomes, you have the help of the Learning Progressions, but, specifically with regard to its development in your schools and wider system, what do you do about *knowledge*? You still develop it—*just more deeply.*

After recognizing the value in finding the bigger ideas in the state and national standards rather than breaking the standards down into a checklist, BESD adopted a Concept-Based Curriculum and Instruction (CBCI) design framework based on the work of Dr. H. Lynn Erickson and Dr. Lois A. Lanning (Erickson, Lanning, & French, 2017). This model allows teachers to capture big ideas and design learning experiences with *conceptual understanding* as an instructional target. Teachers draw disciplinary concepts from the standards and craft the concepts into generalizations or big ideas that transcend time, place, and situation. This approach grounds the unit in standards while leaving space for equitable learning design capable of responding to the needs of diverse learners, levels of learning, and learning styles (Lanning & Brown, in press). That "space" proved a

Figure 6.2 • Generalizations Used in BESD to Ground and Deepen a First-Grade Social Studies Unit

What Do You Really Neeeeed?

Conceptual Lens: Choices

Social Studies—Grade 1

Generalizations

1. People's roles and responsibilities help accomplish tasks in their homes, communities, and schools.
2. The environment shapes the way families live.
3. Families make choices in order to meet their needs and wants.
4. People make informed choices by weighing the benefits and costs.
5. Maps and globes provide information about new and familiar places.

Source: Burlington-Edison School District

perfect place for deeper learning. By merging the CBCI with the deeper learning framework, the district gave life to its idea of an idea-centered and student-centered core curriculum—the standards provided the ideas, and deeper learning provided the central focus on the students and their needs. Figures 6.2 and 6.3 offer examples of how the generalizations can come together under a "conceptual lens" to provide a framework for deeper learning experiences.

Taking Figure 6.3 as an example, think about how this framework supports the embedding of deeper learning outcomes and how the elements of authentic practice might come together in the context of this unit to develop them. There are countless opportunities for students to

- think about and engage with what's important to them and to others;
- connect and collaborate with government representatives and other community members around relevant issues;
- study the impact of the media, economic causes and effects, and how to best write for or otherwise communicate with a range of audiences; and
- take action to solve issues of importance in their local and global communities.

Students may form partnerships and share their learning with the support of digital tools, design their own assessments ("solutions") and self-assess their progress toward deeper learning outcomes, and expand their learning environments to further an experience in which they're the true drivers of their own learning. All the while, in the specific context of social studies, students

- learn about what others have done and are doing to enact positive change,
- make connections between historical and current reform efforts, and
- use successes and setbacks to inform their own efforts to make a difference in their communities.

Figure 6.3 • Generalizations Used in BESD to Ground and Deepen a Seventh-Grade Social Studies Unit

If You Don't Like It, Change It!

Conceptual Lens: Reform and Responsibility

Social Studies—Grade 7

Generalizations

1. Engaged citizens analyze community problems, engage in discourse, and view issues through multiple perspectives.
2. Civic action drives reform of local, state, national, and global policy, practices, and institutions.
3. Consumers' economic choices drive companies to change practices.
4. People protest to signal dissent around a practice or policy and to attempt to bring about change.
5. Groups of people organize to gain collective power to secure and continually improve upon desired working conditions.
6. Media promotes civic discourse by creating connections between people, disseminating information, and calling for collective action.
7. Writers develop arguments to promote their cause, thinking, or choices and to encourage civic action.

Source: Burlington-Edison School District

Learning about what others have done for positive change doesn't have to be the final step, and your learners won't want it to be. Support them to use their learning to contribute back. For now, take some time to think about the generalizations framing both units (Figures 6.2 and 6.3), focusing on the potential for embedding deeper outcomes and practices. What might related learning experiences look like in your own context? Use the excerpts from BESD's Unit Design Template (Figure 6.4) to spark your imagination and frame your design.

Notice the focus of these tools on who each of your learners is, each of the elements of authentic practice, and how AMMA brings it all together in equitable learning experiences tied to what matters for students and the many ways they can demonstrate and further their learning. These are powerful tools no matter what standards you're expected to meet, because they aptly connect key curriculum content to learning that's—in the words of BESD—idea-centered *and* student-centered.

Figure 6.4 • Excerpts From the BESD Unit Design Template

Student-Centered Design

This section of the unit is developed based on the strengths, needs, and interests of your current classroom of students.

Cultures, Perspectives, Funds of Knowledge	Language Development
• Who are my students? • What perspectives/biases are present? • What skills, background knowledge, and understanding can my students bring to this unit? • How will you create a learning partnership with students and families?	• What languages are spoken in my classroom? • What are the language levels within my classroom? • What are the opportunities for translanguaging? • How will I provide intentional opportunities for receptive and productive language development? • How will I ensure that input (what students are hearing, reading, and seeing) will be comprehensible for all of my students?
Learning Environments	**Social-Emotional Learning**
How are you optimizing the learning environment for success? **Physical Space:** • In what ways will the learning environment support learning through inquiry? **Classroom Culture That Promotes:** • Opportunities for all students to flourish • Equity for all students • Social responsibility • Safety • Autonomy • Agency	How are you meeting where students are and helping students develop skills in these areas? • **Self-Management:** *Managing emotions and behaviors to achieve one's goals* • **Self-Awareness:** *Recognizing one's emotions and values as well as one's strengths and challenges* • **Social-Awareness:** *Showing understanding and empathy for others* • **Responsible Decision Making:** *Making ethical, constructive choices about personal and social behavior* • **Relationship Skills:** *Forming positive relationships, working in teams, dealing effectively with conflict*

Learning Partnerships

Learning Partnerships/Community Connections

How can we engage family and community partners to deepen understanding and bring relevance to the learning experiences?

Opportunities:

- For guest speakers? Family or community experts?
- To establish real-world connections and authentic opportunities for learning?
- For civic engagement and contributing back to the community?

Field Experiences

How can we provide opportunities for students to go into our community to deepen understanding and bring relevance to the learning experiences?

Opportunities:

- For common experiences?
- To establish real-world connections and authentic opportunities for learning?
- For civic engagement and contributing back to the community?
- To apply understanding in a relevant real-world context?

(Continued)

Figure 6.4 • (Continued)

Mini-Inquiry: Exploring ______ (Concept 1) and ______ (Concept 2)

<table>
<tr><td colspan="5">Inquiry Into Generalization _____:</td><td></td></tr>
<tr><td colspan="3">Guiding Questions</td><td colspan="2">Guiding Questions: Global Competencies</td><td>Resources: Learning Partnerships and Field Experiences</td></tr>
<tr><td colspan="3"></td><td colspan="2"></td><td></td></tr>
<tr><td>Case Study</td><td colspan="4">Possible Learning Experiences</td><td>Resources</td></tr>
<tr><td rowspan="3"></td><td></td><td></td><td></td><td></td><td rowspan="3"></td></tr>
<tr><td></td><td></td><td></td><td></td></tr>
<tr><td></td><td></td><td></td><td></td></tr>
</table>

Mixed-Method Assessment *How am I going to gather a full range of evidence—qualitative and quantitative—that provides a holistic understanding of the learner?*	**Differentiation/Ensuring Equitable Access** *In what ways are the learning experiences providing varying entry points in which every student is able to experience progress and challenge?*

Source: Burlington-Edison School District

In BESD, an important lever for supporting teachers to make this shift in their unit and lesson planning and implementation are district-wide "consultant teachers."

We developed the role of a consultant teacher—an embedded teacher in each of our schools [who doesn't] have direct service responsibilities for students. Their job is to provide that follow-up professional learning support in the schools [and] in the classroom. . . . They're doing that on the ground, day-to-day capacity building for making deeper learning a reality. We have a theory that if you have a role, you have a learning community. Our consultant teachers are a learning community, and they support each other in their own capacity building.

—**K. C. Knudson**, Executive Director of Teaching and Learning, Burlington-Edison School District, United States

We're fortunate enough to have two consultant teachers [who] meet weekly with all the grade levels to talk about the work of deeper learning, [especially] unit planning, and that's been a huge lever in the work, having that check-in every single week. . . . Those two teachers [are] a part of the change team, because they're such good communicators of the work to everybody they work with each week. . . . [They've supported us with] lots of planning on how to create all of our learning opportunities here at Bay View and how to learn about mixed-method assessment.

—**Amy Reisner**, Principal, Bay View Elementary School, Burlington-Edison School District, United States

We started creating actual units that were based around different concepts, [and] from there we started to have more of a structure for unit development. When I meet with teachers, we look at . . . how the unit is laid out. We start with a generalization that teachers created . . . and then we try to design lessons that go with the generalization. We [also] share ideas with teachers: "Oh, well, *this* worked in *first* grade," [when we] might be [working with] a fifth-grade class. I also volunteer to come in and model things, so I'll come in and either team-teach with someone or model a lesson or activity.

—**Erica Tolf**, Consultant Teacher, Bay View Elementary School, Burlington-Edison School District, United States

We've talked about the importance of change teams in establishing clarity around and helping to lead your work with deeper learning. As the preceding quotations show, there's incredible value in purposing or repurposing specific roles around building and sustaining teachers' capacity to engage with their students in learning experiences that bring deeper outcomes to life. And even without a consultant teacher or similar role, if you have a change team, *you have a learning community*.

CHAPTER 6

As illustrated by the case of BESD, alignment between deeper learning and existing standards results in learning experiences that link to students' interests and needs and deepen their outcomes. Deeper learning doesn't mean you can't teach the curriculum. Rather, deeper learning supports you to engage with the curriculum more deeply, developing important outcomes that may *not* be explicitly included in its text in conjunction with those outcomes that *are*. Curriculum provides the content, and deeper learning provides the framework, for embedding the breadth of desired outcomes.

Putting Depth Into Practice

Activity 6.2: Create Alignment

Think about your own classroom, school, district, or wider system in relation to deeper learning, focusing on the curriculum and other standards and expectations. Knowing what you know now, how well is the system aligned with the development and measurement of deeper learning outcomes? Where are there significant gaps or points of misalignment? Drawing from identified gaps or points of misalignment, and from the steps that learning partners have taken to establish alignment in BESD, formulate what steps you can take right now to create better alignment at your level of the school system or any other. Remember that deeper learning isn't an add-on. Frame your alignment around how deeper learning can enhance what you're already doing, as well as how it can enable you to do what you want to do.

Reflect

Before we dive headfirst into full-on inquiry, take one final opportunity to slow down, look back, and act on what you've learned so far. Think about where you were and where you are now in relation to developing all the outcomes that matter for your learners. What have you learned? What have you already done to bring yourself, your learners, and anyone else closer to deeper learning, and what can you do now? What do you still need in order to be able to use deeper learning measures and other tools most effectively?

Activity 6.3: Evidence Matching

Refer to the *environmental* dimension of the Connection progression (Appendix D.2). What does it ask you to find evidence of? Write down the questions you'd need to ask your learners or otherwise answer in order to develop a complete picture of their progress on that dimension. What do you already know about individual learners' levels of learning, and how did you gather that evidence? How might you, your learners, or other learning partners *tell*, *show*, *demonstrate*, or further *develop* the additional learning specific to this dimension? If it's helpful, repeat this process for each or any of the other dimensions across the three Learning Progressions.

Once you know what evidence you need, you just have to find a way to gather it, further developing learners' outcomes in the process. Enter *inquiry*, the focus of Part III.

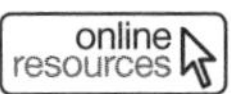

Access the appendices at
resources.corwin.com/MeasuringHumanReturn

Final Reflections on Part II

Throughout this book, we've emphasized the importance of slowing down and celebrating your own and your learners' progress every step of the way, and now is a great time to do so. After getting to know your system and its capabilities in Part I, you've deepened your capacity to *improve* your system by engaging learning partners around what's important, developing the tools to measure it all, and building clarity around the language, intent, and framework of deeper learning and its alignment to existing frameworks, standards, and expectations. Together, the frames of *engagement* (Chapter 4), *development* (Chapter 5), and *clarity* (this chapter) will get the wheels turning and lay the foundation for action.

That's not to say these frames aren't action-packed in their own right, and their importance in establishing and sustaining deeper learning can't be understated. But leveraging the inquiry process in the direct development of both student and professional learning will be, in many ways, a culmination. It'll focus everything you've learned so far within a constant process of continuous improvement and support you to develop and measure the impact of your up-front and ongoing efforts to deepen outcomes for all. As mentioned at the end of Chapter 3, you've been using inquiry all along. Now, you're in a position to do so at wider and deeper levels, using the clarity and understanding you've established to fully inform the use of your measures in a way that enables the outcomes that matter.

You're well on your way to depth. Next, let's move to the frame of inquiry—to the process and practices that take learning deeper—and what it actually looks like in schools, in communities, and in the lives of your learners.

Part III

AUTHENTIC INQUIRY PRACTICE

Chapter 7

PROFESSIONAL LEARNING AND INQUIRY

Drilling Down Into Inquiry

By now, inquiry is a process that needs no introduction—its reputation precedes it. You're familiar with its crowd, and you've seen it around the other elements of deeper learning and their individual components. But if inquiry operates interdependently and never in isolation, why is it one of the five frames of measurement? We emphasized from the outset of this book that there aren't any "steps" for setting up and sustaining this overall measurement framework. Instead, there are "frames" that provide ways of continuously thinking about and adding depth to the full breadth of activity in your school system. We noted that these frames are *continuous*, and they're also deeply *connected*. The descriptions below illustrate how.

- *Engagement*. All learning partners are actively engaged in identifying and describing the outcomes that matter, developing measures and other deeper learning tools, establishing clarity and building deeper learning capacity, every element of inquiry, and working constantly toward greater depth. Engagement (and each other frame) isn't a one-off effort—it's never-ending.
- *Development*. Ongoing engagement and inquiries support you to develop tools, examine their effectiveness, and then fill gaps and refine or add to them as necessary. New tools and new learning require that you share and establish clarity around that learning system-wide, driven by the knowledge that you can always go deeper. The world changes with the learners within it—how can your development not only keep up with these changes but also further support that progress?
- *Clarity.* Because inquiry supports you to add depth to your systems and other processes through ongoing learning and development, your knowledge and understanding are never static. Learning partners have to be supported to find clarity around

new learning, as well as to develop that learning. If clarity once is clarity always, you're not progressing in the ways you need to be.

- *Inquiry.* All *action* or *movement* within a deeper learning system has to be true to the process of inquiry. If you want something to improve, you design and implement "assessments" (any way of collecting evidence) that'll support you to measure where you're at, learn from it, and then make the necessary change. Inquiry facilitates the processes of engagement and development, the embedding of clarity, and the pursuit of greater depth. Don't assume—*inquire.*
- *Depth.* In a deeper learning system, depth is the North Star. It's your guiding light—you have to frame everything, at all times, in relation to depth. It's the collective focus of and the reason for each of the processes above. And there's a reason for that: depth reflects learners and their humanity. A system that has achieved depth supports all learners to achieve it—not just now but throughout their lives.

Given this level of continuity and connectedness, it's impossible to think (or write) about one of the frames as isolated from any other. Even when you're just beginning to set up a system of measurement, it's important to establish (*ahem*) clarity around each of its frames and how to understand them in relation to one another. Since each informs the others, a sound understanding of and capacity in one of these frames means a sound understanding of and capacity in them all. This connection has been visible throughout our discussion of measurement and largely in relation to the individual elements of inquiry.

Inquiry is a beautiful thing. Even when we aren't talking about it in *direct* relation to students and their outcomes, it's supporting their development by focusing all our activity on their fulfillment and success. The next chapters will increase your clarity around each of the individual processes that make up inquiry, which we've touched on already. By now, you know what goes into developing deeper learning measures and other tools, and you've already used them for a variety of meaningful purposes, including (a) building a shared language and understanding, (b) forming alignment between deeper learning and your system, and, in Chapter 2, even (c) *measuring* your system's current capabilities and levels of deeper learning development—measures are versatile tools. Although their value extends well beyond measuring and developing *students'* learning, that's what they're ultimately designed to do, and it's what you're prepared to do now in Part III. In the pages to come, you'll apply everything you've learned and will learn to better develop and measure deeper learning outcomes and enablers and bring them to life at every level of your system. Following Activity 7.1, we'll start by examining inquiry through the lens of authentic assessment.

Putting Depth Into Practice

Activity 7.1: Inquiry Mapping

Deeper learning requires constant improvement. For that reason, assessment, design, implementation, measurement, and reflection and change may occur together and at any time in the learning process. In this way, similar to the five frames of measurement as a whole, the inquiry process is *fluid*—not *linear*, or even *cyclical*—in that the individual processes may be required and carried out simultaneously, at any time, and in any order. What you *do* is inquiry—your entire range of activity can be understood as an ongoing, overlapping series of inquiries within inquires. To help illustrate this concept, this activity asks you to develop an "inquiry map" that frames any number of your current activities (inquiries) and their desired outcomes in relation to one another.

To kick off the process, it might help to start at the level of a single academic year. Each year is an inquiry, complete with unique goals, learning experiences, and learners. (Why is a year an inquiry? It's a vehicle for assessment, design, implementation, measurement, and reflection and change.) Those goals are the overarching outcomes toward which all your activity aspires. Collectively, students' learning experiences, along with any professional assessments, are designed to develop those outcomes. They're inquiries within the wider, yearlong inquiry. Where do they fit in relation to one another, and do they combine to develop the full range of desired outcomes? If they don't, that's okay at this stage—just remember that, like everything else you've designed, created, or measured over the course of your reading, your inquiry map should be dynamic. It's an effective planning tool, but, rather than be static, it should change over the course of the academic year to respond to your learners, anticipate their needs, and ensure the development of intended outcomes. You can always start bigger (e.g., multiple years) or smaller (e.g., a single learning experience or professional assessment). What's important is that you understand your activity as interconnected inquiries and that you be designing, implementing, assessing, measuring, and reflecting and changing at every step of the way.

At this particular step of the way, *reflect* on what's been presented earlier, *design* an inquiry map based on available *assessment* evidence, use the elements of your map to *measure* its comprehensiveness and effectiveness in relation to desired goals, and *change* as necessary, reflecting those changes in your inquiry maps, your learners' outcomes, and the world.

Making Sense of Assessment Evidence

In the sense of the word most suited to deeper learning, "inquiry" can be thought of as an investigation. The cornerstone of any successful investigation is *evidence*. It's important not just for the assessment of student learning, but for all assessment practice at any level of the system. Fortunately, evidence is everywhere. You just have to know how to find it.

Whatever tools you use (e.g., the Learning Progressions, the Capability Rubrics, or the Authentic Inquiry Guides) must reflect everything you've identified as important in your system's ongoing engagement process. The deeper learning outcomes and enablers are global and comprehensive, meaning that whatever your learning partners identify has a home within these tools and their dimensions. While the deeper learning outcomes aren't unique to your system, remember that *the learners* you're measuring are unique, down to every last one. Since no two students are the same, and since different learners demonstrate deeper learning outcomes in different ways, the *evidence* that informs the measurement of their outcomes will be different in every system, too. The same goes for system capabilities and professional inquiries—your learners make your system what it is, and how you operate within it will vary to the extent that your learners' identities, interests, and needs do the same.

To further illustrate the relationship between outcomes and evidence, think about the contextual differences spanning the United States. Starting at the top, every state has different cultures, different natural and built environments, different standards and curriculums, and any number of nuances in relation to their inhabitants' overall ways of doing and being in the world. These circumstances shape the way we engage in education, influencing everything from statewide standardized assessment to personalized assessment of individual students. Depending on who and where you and your students are, your students evidence learning in any number of ways. What matters is that you support them to evidence their learning in the ways that reflect their humanity—who they are, what they know and can do, how they connect with others and the world, and how they contribute back. When learners' humanity is reflected in the evidence you gather, you're supporting them to reflect their learning in the lives of others and the world. When you assess in ways that let learners and their outcomes shine, you're supporting them to contribute back.

Authentic mixed-method assessment (AMMA) has to be understood both in relation to student learning (outcomes) and in relation to professional learning (capabilities and practice). We need to design and implement assessments that develop outcomes *and* enablers and then synthesize assessment evidence to measure them. Assessment may be a "holy grail" (see Chapter 2), but, at the same time, it's one element of a wider inquiry process. It's nonexistent without design and implementation, static without reflection and change, and limited in scope if it's not leveraged in the measurement of learning. These elements are truly meaningful only in a collective process. Figure 7.1 breaks down their relationship in yet another way.

Figure 7.1 • Breaking Down the Relationship Between the Elements of the Inquiry Process

1. Measures describe the outcomes and the enablers that we want to develop and measure.
2. The development of those outcomes and enablers can be measured only with assessment evidence that directly informs our use of the measures.
3. Therefore, we have to design and implement assessments that collectively capture the complete picture of progress in direct relation to what we're trying to measure, reflecting on and changing our practice as necessary to fill out the picture.

Source: The Learner First, 2018

Assessments should be designed to tell us exactly what we want to know. Collectively leveraging learning partnerships, environments, technology, and the individual elements of inquiry enables a wealth of opportunities to develop and evidence intended learning. Before we explain how to use your measures and other tools to bring authentic assessments to life, let's consider the role and power of AMMA in relation to some other foundational measurement concepts, starting with making individual and overall ratings.

Think back to your measurement of your system's capabilities and deeper learning development in Part I. You used the rubrics to first determine a *dimension rating* for each of the rubrics' dimensions and then to determine an *overall rating* across dimensions. To determine the level of evidence currently demonstrated by students, systems, or any other focus of measurement is to determine a *rating* of their progress. Let's use the Leading for Deep and Sustainable Change Capability Rubric (Appendix A.4) as an example. The rubric has four dimensions:

- ✓ Focusing every action and decision through the lens of the least-served learners
- ✓ Prioritizing what needs to change and collaboratively designing solutions
- ✓ Leading change all the way through to measured, sustainable outcomes
- ✓ Fostering and supporting student, teacher, system, parent, and community leaders

Using the complete range of evidence gathered from throughout your system, you determine a rating for each of these dimensions, or at least those that you're focusing on. Based on these dimension ratings, you determine an overall rating of your development of the capability as a whole. Given the diversity of what's required to successfully develop these capabilities throughout a system, or to develop an outcome like self-understanding, connection, or collaboration, it's not uncommon for dimension ratings to vary, even significantly, within a single measure. And that's okay—it demonstrates areas in which you need to grow and on which to focus your professional learning or instructional efforts. Understandably, it also increases the complexity of determining an overall rating. The same is true for determining dimension ratings: when the evidence informing a single dimension rating varies, how can we go about determining a rating?

Whether you're determining an overall rating based on your dimension ratings and their underlying evidence, or determining a single dimension rating based on the range of available assessment evidence, it's important that you take a structured and consistent approach to the synthesis of that evidence and your subsequent measurement. The CORE approach (Figure 7.2) describes this process of synthesis and decision.

Figure 7.2 • The CORE Approach for Synthesizing Evidence to Make an Overall Judgment

C	Center of gravity	Start by looking at where the "center of gravity" is for the points of evidence within your gathered *performance picture*. Taken together, what does the evidence tell you?
O	Outlying ratings	Look for any extreme differences within the performance picture. Are there ratings or pieces of evidence that indicate progress to a point further than or not as far as the center of gravity? Look at the strength of your evidence to determine how "gravitational" these ratings or evidence points really are. How far in their direction should they pull the overall rating? Note that strengths in one aspect of learning or development don't necessarily compensate for weaknesses in another.
R	Reflection and discussion	Step back and look at the overall picture of strengths and gaps for the measured element of deeper learning to come to an overall rating decision. Does this rating make sense and "add up," given the complete picture of performance provided by gathered evidence? If evidence reveals significant variations in performance, why do these variations exist? Might someone else come to a different rating? If you have the opportunity to synthesize evidence with other learning partners, explore the reasons behind any varying perspectives and decisions and refine your rating as necessary based on your collective knowledge and understanding.
E	Explanation and feedback	Identify the most important information and evidence to share with your learning partners. Determine how to best explain the performance picture and the reasoning behind overall decisions. Discuss strengths as well as areas for improvement, what you need to work on next, and how you can work on it together.

Source: The Learner First, 2018; adapted from New Zealand Qualifications Authority (NZQA), n.d., p. 9

Putting Depth Into Practice

Activity 7.2: Synthesize and Decide

The pieces of evidence in Figure 7.3 represent a learner's performance on a range of math-related assessments over the course of an academic year. Use the relevant Learning Progressions and the CORE approach described earlier in conjunction with the following performance indicators to indicate, rate, or otherwise describe the student's overall "performance picture." Then, drawing on what you know about the given indicators and relevant Learning Progressions, write a narrative that tells the story of this learner and her or his learning, referencing "evidence" about the learner collected from specific assessments and the full range of learning partners.

Figure 7.3 • Sample Ratings and Other Math-Related Evidence Points for a Single Learner

STAR Math:	Urgent Intervention Intervention On Watch At/Above Benchmark
School Math Test:	85%
In-Class Work and Homework Average:	70%
Participation:	Low
School Math Relevance Survey:	Seeing math as completely pointless Seeing math as mostly irrelevant Ambivalent about math Seeing math as somewhat relevant Seeing math as relevant
Identity Dimension (Self-Understanding):	Looking Promising
Conceptual Dimension (Connection):	Substantially off Track
Universal Dimension (Connection):	Well on Track
Overall Rating (Collaboration):	Well on Track

Source: The Learner First, 2018

CHAPTER 7

Reflect

In US educational systems, evidence labeled as "subjective" is often also labeled as "invalid" or "unreliable." Reflect on some of the potential reasons for this. What specific types or forms of evidence do you or might others see as invalid or unreliable, and why is or might that be the case? In principle, do you believe that using wide-ranging, varied pieces of evidence to arrive at an understanding of performance is better than using one or two? In what ways might evidence be a barrier to your work toward deeper learning, and how can you push through it? Reflect on your experience with the preceding activity and your initial confidence with regard to using the CORE approach to make overall judgments.

For Your Consideration . . .

One of the most basic and fundamental privileges of being a professional is being trusted to make the right decisions in accordance with a given responsibility. In the same way that it's the responsibility of a doctor to synthesize the full range of a patient's quantitative and qualitative medical evidence to come to an overall decision about health or treatment, or in the same way that it's the responsibility of a district superintendent to assess every aspect of the school system and its needs when determining a course of action, it's the responsibility of a teacher to determine individual learners' levels of development. You have to give other professionals space to make evidence-based professional judgments. When you do, the range of evidence you gather will say a whole lot more about who your learners really are and what they're really capable of than any single test or other assessment ever could.

Learning partners working to measure deeper learning have noted difficulties in determining ratings due to variation in development across classrooms or across schools. The CORE approach provides a process for determining ratings in these cases, but the challenge itself begs an interesting question—why the variation? No matter the measure at hand, it's critical that you examine any variations in performance or levels of development across school systems, schools, or learning partners. Performance always varies, but you have to be able to understand the reasons behind that variation and to begin that process by looking first at *yourself.* What are the reasons or conditions influencing varying performance, and how can they be addressed? As always, refer to the evidence.

When using the measures in this book to determine ratings, it helps to keep the following in mind:

1. The measures are designed to describe progress levels in relation to a target. The five-point **rating scale** gives you the precision you need to accurately determine how well your approaches are moving you or your learners toward that target.

2. The descriptions paint a necessarily broad picture of performance—while you and your learning partners are all working toward the same outcomes or targets, different learning partners will use different evidence to inform levels of progress. We kept the descriptions of progress from being too specific in order to allow all learning partners to match widely varying pieces of evidence to the same description, a feat that's immensely important and valuable in collective work toward deeper learning.

3. When making ratings, draw on whatever evidence is available. Evidence will always be "lighter" early on in your work with individual students or toward certain capabilities, but there'll never be a time when you don't have enough evidence to use deeper learning measures. Use them in order to see, and design ways to find, what you're missing.

4. As briefly noted in our discussion of the measures developed in OKCPS (Chapter 5), and specifically in relation to the Learning Progressions, you should use measures of student learning to determine a student's level of progress relative to where you are *now*—not relative to the standard he or she is expected to achieve by the *end* of the school year or at any other time in the learning process. For this reason, a change in level of progress (e.g., from *getting started* to *looking promising*) is reflective not of normal or standard progress but of *acceleration*. To illustrate this, just because students haven't learned everything they will learn over the course of a school year doesn't mean they can't be *geared for success*. You have to focus on where you are now, and you have to leverage ensuing learning experiences to accelerate every student along the progression.

5. These measures are designed to be used by professionals trained to make professional judgments based on a synthesis of a range of professional evidence. Using change teams as an example, while the students, parents, and community members both on and outside of change teams provide necessary and invaluable evidence to inform ratings of progress, it's important that those ratings be ultimately determined by teachers, school and school-system leaders, and other learning partners professionally trained to use measures of learning. Remember that the ratings themselves aren't inherently valuable—they're only as good as the

evidence that informs them, which itself comes from the full range of learning partners and their collective experiences.

6. Last, as evidenced in the CORE approach, there's the possibility that ratings will vary among learning partners. The nature of deeper learning makes it a clear target for variation—deeper learning requires the synthesis of a range of quantitative and qualitative data. Building clarity around assessment and the synthesis of evidence will go a long way to limit discrepancies and establish the inter-rater reliability you need. Even with this shared understanding in place, slight variations in ratings are likely to occur. Why? Because educators and other system leaders are professionals. They make professional judgments, and sometimes those judgments differ. That's okay—what's important is that you talk through differing ratings or decisions whenever possible, sharing your thoughts and perspectives and finding a way to a collective decision. Again, if you want your learning partners to agree with your decisions, you have to back them up with evidence.

Putting Depth Into Practice

Reflect

Reflect on your understanding of how to work with these measures of deeper learning and of what's required to determine accurate, evidence-based ratings. Are there any measurement concepts that you're not quite clear on or that you'd need to engage with more deeply to better reflect the concept in your practice? What might it take to establish inter-rater reliability across your school, district, or wider system? Are there certain processes already in place but others you still require?

The CORE approach, AMMA, and the inquiry process as a whole are all about the evidence. If you don't take the time to use your measures to build clarity, language, and capacity all throughout your learning journey, you won't know how to capture the evidence you need, and it's likely your measurement will be misinformed. With deeper learning, you're moving away from traditional measurement—which we consider "malnourished" and misinformed—to deeper measurement—which is well nourished, fully informed, and overflowing with life and humanity. You've taken the time to lay the foundation for gathering deeper and more authentic assessment evidence. Now, what does that evidence look like at varying levels of your system, and how can you gather and synthesize it to develop in ways that enable deeper learning for all?

Engaging in Professional Inquiry

Student inquiries are aimed at the direct development of students' deeper learning outcomes. In comparison, *professional inquiries* are aimed at the development of the capabilities and practices that *enable* those outcomes. We're all learners—professional and student learning are equally important for the development of the outcomes we want for our students. For this reason, and as discussed in the development frame (Chapter 5), we need both *professional inquiry guides* and *student inquiry guides* for use alongside rubrics and progressions. What we're ultimately striving for are deeper learning experiences for our students, but we have to develop the capacity to embed the practices that will enable those experiences to occur. That's why we'll start on the "back end," with the professional inquiries that'll take you and your system deeper and support your students to move even further in that direction. Let's take a look at dimensions of each Capability Rubric to deepen your understanding of the relationship between inquiry and the system.

Understanding Your System

Developing a systemic professional learning strategy that addresses the real causes of underachievement. We can't talk about professional learning (or development, for that matter) without talking about inquiry. As long as you form and fully embed this connection in your mind, your professional learning strategies will be built around your measures, derived from a comprehensive assessment of your system and its needs, and developed in light of learners and their outcomes.

Gathering meaningful, collective evidence in the system and in the community. There's that word again—need evidence? Think *inquiry*. This dimension will support you to engage learning partners in inquiry at any level of the system and will support you to understand who your learners are and what really matters for them.

Engaging Learners, Parents, and Communities as Real Partners

Partnering in every aspect of the inquiry process. Partnering in learning assessment, design, implementation, measurement, and reflection and change speaks to how not only learners, but also their parents and community members, can be engaged as partners in every aspect of learning.

Providing opportunities for technology-enhanced, connected learning anytime and anywhere. How can you enhance learning experiences by incorporating digital and other technologies throughout the inquiry process in ways that connect learning partners, expand your learning environments, and directly deepen learning as a result?

Identifying and Measuring What's Important

Engaging in authentic assessment that fully informs the measurement of learning. As you know, there's no measurement without assessment, design, implementation, and reflection and change. Whether we're talking about student learning or professional learning, you have to gather the assessment evidence that'll tell you how you're doing and how you can improve. This process is inquiry.

Moderating exemplars to ensure inter-rater reliability and to identify and spread best practices. We're talking about measuring not only outcomes but their enablers as well. Measuring the effectiveness of your inquiry and other practices through the process of collaborative moderation will support you to reflect on and change your practices as necessary.

Leading for Deep and Sustainable Change

Focusing every action and decision through the lens of the least-served learners. This is like a muscle—and you flex it every time you use the process of inquiry to take an action or make a decision. The stronger the muscle gets, the deeper the outcomes will be.

Prioritizing what needs to change and collaboratively designing solutions. Knowledge of your learners and the measurement of their outcomes will demonstrate where you are as a system and where you can improve. You have to collaboratively design solutions (*inquire*) with a clear line of sight to the learner—how will this specific change foster the conditions that will enable intended outcomes?

Creating a Culture of Learning, Belonging, and High Expectations for All

Providing the freedom to learn, share, celebrate, and improve. Inquiry is built on a foundation of *learning*—not just for students, but for everyone. It's not enough to take one shot at this. You have to engage in constant, overlapping, and overlaid series of inquiry that'll ensure you learn from your actions (reflection) and improve your practices (change). With inquiry, there's no limit to your own or your learners' improvement.

Engaging in deeper learning experiences and teaching for 100 percent success. Assessment design will take you only as far as its implementation. Remember that instructional practice is a partnership—are students active "partners in practice," and do they demonstrate a commitment to not only their own success but also the success of every learner? Supporting the learning of others gives students a way to contribute back.

Putting Depth Into Practice

Reflect

Looking back over these examples from the Capability Rubrics, which dimension most resonates with you based on your current capability ratings, your roles and responsibilities, your understanding of where you are personally and as a system, and your knowledge of and excitement around what needs to change for your learners? Where do you—personally or as a system—need to *start* in order to develop in the ways that'll fill the gaps in learning you've identified?

A Recipe for Return: Models of Practice From BESD

Digital Inquiry

Professional inquiry is a logical entry point for your work toward deeper learning—it's about looking for evidence of what's working and what needs to change to enable deeper learning and then making those changes happen. Following the thread of professional inquiry as presented in our ongoing exploration of Burlington-Edison School District (BESD), the first inquiries explored in the district's narrative were around how to respond to the introduction of the CCSS. District and school leaders had to ask themselves, "What will work and what will need to change in order for us to meet these standards while also meeting the standards of our learners and their humanity?" The second half of that question led them to embed emphases on a deeper set of learning outcomes, emphases that necessitated a Concept-Based Curriculum and Instruction (CBCI) design framework for picking out big ideas and leaving space for learning that wasn't explicitly focused on in the standards. Learning partners soon realized that they wouldn't be doing all they could to develop these broader outcomes unless they were measuring them, too. Inquiry led them to another solution—a deeper learning framework, complete with measures of the outcomes that matter for their learners. But in order to build their capacity to use deeper measures, they had to build their capacity to design assessments that effectively evidence and develop deeper learning outcomes. Additional tools and supports were designed and implemented, and the cultural and consequent outcome shifts continue. . . .

This broad-stroke narrative paints only a small piece of the picture of "inquiries within inquiries" that has guided BESD and a range of other districts both to and throughout their deeper learning journey—or *deeper learning inquiry*. But it does depict a district working to develop the capabilities and foster the conditions that enable deeper learning. Each capability plays a part in our stories, and though each system has a different path to developing them, the practices that'll help bring them to life are the same in any classroom, school, or wider system.

We've already learned a good deal from BESD's inquiries into deeper learning partnerships with learners, parents, and the community and in environments in which learners are supported to run with, design, and see themselves reflected in their learning, both inside and outside of school walls. As we turn now to BESD's "digital inquiry," reflect on the ways in which you, your school, or your school system already use or can better leverage technology to develop system capabilities. Reflect on how technology, like every other element of authentic practice, enables, enhances, and deepens the others.

> If it was easy work, people would have done it before, and people like to be challenged, but they like to be supported in the challenge, too. We need to be able to support our system to . . . take that leap of faith with us and [to] provide the supports and tools necessary to do the work.
>
> —**Bryan Jones, EdD**, Director of Equity and Assessment, Burlington-Edison School District, United States

CHAPTER 7

The Capability Rubrics and professional inquiry guides will help you identify the supports you need to continue to build your deeper learning capacity. First you assess and measure your capabilities, and then you design solutions.

To guide our exploration of BESD's approach to leveraging technology in the development of key system capabilities, let's focus on three of the dimensions showcased earlier in this chapter: developing a systemic professional learning strategy that addresses the real causes of underachievement; providing opportunities for technology-enhanced, connected learning anytime and anywhere; and engaging in authentic assessment that fully informs the measurement of learning. In what ways might digital and other technologies support the development of these dimensions? For answers, let's turn to an assessment of BESD's approach to professional learning and the district's response to its learning partners' needs.

> It shifted when we started doing deeper learning, because we were doing an old-school model where basically you come in and we'll do an hour of "How do you make a slideshow?" an hour of "Here's how you build your website," and now we've shifted the whole thing—now we actually use the 6Cs. . . . We just had a training that was all about communication and collaboration . . . how do you support communication? How do you support your students? And so [teachers] dig into all these materials, they use tech tools, and it's not about just how you make a website. You might learn that . . . but that's not the focus. The focus is communication or collaboration, and they get to explore what makes sense.
>
> —**Tracy Dabbs**, Coordinator of Technology and Innovation, Burlington-Edison School District, United States

Notice the professional learning shift—from the *technology* itself to the *outcomes* it develops, and from *jamming* technology into our learning experiences to *selecting* the tool best suited for developing a specific outcome at a specific time. BESD implemented yearly collaborative learning sessions in which teachers in similar grade levels throughout the district can learn about new tools and share successes and challenges, with a clear and driving focus on teaching practice. One of the biggest successes that teachers have shared involves how technology has shifted the role of the students and the environments they learn in. Instead of telling students what technology to use at what time and to what purpose, teachers are allowing them to determine for themselves what they need and when they need it in order to meet learning goals. In addition to supporting self-direction and the pursuit of personally relevant and meaningful learning opportunities, empowering students with technology has solved one of BESD teachers' most significant problems in providing opportunities for digital learning.

> One of the pieces I think is tricky for some [teachers] is they feel [as though they're technologically lagging] behind their students. "Oh, my students know how to make these YouTube videos, and they want to do this and that, and I don't even know how to help them with that," or "I really want to build a website, but I haven't done it enough," so [feeling] like they [have to] keep on top of every tool and every little thing. So we have this model where we've told them they're building "student coaches." What's pretty exciting is they've turned their rooms more over to students, [so that] they don't have to be the expert. Have the student teach you how to do it. So I think our student tech coaches—tech leaders in the classroom—have really shifted [teachers'] need to feel like "I have to know everything," because the teacher can't do that. . . . You're not going to be the expert in everything. You want students to drive and be pushing on what could and should be, and we all know that you learn the most when you teach other people something.
>
> —**Tracy Dabbs**, Coordinator of Technology and Innovation, Burlington-Edison School District, United States

From kindergarten onward, whenever BESD students or teachers have a question or a problem they want solved with technology, they consult their class tech coach—a role that rotates between interested students throughout the school year, and one that's awarded by, understandably, a competitive application process. Along with a multitude of additional tools, videos, frameworks, and other resources hosted on the district's dedicated "Ed-Tech Tools" website, teachers can access a guide to implementing the tech coach role in their own classes (Figure 7.4) and a sample application for the position (Figure 7.5). Where are there opportunities to implement tech and other student-held coaching roles in your own classes or your school system?

Figure 7.4 • BESD's Tech Coach Implementation Guide

Creating a Plan:
Classroom Tech Coaches

iStock/BeholdingEye

A big frustration with added technology tools in the classroom can be the added management and student questions that arise. You thought that more tech would make your life easier and now there are just more questions and more tools that need care.

Not to worry . . . you have all you need right in your classroom. You can start your own team of tech coaches using your own students. What? You teach primary . . . not to worry. Even our Kinder students have been trained to be quite a help with technology. Check out the tips and tricks below and please share your progress and ideas.

How to Begin

There are several things to consider as you develop your student tech coach plan. Remember, you can start small, but make things easier on yourself by outlining some starting ideas:

- Come up with a clever name or have the students help you come up with something. I know, it might sound silly, but naming the job is really fun.
- Have a way to identify when a student is acting as a tech coach. Consider lanyards and badges for students. I have seen some students that can earn stickers or stamps on their badges as they master various skills.
- Develop your routine of how you will use your coaches. Will they work only during certain times, or will they be on call throughout the school day? Will you consider loaning your coaches to other teachers? Sometimes this can be super helpful when other classrooms are trying to develop or train their own coaches or have very young students working with a brand-new tool.
- Come up with a training plan. I have provided a sample application if it works for you, but you will also need a plan for training your coaches. We are trying to work on some video lessons, but this is still a work in progress.
  - Contact me at tech for some training support ideas.
  - Remember, after you train one set, they can be your trainers.

What Should Student Coaches Do?

There are a lot of things that tech coaches can do to support your room, but remember: they should be making your life easier, and they should be learning some skills too!

- Manage classroom devices:
  - Safely distribute and collect devices.
  - Ensure devices are stored properly and plugged in.

(Continued)

Figure 7.4 • (Continued)

- Check for proper sign-off (especially on iPads with Google Drive sign-in).
- Take care of headphones and mice (returning to bags and tubs).
- Properly clean screens, keyboards, and carts, and ensure labels are intact.

- Support students with new tools:
  - Give tech coaches time to explore and learn about new tools before the whole class begins use. Coaches can watch YouTube how-to videos and learn how tools work. They should collaborate together and ensure that the whole coaching team understands the tool.
  - Coaches can move about the room to support students or just be ready to support students at their table when needed.
  - You could have coaches provide mini-lessons for students in various parts of the room, to which other students can drop by for tips.
- Create training docs and videos:
  - Provide your coaches with training on creating docs with images or skills with video creation. Your coaches can create a bank of support materials for your students and even for other classes to use.
- Problem solve:
  - Is a tool or device not working? Ask your tech coaches to take a look and provide support. It would be great if student questions on devices or tools always went through at least two tech coaches before coming to you.
- Preview and review tools:
  - If you find an interesting app, have your tech coaches try it out first. How does it work? Does it do what you thought it would? Students can provide wonderful reviews.

Things to Remember

Maybe I should have put this at the top of the document . . . but read on—these are pretty important things to consider that could help your classroom coach plan really work for you.

- Before students work with peers, be sure that you train students on how to provide support. This is really important and will keep students from getting frustrated with each other.
  - Coaches should NEVER take or touch the device of the person they are helping. I know, it is super hard, but they should only instruct and tell the student what to try. Taking and doing for the student will never help them learn to do it themselves.
  - Coaches need to practice asking LOTS of questions. Think about providing some script ideas for coaches to use, such as the following, until they get more comfortable.
    - What are you trying to do with this tool or device?
    - What steps have you already tried?

- What happened when you tried that?
- What worked in the past?

- Student coaches should never be given other students' login information or be allowed to work on a device that another student is logged in to.
- Remember to start small: Maybe all your student coaches do at first are some management tasks. Even these jobs will help you a great deal and allow the students to build some ownership and responsibility.
- Coordinate with other teachers in your building. Teachers have great ideas. Work together and make your coaching plans even better. Consider swapping coaches and allowing students to work in other classes or make support materials for other classes.
- Try and find a way for all students to have a turn as a tech coach in your classroom, and find ways for them to reflect on what they learned as a coach and how to improve their skills.

Good luck! Please contact me with questions and ideas.

Source: Burlington-Edison School District

Figure 7.5 • BESD's Sample Tech Coach Application

BESD Student Technology Coach Application

Place an X on the line below to share:

How comfortable are you with technology/digital tools on a scale from 1 to 10 (1 = not at all comfortable and 10 = extremely comfortable)?

1---5---10

Place an X in the box to show:

What types of technology/digital tools do you use at home or at school?

	Tablets (iPad or Android)
	Computer laptop or desktop
	Chromebook
	Projector or TV setup with multiple inputs
	Gaming system
	Speakers or other sound equipment
	Cell phone
	Virtual reality headgear
	3D printer
	Other (please list):

(Continued)

Figure 7.5 • (Continued)

Fill in the table to share:

List some applications, add-ons, and games that you use on a regular basis. These would be resources you are so comfortable with, you could teach someone else. They could be tools you use at school or home.

School Use	
Home Use	

When you experience a challenge or frustration when using technology/digital tools, what steps do you take to work through it?

When a friend or classmate has a challenge or frustration when using technology/digital tools, what steps do you take to support them?

Why do you think you would make a valuable part of a student technology coach team? Which of the 6Cs do you think would support your work in this position?

You will need to print your completed application for these next steps:

I am aware of and support my child in applying to be a Student Tech Coach:

Parent signature ______________________________

Please provide the signatures of at least 1 staff reference who supports your application. There is a spot provided for staff to write a short note of support.

Staff signature ______________________________

Staff signature ______________________________

Source: Burlington-Edison School District

CHAPTER 7

The thing that I've noticed that's way different now . . . [is that schools] bring us in when there's a specific thing they want to talk about, and it makes the whole time more purposeful because they've chosen what they're interested in. . . . The teacher training part is really important, because it seems like there's a lot of times when we get the technology, we got the money to spend on technology, but then there isn't the training part. But I've seen, as we've gone through our technology learning here, teachers [who] have gone from deer in the headlights—they don't know what's going on—[to] now feeling comfortable. It's not like they have to be an expert on how to do everything, [they] just [have to] manage the stuff that they have—be a facilitator.

—**Jim Logan**, Programmer/Database Analyst,
Burlington-Edison School District, United States

[The professional learning model] is all inquiry-based. It's really changed how we teach our teachers, and it's changing what's happening in our classrooms. . . . The teachers are telling us that the capacity of their students is like nothing they thought could ever happen. The way they are engaged and pushing on what's supposed to happen, or what their learning should be, has really become amazing. [In classes, it's] not like, "Okay, today we're just going to learn how to use Google Docs and word process"—that's not it. It's, "Okay, today we're going to write this letter because we all really care about this issue of having trash on the playground, so how can we communicate that with everyone? Should we build a website, should we do a blog, should we make some posters, what can we do?"

> The partnership of having teaching with tech—that has made all the difference for us. That it's not this separate thing and we just tell [teachers] what we want and it'll magically happen. It's been intentional planning all along, of "What do we think is really going to be the best for our students?" and tech is right there at the table from step one, not a cleanup after the fact . . . That's been such a pivotal shift for us to really make things happen. Now I don't even think of it as separate departments—it's teaching, learning, tech all together.
>
> —**Tracy Dabbs**, Coordinator of Technology and Innovation, Burlington-Edison School District, United States

Think about all the opportunities that technology provides for assessing and developing your own and your students' learning. As professionals, educators leverage technology to develop capabilities that enable student outcomes, and so that students can leverage it to directly develop their own—and others'—outcomes. From there, it's a matter of capturing that evidence—and, luckily, there are tools for that, too.

BESD's Technology Department recently created a powerful and flexible online assessment system to capture a range of student demographic, testing, attendance, discipline, and other data, providing a wealth of assessment evidence with which to begin to inform a complete picture of student success. What will their next steps (or, rather, *inquiries*) be? While the focus, for now, rightly remains on more authentic instruction, learning partners are beginning to integrate deeper learning measures into their online assessment system, providing for more meaningful tracking and reporting of students' development of the range of deeper learning outcomes. Learning partners have cautioned against putting the focus on capturing data before allowing deeper learning culture and other capability shifts to take a firm hold, but it's a worthy goal for any system committed to taking the measurement of deeper learning outcomes to the greatest possible depths. Getting there requires *inquiry*.

> Hopefully, as we learn more on how to have [deeper learning] transfer into all our thinking, the system will be able to collect [that data] and then we can report that out as part of our reporting process. We're not there yet, but as I work with the school board, we've shown them the [measures] and we want them to see that we want [these outcomes to] be part of the story that people would see when we're talking about their students, when we're talking about their school, and [when we're] talking about the district—[that] we're more than a single-digit number from a state exam . . . I visualize that's how it'll be eighteen months from now—we'll have a way to communicate at the classroom level, at the school level, and then at the district level. Our change teams are going to help us with that.
>
> —**Laurel Browning**, Superintendent, Burlington-Edison School District, United States

There's a ton going on in our schools and wider systems—the Capability Rubrics, within the inquiry process and a wider system of tools, add depth to it all. Inquiry is the way we think; it's the way we *do*—but we have to use it *deliberately* in our school systems to ensure we never lose sight of why, and for whom, we're doing it.

Before we move on to inquiries at the level of student learning, use the following activity to explore how the Capability Rubrics and the professional inquiry guides come together to develop and measure the capabilities that enable deeper learning.

CHAPTER 7

Putting Depth Into Practice

Activity 7.3: Professional Inquiry in Practice

Look at your ratings of your system's current capabilities. Whether they're the initial ratings you determined in Chapter 2 or ratings that you've updated any number of times since that first "rating period," make sure they accurately reflect where you are now. Thinking back to the preceding reflection and the dimension you determined as that which most resonates with you at this point in time, use the professional assessment guide (Appendix F.1) to reflect on and identify the evidence of that dimension in your system. Then, use the CORE approach (Appendix C.7) to synthesize that evidence and come to an overall rating for the given dimension. (It may be the same rating as your initial rating, or it may have changed with the inclusion of altered or additional evidence or with shifts in understanding and practice.) Record this "pre-rating" in the professional measurement guide (Appendix F.2) and reflect on the corresponding pre-rating questions.

Drawing from the evidence detailed in your assessment guide, with special attention to any missing evidence or evidence of relatively low development, use the professional design guide (Appendix F.3) to design one or more solutions to evidence gaps and evidenced needs. How can you leverage partnerships, environments, technology, and the elements of inquiry to enable and deepen learning? (It might be best if you focus on a single element of authentic practice.)

Once designed, your solutions (assessments) will be ready for implementation. It's likely these changes will take time, but you have the understanding and tools you need to make them happen. As you go, record the evidence you capture using the assessment guide, and use the measurement guide to track your progress and ultimately determine the overall effectiveness of the solution by using the Capability Rubric again to make a "post-rating." Based on your rating of the

(Continued)

(Continued)

inquiry's effectiveness, reflect once again on the process and its outcomes, and use those outcomes to help you determine what steps to take next. What worked well, what was ineffective, and what do you need to do now to add even greater depth to your system and your practice?

Reflect

Whether or not you've kicked off the process described in Activity 7.3, what about it has been or looks promising, exciting, or challenging, and how did or can you celebrate and expand on those successes and work through those challenges? What indicators were you using or will you use to evidence learning and growth? Is there a strong balance between indicators that *demonstrate* levels of development and those that also *facilitate* it? In light of AMMA, is your system using the right range of performance indicators for measurement *and* development? Think about how you could change, expand, add to, or otherwise deepen these assessments to inform the measurement and development that your system and its professionals require, keeping all eyes on learners' outcomes.

Access the appendices at
resources.corwin.com/MeasuringHumanReturn

Chapter 8

INQUIRING INTO OUTCOMES

Assessing and Measuring Student Outcomes

At our change team meeting yesterday, a teacher shared that they're becoming more proactive in actually teaching communication versus just looking at the progressions and saying, "Oh, yeah, we do that," and that's a huge step. It is easy to say, "My students already communicate" or "They're already collaborating," but when you actually look at the progressions it becomes so much more precise. . . . As teachers are growing more comfortable with the tools, they are beginning to understand the nuances in the progressions that help move students along the continuum.

—**Tiffanee Brown**, Instructional Design Team, Burlington-Edison School District, United States

CHAPTER 8

Up to now, we've primarily viewed student engagement through the lens of *professional* learning: what role do students play in supporting educators and system leaders to build the capacity required to develop the outcomes that matter for learners? Still, notice the loop—even in reference to professional needs, it has to come back around to student outcomes. Our constant and collective "why" is *student* learning—what does it actually look like when students are developing deeper learning outcomes, and how can we make it happen?

The vehicles that bring this into focus are deeper learning experiences. Like all other activity, learning experiences can be understood as *inquiries*, in that they're a vehicle for learning assessment, design, implementation, measurement, and reflection and change. Also, like all other inquiries, these experiences can be large or small, they can be short or long, and they may involve multiple intended outcomes and assessments or a single assessment and aim. Since any activity evidences learning, what students *do* all throughout these inquiries are the authentic assessments that demonstrate deeper learning and bring it to life. With regard to implementation, remember that it's *responsive*. Because learning needs and goals often change mid-learning, when you perceive that the learning needs to be enhanced or when students want to take it

Figure 8.1 • **Lines of Sight in a Traditional Education System**

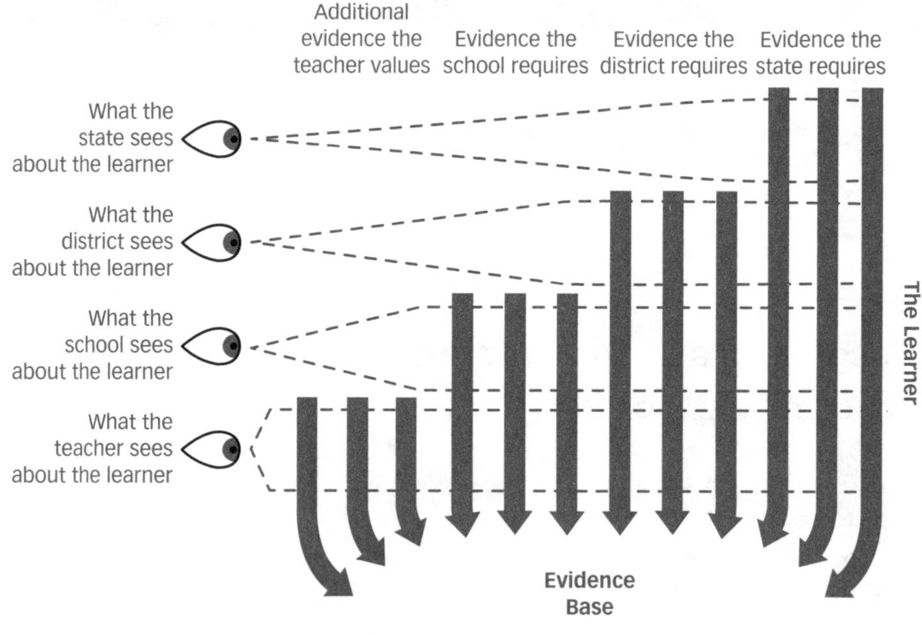

Source: The Learner First, 2018

CHAPTER 8

in exciting new directions, you have to be prepared to design and implement assessments to meet those needs in real time.

Traditionally, as we move up through the levels of our educational systems, the view of learners and their outcomes narrows (Figure 8.1). Teachers see the full range of important outcomes, but if only a small piece of the picture is seen as important at higher levels of the school system, teachers and other learning partners won't be fully supported to meaningfully gather and act on evidence of deeper learning, and learners won't be fully supported to develop its outcomes.

What's important is that you collect the wealth and variety of evidence at every level of the system that informs a full understanding of, and establishes a clear line of sight to, everything your learners are and everything they're capable of. It's unacceptable for any level of a school system to see a student as a test score. You have to see your learners for who they really are and how they can contribute back, and it starts with a commitment to collecting deeper and more authentic evidence.

I hear a lot of "I didn't know my students could do this" or "I didn't know my child could do that." [With deeper learning,] students get to be smart and good in different ways, and traditional school doesn't always provide them with those opportunities. [Deeper learning] gives all kids the chance to be amazing and show the gifts they bring. The way we view our students is changing, along with the opportunities we give them to be great.

—**Anita Simpson**, Elementary Principal, Dubai American Academy, Dubai, UAE

It's always possible and important to gather a complete range of learning evidence, whether it's important at higher levels of your school system or not. For starters, and most importantly, these are the outcomes your learners need now and throughout their lives. If your system doesn't see or recognize that yet, it doesn't mean you can't act on what you know is right and best for your learners. Change your practice, and set an example for others—teach and learn in ways that are impossible to ignore.

Although gathering the AMMA evidence required to measure deeper learning outcomes may seem daunting, *every interaction with a student and his or her learning is an opportunity for assessment*. Take a quick look at some of the types of assessments that teachers and other learning partners are designing and implementing to evidence and measure deeper learning outcomes (Figure 8.2).

The list goes on and on. What are the benefits of presenting these assessments in this format? Well, a few are evident right away:

- *They're familiar*. It's likely that you or learning partners you work with already use a lot of these assessments, in some form or another, on a regular basis to meet existing curriculum standards.
- *They're implementation-ready*. Every day, wherever you are (often with the help of digital tools), you and your students have the opportunity to leverage these assessments in ways that develop learners' outcomes and inform a complete picture of where learners are and how they're progressing.
- *They're assessments*. Blog posts, conversations, tests, drawings, portfolios, games, observations—every engagement with students and their learning is an opportunity to gather valuable assessment evidence.

Remember that we as teachers, school leaders, and other systems-level learning partners are professionals—*our experiences and observations are evidence*. As explored in Figure 8.3, professional judgment, when informed by a rich mix of qualitative and quantitative evidence matched to a rubric or progression, provides a valid and reliable measurement of learners' success.

Figure 8.2 • Sample Assessments That Have Informed the Measurement of Deeper Learning

This is an adaptation of a list of assessments implemented by teachers and compiled by the Department of Education and Training, Australia.

Graphs	Blog posts	Oral/written presentations
Exhibitions	Journal entries	Photography
Coding	Website development	Conferences
Modeling	Games	Volunteering
Research	Observations	Experiments
Literature reviews	Infographics	Reports
Writing pieces (persuasive, creative, procedural, etc.)	Maps (concept, inquiry, geographical, etc.)	Graphic organizers (e.g., Venn diagrams)
Exit tickets	Drawings	Animations
Comics	Plays	Reflections
Sculpture	Podcasts	Self- and peer-assessment
Worksheets	Publications/e-Pubs	Charts
Simulations	Tests	Web quests
Checklists	Cheat sheets	Word problems
Socratic circles	Articles	Annotations
Competition submissions	Essays	Quizzes
Contracts	Role-plays	Portfolios
Projects	Radio/TV productions	Movie making
Online courses/MOOCs	Questioning	Interviews
Rubrics	Storytelling	

Source: The Learner First, 2018; adapted from McEachen, 2017

CHAPTER 8

Figure 8.3 • Synthesizing Assessment Evidence to Make Progression Ratings

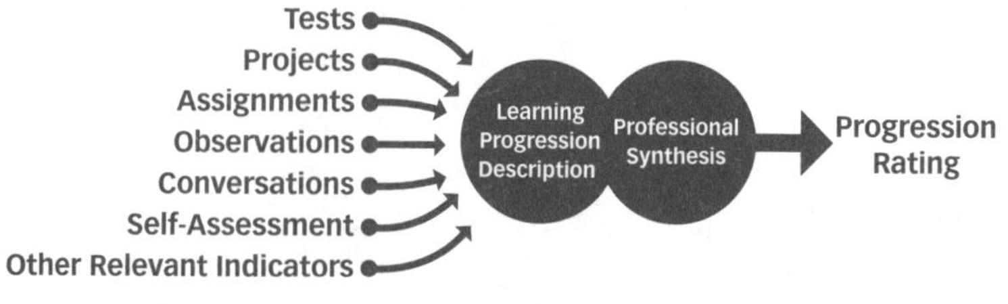

Source: The Learner First, 2018

Putting Depth Into Practice

Activity 8.1: What Do You See?

Draw or put together a "picture of student success" based on your knowledge of your learners and the full range of deeper learning outcomes. What does it look like when learners are really and truly succeeding? Referring back to Figure 8.1, think about your picture as a way of seeing and representing the whole learner. Then, think about the performance evidence currently required at your school, district, and state levels, respectively, and overlay your picture of success with an "evidence picture" or representation that captures the evidence, if any, currently being collected to determine each aspect of success.

Reflect

Think about the evidence of learning demonstrated by your students over the course of an academic year. What important learning do they demonstrate in relation to self-understanding, knowledge, competency, and connection? Is there a difference between this evidence and the evidence that is viewed as important at other levels of the system? How might you bridge any gaps? Reflect on the evidence you view as important. Where is there room to go deeper?

Designing Authentic Assessments

Listing assessments is one thing. Leveraging them within inquiries in ways that develop self-understanding, knowledge, competency, and connection is another. Fortunately, *you're already doing it*. Now, with the added support of deeper learning frameworks and tools, you have the opportunity to assess more intentionally, purposefully, and deeply in your everyday practice. When thinking about designing deeper and more authentic assessments, keep the following in mind: this is the way learning was meant to be designed—it's what we all want for our learners, and it's what our learners and our communities need. The following discussion and ensuing activities will further support you to design assessments that match your students' needs.

Think back to Activity 6.3, "Evidence Matching," in which you examined the *environmental* dimension of the Connection progression to determine what exactly it asks you to find evidence of and what you'd need in order to develop a complete picture of a learner's progress on that dimension. It's clear that there's a wealth of components wrapped into not only each outcome as a whole but each individual dimension as well. It's important to dive into the language of each dimension to find out what, specifically, it's asking you to measure. The individual components wrapped into the *environmental* dimension, taken directly from the language of the measure, include the following outcomes in relation to natural and built environments: interest, respect, balance, health, safety, sustainability, mindfulness, knowledge, understanding, practicality, creativity, sharing, purposeful action, assessment of impact, positive impact, symbiosis, and interdependence.

There's incredible value in working through each of the measures in this way, since it makes you think about the depth of each dimension and the depth of assessment required to measure their outcomes. Whenever we think about designing and implementing assessments, we have to think about the elements of authentic practice. The practices that embody them are the practices that bring deeper learning to life. We can find out what those practices are through the inquiry process—designing and implementing assessments that embed a range of proven or prospective practices, measuring those practices' effectiveness in light of their impact on learners' outcomes, reflecting on their impact, and acting on what we find. Needless to say, it helps if, at the outset, you have an understanding of effective practices for application in the ways most suited to your learners and their needs. The following questions linking assessment and each respective element of authentic practice (partnerships, environments, technology, and inquiry) will help introduce the practices already making a difference for learners in school systems in the United States and other countries. They're intended to get you thinking about where your system is now and where it needs to be.

Partnerships

Are students engaged as active partners in the assessment of their own and others' learning? Is there assessment of students' partnerships with teachers, parents, community members, and others? How are learning partners assessing students' capacity to learn both from and with other learning partners?

Environments

Are students taking responsibility for their own learning, and are they pursuing questions that are meaningful and important to them? Are students exploring natural and built learning environments most suited to the learning at hand? Do students demonstrate the motivation and capacity to learn anytime and anywhere?

Technology

Are students leveraging digital and other technologies in the direct development of deeper learning outcomes? Are students leveraging technology in the activation of learning partnerships, learning environments, and the elements of inquiry? Do students recognize digital technology as an enabler, not a driver, of their learning?

Inquiry

To what extent, and how well, are students assessing their own and others' learning? Are students taking on active instructional or teaching roles in all phases of the learning experience? Are students able to draw from a range of assessment evidence to measure their progress and performance?

The overarching theme—or, in this case, *practice*—embedded in each of the questions above has to do with *students* taking on roles traditionally associated with *teaching*. The widening of students' role into the realm of instructional practice creates exciting opportunities for assessing their deeper learning progress. At the deepest levels of learning, students

- seek out and form partnerships that directly accelerate the development of ideas or solutions,
- take ownership of their learning both inside and outside of school walls and directly contribute to others' learning,
- leverage and create digital tools that directly deepen aspects of the teaching and learning process, and
- partner in designing, implementing, assessing, measuring, reflecting on, and deepening their own and others' learning.

(Similar learning has been shared by NPDL and published through the Organisation for Economic Co-operation and Development by Alejandro Paniagua and David Istance, 2018).

It's easy to see why this shift has a positive impact on students' outcomes: Teaching is about using our learning to contribute to the lives of others and the world—teaching is contributing back. When students are at the center of and active partners in their learning, there's no limit to the self-understanding, knowledge, competencies, and connections they'll not only develop themselves but support others to develop, too. The deeper the learning, the more *learning* resembles *teaching*. In other words, the more it resembles *contribution*. As educators and other learning partners, our ultimate contribution is to partner with our learners in ways that support them to contribute back. Education doesn't get any better than that.

Putting Depth Into Practice

Reflect

Reflect on the questions above under each of the elements of authentic practice. What opportunities do these practices open up for the development and measurement of deeper learning? Take the time to

(Continued)

(Continued)

consider and answer each question as it relates to your or your system's general assessment practice. In what areas are you most successful; conversely, what areas demonstrate the most opportunity for growth? Reflect on the discussion of teaching, learning, and contribution. Do your students consistently engage in learning that resembles the previous bulleted list? Assess your comfort level with regard to *diminishing the division between teaching and learning*. Do you agree that this shift enables deeper learning outcomes? What might this shift look and feel like in practice?

For Your Consideration . . .

The deepening of learners' roles in the teaching and learning process involves a greater emphasis on *self-assessment*, which traditionally refers to the process of drawing on evidence of your own learning to determine your levels of performance. It's an important process, since it's important for learners to understand where they are and how they can improve. But there's more to learning than assessing current levels of performance. In addition to knowing where they are and where they can improve, the goal is for learners to know how to "give life" to that improvement *and then make it happen*. Support your learners not only to assess their own performance but also to bring their own assessments to life. Evidencing, measuring, and giving shape to our own and others' collective learning in the ways that best develop and support us to measure intended outcomes is not just self-*assessment*—it's deeper. In the remainder of this chapter and in the next, we'll explore examples of students and others bringing this depth of learning to life.

Deeper learning experiences are aimed at developing any number of outcomes and solving any range of academic, local, and global problems. They reflect a deep commitment to learners' self-understanding, knowledge, competencies, and connections, either directly or indirectly supporting them to contribute back to others and to their communities. It's important to note that even if a learning experience doesn't involve a direct, explicit, or external "contribution," as long as it supports learners to develop these outcomes it'll support them to make a difference. In other words, it'll still be *deep*. And remember that contributions come in all shapes and sizes. When students actively partner in their learning, contribution—like the inquiries that support it—will show up everywhere. And students will naturally want to take that learning as far as it can go—to the deepest possible ends. With deeper learning, those "ends" are contribution, meaning, and fulfillment.

A Recipe for Return: Models of Practice From BESD

From Standards to Experiences

In Chapter 6, we explored how an overarching conceptual lens and underlying generalizations drawn from our school systems' standards can create a framework for a deeper learning experience. We broke down the generalizations for a social studies unit in light of its opportunities for embedding each of the deeper learning outcomes and leveraging authentic practices to develop them. Figure 8.4 provides another example, this one from an implemented fifth-grade science unit.

Figure 8.4 • Generalizations Used in BESD to Ground and Deepen a Fifth-Grade Science Unit

Energy's Epic Journey

Conceptual Lens: Interdependence

Science—Grade 5

Generalizations

1. Movement of matter and energy through and among systems supports life.
2. Sustainable ecosystems allow energy and matter to flow through multiple organisms who are interdependent with each other.
3. The interaction of Earth's systems shapes surface materials and processes.
4. Human activities alter Earth's systems in ways that can be either beneficial or harmful to humans and other organisms.

Source: Burlington-Edison School District

Again, think about how framing the learning in this way lends itself to deeper learning experiences that embed clear content and conceptual focuses and further them alongside a range of additional outcomes. The identified conceptual lens, "Interdependence," already does a lot to link this content with our ongoing exploration of the Connection progression's *environmental* dimension. In BESD, it did a lot to open the door to a range of learning opportunities and new experiences for students and, as a result, to a wealth of opportunities to assess students' learning and fill evidence gaps.

One of the vehicles for this greater depth of assessment was a new third-grade outdoor learning program, "From Summit to Sea" (Cauvel, 2017). BESD's Lucille Umbarger Elementary launched the new program in order to (1) connect what learners engaged with in the classroom to the natural environments in and near their own community and (2) connect *students* to those environments and their inhabitants. During a "field experience" in Washington's Deception Pass State Park, third-grade students and their teachers explored a forest and a beach, partnering with college-level researchers to learn about the environments and their wildlife. They learned about the importance of salmon both as a food source and in relation to the area's history, which linked to learning about Native American history and the Upper Skagit Indian Tribe's connection to Deception Pass.

> Getting them out into the woods, here to the bay, [and having them experience] the amazing ecosystems that we have outside our back door [enhances the learning]. This just keeps them asking questions.
>
> —**Andrea Lemos**, Teacher, Lucille Umbarger Elementary School, Burlington-Edison School District, United States

> There's nothing that compares to the way a child's eyes light up the first time they see a crab or a barnacle. . . . We wanted to make the connection between the North Cascades and Deception Pass State Park and the interconnectedness between the people, the animals, and the plants.
>
> —**Julie Soiseth-Farmer**, Teacher, Lucille Umbarger Elementary School, Burlington-Edison School District, United States

CHAPTER 8

> Today I learned I love nature.
>
> —**Student**, Lucille Umbarger Elementary School, Burlington-Edison School District, United States

Today I learned I love nature—that statement alone is invaluable assessment evidence. Think about all the opportunities that an inquiry like this provides for learning partnerships between students and others (including plants and animals) and for assessing students' interest in and respect for their environments and the plants and animals within them; mindfulness and understanding of the balance between and interdependence of humans and our environments, the life cycles, health, and safety of animals, and the sustainability of their and our own natural habitats; and knowledge of the characteristics of varying organisms in relation to changing environments.

It's the language of the progression and the standards all in one—they're more connected than they may appear.

> It goes back to that mixed-method of assessment. If you're giving students lots of opportunities to share what they know in different ways, [and] you're

gathering these different types of data from them, you have a much richer understanding of what they know about that content [*and* about] skills they need to work on—they're not losing out on any content.

—**Tracy Dabbs**, Coordinator of Technology and Innovation, Burlington-Edison School District, United States

It's important to remember that this and the other learning experiences you've engaged and will engage with aren't isolated experiences. As part of the ongoing inquiry, Lucille Umbarger Elementary students spent time throughout the year engaging in additional in- and out-of-school learning experiences focused on the salmon and other sea life and mammals, along with the resources, economics, and recreation opportunities, of the Skagit River area. They tested water in the Skagit River and took action to rehabilitate the shoreline, and the school built on that learning later in the current school year by hatching salmon in tanks out in common hallways, with the plan to release the salmon into the river when they were old enough to survive on their own.

When we're intentional about what, why, and how our students are learning, any of their learning experiences—whether they take place in state parks, community parks, car parks, or classrooms—can be a *deeper* learning experience.

One challenge we've experienced is helping teachers see that a deep learning experience doesn't always have to be something major; it can be simple and naturally happen through the structure of learning on a daily basis. Deep learning occurs in the little moments as students engage in personally meaningful and relevant experiences, and with this comes a conversation about how we can assess students in a more authentic way: "What are the things students are engaging in in the classroom, and how do we learn from that?" Data includes so much more than a standardized test or a "formal" assessment; teachers are exploring new ways to measure and monitor growth.

—**Tiffanee Brown**, Instructional Design Team, Burlington-Edison School District, United States

And another layer—[say,] with the Learning Progressions—you're really focusing in on communication. It doesn't have to be during this one, set-day learning experience that you're assessing where kids are at. You're watching that at all times, and you can notice things, and that is valid information to inform the final synthesis of where the child is. . . . It is contagious, and once teachers get a taste, they love it and they can't go back.

—**Brenda Booth**, Instructional Design Team, Burlington-Edison School District, United States

Putting Depth Into Practice

Activity 8.2: Student Inquiry in Practice

Think back to Activity 6.3, "Evidence Matching," the discussion of the *environmental* dimension in this chapter, and how the environmental dimension came to life in the learning experiences at Lucille Umbarger Elementary. Building on this and on everything you've learned to this point, design an assessment that evidences and further develops students' progression on the environmental dimension of the Connection progression. (Alternatively, you can focus on additional dimensions or another dimension/progression entirely. In that case, go through the same process of developing understanding around the dimension[s] you're focusing on.)

You've already developed a deeper understanding of this dimension and what it's asking you to find, and you've seen examples of assessments and practices that have successfully developed these outcomes for learners. Now, use the student design guide (Appendix E.3) to start to give life to a deeper learning experience.

If possible, first use the student assessment and measurement guides (Appendices E.1 and E.2) to assess and measure one or a small number of your learners' development on your chosen dimension(s), evidencing current levels of progress and areas of greatest need. Then, as you design the assessment, keep the following in mind:

- You might choose to design a single assessment or to design a number of connected assessments within a wider learning experience. "It doesn't have to be something major"—any single assessment, at any day and any time, can be deep.
- You might design a worksheet, a survey, a project, a field experience, a conversation with a student or parent, or an opportunity for observation—it's all assessment. Refer back to the list of assessments in Figure 8.2 to spark your imagination. How might you incorporate some of these and/or other assessments?
- The elements of authentic practice are a valuable frame. How might they link with those listed assessments and with any assessments you design in the direct development of intended outcomes?
- Standards are a valuable frame, too. You may choose to start with generalizations similar to those in Figure 8.4 or with others aligned to your own standards, whatever they may be.
- You, your context, your environments, and every one of your students are unique. Draw on what *your* community

and environments have to offer, and draw on what you and your learners have to offer in return.

You may also want to continue to build on the capability dimension of focus identified in Activity 7.3, "Professional Inquiry in Practice" (or another dimension), using the Capability Rubrics (Appendix A) and the Learning Experience Rubric (Appendix G) to assess the impact of your own capabilities and practices alongside the development of your students' outcomes. Although that's what you're ultimately working toward, it's important to start small, as evidenced in the discussion immediately following this activity. Most important, remember why you're designing, assessing, and measuring deeper learning in the first place. When what you're working toward is your own, your learners', and collective success, every moment is meaningful, and your work is fulfilling.

Reflect

Whether or not you've kicked off the process described in Activity 8.2, what about the process has been or looks promising, exciting, or challenging, and how did or can you celebrate and expand on those successes and work through those challenges? Do you have some understanding of how all the tools work together toward the development of deeper learning outcomes? Reflect on major points of learning, and jot down any questions you still have.

Just as we did with the *environmental* dimension in the preceding activity and in earlier activities, it's important to begin your measurement of deeper learning with a small number of focused measurement objectives. We've emphasized the value of going slow to go deeper; similarly, you should start by "going *small*" to build your capacity for measuring depth. This might mean focusing on a single rubric or progression, or even a single dimension of those measures, to build your capacity to match evidence to measure.

In our initial discussion of change teams (Chapter 3), we mentioned that teachers start with a small number of students (e.g., three to five of the least-served learners) when beginning to measure and track learners' progress. Why? In order to learn how to measure the development of deeper learning outcomes (or any other element of deeper learning) in a way that's valid, reliable, and meaningful, you have to learn how to go deep at an individual level. As you've likely gathered, it takes time at first—for many learning partners, the process is new and unusual, and it requires a sharp focus on and understanding not only of learners but also of every detail of their learning. You don't have to be an expert in the use of every tool from the get-go. When thinking about where to begin, remember that, with deeper learning, "it's all good"—start with your own and your learners' interests, passions, and needs, taking the time to get used to this depth of measurement and working more closely with additional tools to fill in gaps. When you start to pay attention to this level of detail, for even a single learner, it's only a matter of time before you do the same for all learners. Eventually, you'll have the capacity to measure each learner's development, too.

With this final measurement concept in mind, you're ready to bring it all together more deeply in practice. Yet perhaps the potential barriers to implementing deeper learning still seem too numerous, or perhaps the depth of practice required by AMMA and the measurement and development of deeper learning outcomes seems impossible. It is possible—*we've seen it*—in any classroom, school, district, or school system that puts the needs of its learners first. You have what you need to make deeper learning a reality. Before you move on to the next chapter, in which we'll celebrate some systems in which learning partners are already making it a reality, look back to the previous activities to start putting the pieces together in the ways that will make it a reality in your own.

Putting Depth Into Practice

For Your Consideration . . .

Deeper learning doesn't come with a checklist, on which you check off specific steps on predetermined days on learners' roads to meaning and fulfillment. That's not to say that lesson or learning planning is impossible. You just need to shift from a fixed and linear understanding of learning and progression to one that's flexible and fluid. The most important consideration for facilitating this shift has to do with your understanding of *evidence*. As educators, we see so much about our learners every day—we have to view it all not only as important, but also as necessary and measurable evidence. Understandably, this shift in thinking requires significant shifts in practice. The diminishing division between teaching and learning doesn't only involve learners taking a more active role in teaching—teachers and all other learning partners take a more active role in learning, too. Every day is an opportunity for professional learning and growth, and there's no checklist for *your* progress, either. If you take the time to go slow and be deliberate, with focused measurement objectives up front, what makes sense and feels right for you as a professional will become clear. Work and grow alongside your learning partners, use the following chapters to continue to reflect on and develop your practice, and come back to these activities and other points of learning as continuous and ongoing resources, remembering and celebrating your role as a learner. In what ways can you develop your self-understanding, knowledge, competency, and connections in partnership with your students and others, and in what ways can you contribute back?

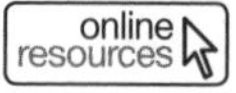

Access the appendices at
resources.corwin.com/MeasuringHumanReturn

Chapter 9

DEEPER LEARNING EXPERIENCES

Practice Applies

It's worth taking a moment to consider everything that's paved the way for the implementation of deeper learning experiences. School systems are centering their learners and engaging learning partners around everything from the identification of the outcomes that matter to developing and building clarity and capacity around tools that support their development. Systems' engagement with key capabilities and practices is fostering the conditions required to bring deeper learning to life. Why have we been building up to deeper learning experiences? They develop and support us to measure deeper learning outcomes—and that's what it's all about.

Shifting in this chapter to a greater emphasis on implementation as well, remember that any learning implementation is assessment implementation. Once designed, the assessment is ready for action. In the traditional learning process, this marks the point of entry—and exit—for students. A learning experience is prepared for them, they work through it, and the teacher assesses their performance. Thus, learning is a single point in a disconnected process. With deeper learning, *entry* and *exit* are replaced by *ongoing engagement*—learners are engaged every step of the way, and the assessments they engage with respond to their needs, reflect their interests, and are marked by their own design. During and after the experience, students assess, reflect on, and measure their learning, identifying ways to change or expand upon the direction of their current and future experiences. If we find that our students are ever exiting the learning process, we have to find a way to bring them back in and make sure they get—and want—to stay.

With any learning, what's most important isn't the context surrounding the experience, but its outcomes, along with the practices that develop them. This chapter draws on learning experiences in communities throughout the world to identify and describe the *practices* that are successfully facilitating the assessment, development, and measurement of deeper learning *outcomes*. By the end, you'll be ready to take your own use of the tools, and your wider professional practice, deeper.

Think back to Chapter 1's discussion of the global nature of deeper learning, and to your own reflection on your willingness to learn from and with learning partners all over the world. A lot (if not all) of the preceding and following experiences we describe take place in schools, school systems, and even countries outside your own. But if you're truly open to each school's and system's experiences, the following will be clear: Every experience in one way or another resembles an experience that could happen in your own classroom, school, or school system. The assessment would necessarily look different—your *place* and every one of your learners is unique, after all—but as long as its intended outcomes are those you want for your learners, the practices embedded to develop them can be leveraged toward the same ends. Think about what these assessments and practices might look like with your learners, and remember that while context frames isolated experiences, *successful practice can be applied in them all.*

With an understanding of the purpose and value of these experiences and what you're looking for in the descriptions that follow (context frames—*practice applies*), you're ready to celebrate deeper learning experiences in light of the impact of their embedded practices on the learner. Pay particular attention to each individual opportunity for assessment—both of students' outcomes and of professional capabilities and practices—embedded within the experiences. Use the activities to reflect on and more deeply engage with each experience, and celebrate the depth of learning experienced in your own system and in others around the world.

A Celebration of Learning and Practice

Deeper learning is a celebration of learners and their identities; of their teachers, families, and all other learning partners; and of the outcomes that contribute to their success. It's a celebration of learners' contributions in classrooms, schools, households, and communities everywhere, and of lifetimes of meaning and fulfillment. It's a celebration of humanity—and of everything that recognizing our humanity can accomplish. Let's kick off our own celebration in Marlborough, New Zealand, with a group of learning partners experiencing the impact and importance of knowing, sharing, and celebrating who we are, both individually and as a whole (Spencer et al., 2017).

Rapaura School is located in the village of Rapaura, New Zealand, in the northeast corner of the country's South Island. In 2017, based on initial discussions and conversations, students and their learning partners realized there was a clear opportunity for them to further their understanding of Matariki, a Māori cultural celebration named for the cluster of stars also known as the Pleiades and that marks the beginning of the new year. One of the four future-focused themes in the New Zealand curriculum is *sustainability*. Linking this theme to the *character* competency and to the social sciences, another curriculum area, learning partners set out on a learning experience designed to sustain and deepen their understanding of themselves, their cultures, other cultures of the world, and the festivals that celebrate them: "We agreed [it] was important that all our students had a sound understanding of this festival as part of Tikanga Māori [the cultural "Māori way"], and as a New Zealand citizen prior to leaving our school" (Spencer et al., 2017).

Learning partners continued their inquiry by identifying students' prior knowledge and understandings, which were then unpacked and analyzed to determine gaps and areas of need. Students participated in a whole-school, daylong exploration of "Cultures and Festivals," in which they engaged in learning experiences designed to introduce them to the reasons behind and diversity of many festivals of the world. At the end of the day, the school and community participated in a Holi festival (the Hindu "festival of colors") to celebrate the beginning of their journey together.

The evidence gathered from these initial assessments, as well as from self-assessments, was used to measure students' current levels of learning and inform the direction of the next phase of the inquiry. With their foundational learning in tow, students in each class had a "wonderings" session to explore any questions they still had and the opportunities to expand their learning, leading to reassessment and the identification of further directions for learning. Students worked in groups to determine and explore a learning area of their choice; their selections included

- "passion projects" relating to a chosen culture or festival,
- a record book of school traditions and a mural to depict them,
- a "Wildfoods" festival,
- digital stories,
- the creation of a school tradition around Matariki, and
- the design of related artwork for a classroom currently under construction.

Teachers engaged students in individual, group, and class-wide inquiries simultaneously, supporting them to apply learning in one area to their work in another, and deepening and expanding individual and collective learning in the process. Teachers described their role as "facilitators" of learning, providing scaffolding and support dependent on students' individual needs. Throughout the learning experience, families and community members worked in partnership with learners through out-of-school excursions, interviews, email, and other forms of connection. At the end of the experience, students and school staff invited their families and other members of the community to a "Night Festival," organized by students and other learning partners to celebrate and share the learning that had occurred:

> It's been exciting to watch the students get excited, drive their own learning, problem solve, and really "feel" it. The culmination of all

> their hard work at our learning celebration, "Night Festival," was very special to witness. Students have worked on learning in the social sciences curriculum, but this learning experience has been very different from the "traditional approach." Teachers scaffolded, supported, and guided students as they took agency over their learning, made connections to our school and wider community, applied these learning concepts in a real-world setting, and used digital technologies to extend their learning further than the classroom walls. We believe this type of learning strengthens our students' understanding of themselves as [learners], increases their ability to focus on their own individual strengths, talents, and interests, and improves learning partnerships [between] our school community and families. . . . This inquiry has also developed a deeper awareness of the different cultures [and] heritages within our school and allowed a great opportunity for them to be celebrated and better understood. . . . Each class now begins each day with a Karakia [Māori greeting], and staff and students now have a deeper understanding [of and] appreciation and respect for Matariki and its importance for us as New Zealanders. (Spencer et al., 2017)

Reading this description, you can already begin to see the practices and outcomes at play in the experience, as well as how it facilitated deeper learning through the ongoing process of inquiry. In sharing the learning that occurred, partners paid explicit attention to the practices that deepened the experience through the successful development of deeper learning outcomes. They described equitable learning partnerships between and among students, teachers, families, and other community members that were formed and leveraged throughout varied assessments, with students engaging a variety of partners depending on their learning needs and then sharing their collective learning in a crowning community celebration. Students were engaged as active partners in all aspects of inquiry, including the design and implementation of layered assessments that facilitated the measurement of deeper learning outcomes. In addition, students were engaged in a range of authentic and virtual learning environments that connected them to learning partners within and beyond their local community. They took ownership of the direction of their learning and explored "meaningful ways they [could] make a difference with new learning" (Spencer et al., 2017). Finally, digital tools were leveraged to "connect with parents, experts, and the wider community at different stages of [the] inquiry" and to "deepen and expand students' learning experiences beyond classroom walls" (Spencer et al., 2017). What was the result? The deepening of students' self-understanding, the development of intended knowledge and competencies, and the formation of powerful, lasting connections for all involved.

I have enjoyed making the Matariki stars this inquiry. I have learned that the Seven Sisters come out once a year. I learned how to celebrate a festival. I

> liked working in a group with other people. I thought that at the learning celebration, it was good that everybody was into different things, [that] every class did different things. Everyone liked it.
>
> —**Student**, Year Two, Rapaura School, New Zealand

> What I liked about this inquiry was that we were all collaborating and working together. I now know about Matariki and festivals that lots of people celebrate in many different ways. Matariki is important to New Zealand.
>
> —**Student**, Year Four, Rapaura School, New Zealand

> I did Stonehenge summer solstice for my inquiry, and I learned that it is basically Matariki, but it's on the ground, so when the sun hits the center rock, that's when you know it's time to plant a crop. I worked with someone on this inquiry, and it was good working together, but some things we didn't agree on, so we had to compromise and add both our ideas together.
>
> —**Student**, Year Six, Rapaura School, New Zealand

Kaia, a year-three (seven- to eight-year-old) student at Rapaura School, described her learning while referring to a book her grandmother had made for the class and to photographs from time spent with her family in Tonga, which were displayed on the classroom wall.

> We learned about cultures, and my grandma came in and she [shared] a bit about Tonga. And she left us this book, and it's got markets and Tongan food in it, and this is an Indian apple. And . . . here is a big bunch of peanuts. And that's my uncle harvesting the manioke. The book's title is called "Kaia's Favorite Tongan Food," and this is the [Tongan] flag. And that's not the only inquiry we've had. We learned about Matariki stars, and we've made some for our learning celebration . . . to show off our learning.
>
> —**Kaia**, Student, Year Three, Rapaura School, New Zealand

Kaia's classmate, Charlotte, expressed the value of learning about Kaia's culture from her and her grandmother, and she shared in Kaia's excitement about Tongan cultural foods.

Forming learning partnerships and communicating our learning in the direct development of cultural knowledge, key learning competencies, cross-generational and cross-cultural connections, and understanding of ourselves and our peers—*that's deeper learning*. The experience at Rapaura

School instilled pride in learners' own cultures, the cultures of their peers, and the Rapaura community as a diverse and collective whole. This level of cultural and self-understanding is fostered by another culture—the school's. We've talked about developing a culture of learning, belonging, and high expectations for all in our schools and our school systems. As evidenced in this experience, belonging runs deeper than knowing and understanding our cultural and individual differences. It's about celebrating them and marveling at their power when paired with another's. There's no better way to engage in education than as an ongoing celebration of ourselves and our learning.

Learning and belonging go hand in hand, and we have to celebrate all the other elements of learning in the same way we celebrate who we are. As discussed earlier, a culture of learning involves the freedom to pursue our interests, share our learning, and improve upon our successes and challenges. It's student-driven, and it embraces—*celebrates*—mistakes and "failures" as opportunities to further deepen our learning. As explained by Rapaura School,

> [l]earning should be not only authentic to us, but authentic to the students—what are they interested in? Where do they want to take it? Students face challenges along the way, as is the nature of inquiry learning, but they are supported to take risks and enter the "learning pit," as this is what helps us to become a better learner. (Spencer et al., 2017)

As evidenced in the Learning Progressions (Appendix D), who we are as individuals has a whole lot to do with others. Along with what we know and can do, who we are involves how we connect with the world—both its people and its environments. Our interactions with and within our everyday environments say a lot about who we are, as does our capacity to *expand* them in the direction of greater depth. Supporting students to take risks and direct their learning in a range of powerful learning environments connects them to a wealth of knowledge and information, to new opportunities for developing and demonstrating deeper learning outcomes, and to learning partners both locally and all over the world.

A Recipe for Return: Models of Practice From BESD

Who We Are and How We Got There

While learning about different cultures and how varying groups of people immigrated to the Burlington area, fifth-grade students at Bay View Elementary wanted to learn more about their own heritage and family histories and to share them with others. After a research process that included interviews with parents and other family members, students chose how to best demonstrate and celebrate their cultures at a family "Heritage Night," where they displayed posters or online slideshows, brought in cultural foods and clothing, and shared about their and their classmates' personal and family histories with their parents, teachers, and other learning partners. After the event, the learning continued, with students volunteering to share their stories at one of the school's weekly student-led assemblies (see "Leadership at Every Level" in Chapter 2) to talk with students at other grade levels not only about who they are but about the importance of understanding it, too.

In kindergarten, it's all about "me." Focusing on individual identities, Bay View kindergarten students set out to discover what types of learners they are, what they're interested in, the ways they most like to learn, and how it all comes together to make them who they are as individuals. They hosted a "Me Museum" for parents, grandparents, community members, and the district office, where they set up trifold-poster and other displays and shared what they'd learned about themselves, including their favorite foods—grapes, Oreos, and tomato soup, to name a few. Of course, since who we are is never just about "me," students learned about the ways in which they were similar to and different from their classmates, as well as how important those both are in "making us '*us*.'"

On a normal year, we'd have programs where parents and families come back into the building, but the attendance [wasn't] really great for learning-centered things. So this year, when we've had something come from *student* interest, [when it] has been planned by students, we get almost 100 percent attendance at every grade level—really bustling, alive with people, and it's been really wonderful.

—**Amy Reisner**, Principal, Bay View Elementary School, Burlington-Edison School District, United States

Spotlight on Evidence

The learning experiences and cases described in this chapter and every other chapter aren't only school-system narratives—*they're assessment narratives*. In the same way that learning partners' descriptions of learning experiences or their stories about other activity in our systems serve as valuable assessment evidence, the narratives throughout these pages do too. They evidence learning that's happening globally and the practices and capabilities that enable it anywhere. As we know, that

(Continued)

(Continued)

evidence makes the greatest impact when it has a measured application. We'll illustrate this with the evidence described in the experiences above and the "measured applications" that follow.

At Rapaura School, the shift to deeper learning started with conversations. That initial assessment of current levels of learning led to the identification of a learning direction and then a whole-school and community celebration to kick off learners' exploration of cultures and festivals. (We often celebrate deeper learning that has already taken place, but what about the deeper learning to come?) Events like these are valuable opportunities for assessment—there's a lot to gather from students' interactions with people and in environments other than those regularly found within classroom walls. Students then self-assessed their learning and had a "wonderings" session to inform the next phase of the inquiry, and then they took "self-*assessment*" deeper: they chose what their next assessment would be, and they designed and implemented it in partnership with others. Throughout the experience, collaboration with classmates, parents, and community members gave life to assessment evidence in the form of interviews, emails, and observations during out-of-school "excursions." After their "Night Festival" celebration, students provided reflections on their learning that captured learning in each outcome area and they explored "meaningful ways they [could] make a difference with new learning." Those are the assessments that tie it all together—*how can students evidence and combine their new knowledge, competencies, interests, and wider self-understanding to connect with others and contribute back*?

In BESD, fifth-grade curriculum learning around cultures and immigration connected with and led to students learning about their own cultures. They partnered and celebrated with parents and one another; chose how best to evidence and share their learning, digitally or otherwise (notice the assessment opportunities provided both by the *choice* and by the *product*); and presented at a whole-school assembly as well. In kindergarten, students learned about, evidenced, and shared their interests, learning styles, preferences, and similarities and differences.

As evidenced here, *assessment is what we do*. Taken together, the assessments respective to each of the examples above are opportunity enough for informing the measurement of learning and practice. Remember to look out for assessment evidence in the examples to come, and use the Putting Depth Into Practice activities to experience how it all comes together.

Putting Depth Into Practice

Reflect

Reflect on the learning experiences described earlier in light of each individual opportunity for assessment, each of the other practices spotlighted above and others embedded throughout the experiences, and your own learners' cultures and identities. What might similar assessments look like with *your* learners? How could an experience like the ones in this chapter serve as a "shell" for an experience that embeds these and other practices in the direct development of self-understanding, knowledge, competencies, and connection? How might your learners use a greater understanding of themselves and others in order to contribute back? Refer to the Creating a Culture of Learning, Belonging, and High Expectations for All Capability Rubric (Appendix A.5) and reflect on the capabilities demonstrated in one of the learning experiences described. How might those capabilities translate to your classroom, your school, or your wider system? What explicit practices might support your system to further develop them?

Activity 9.1: Assessing Learning—Self-Understanding

Consider either the *identity* or the *place* dimension of the Self-Understanding progression (Appendix D.1), Think about how, for any or all of the learning experiences above, individual assessments might evidence this dimension. (For example, how might you leverage conversations, celebrations, or students' trifold-poster displays to evidence students' understanding of identity?) What evidence do you need to measure a student's progress on the dimension, and how could these or similar assessments bring that evidence to life in your own classroom, school, or wider system?

Activity 9.2: Measuring Practice—Environments

Rate the "Cultures and Festivals" learning experience on the *environments* dimension of the Learning Experience Rubric (Appendix G). What evidence of practice are you using to determine your rating? Where are there evidence gaps, and what's needed to fill them?

In Åbo, Finland, Cygnaeus School is engaging in the same process of developing a culture of learning and belonging (Muallim, 2017). In order to sharpen their understanding of learning goals, and of themselves in the process, fifth-grade Cygnaeus students set out to learn more about their country's new competency-based curriculum, which comprises the following elements:

- Thinking and learning to learn
- Cultural competence, communication, and expression
- Taking care of oneself and others, managing daily activities, and safety
- Multi-literacy
- Information and communications technology (ICT) skills
- Entrepreneurial and work-life skills
- Participation and influence—building a sustainable future

The students began by thinking and talking about what each competency meant to them, and then they used their understanding as a starting point for writing a play to celebrate Svenska Dagen (Finnish Swedish Heritage Day). Over several weeks, they used the competencies to frame their own interests and needs, reflecting on how they as individuals fit into the curriculum and on how their identities would be represented in their learning. The learning experience was designed to support learners to see themselves reflected not only in the learning *process* but in the actual learning *content* as well.

> The learning design ends up connecting to curriculum expectations. The core curriculum becomes an everyday instrument. The students can internalize the curriculum and make it their own.
>
> In this task, it's not only the students who learn about learning and themselves. In the deep discussions, they learn about each other. This is also a rewarding way for a teacher to get to know the students even better. This information can be used when planning future tasks [that] thereby increasingly take into account every student's "world."
>
> It is the process that matters: At the moment, I think this way, but tomorrow the answer could be another! "School" has, for a long time, been the sole [time and place] for "learning"—it is not that anymore. We learn all the time, everywhere.
>
> —**Minna Muallim**, Teacher, Cygnaeus School, Finland

When students internalize the curriculum in this way, *it's with them all the time*, opening the door for explicit curricular learning everywhere and at any time. Van Randwijkschool in Ilpendam, in the Netherlands, engages learners in the same process of internalizing deeper learning outcomes, reflecting on their importance, and celebrating their impact on both present and future learning (Turning Learning, 2017).

We had to start a company, and we decided that we wanted to sell services rather than products, like chores and that kind of stuff. We had to write down what we wanted to do with that company and what our plan was. A part of how we learn is using the 6Cs, and one of them is critical thinking. Especially when learning this way, you have to discover and do research by yourself. This makes you think critically, [so] that when you read a book, you think: "Yeah, but somewhere else they said something different. So what's true? How can you be sure if it is the truth?" This way of learning is beneficial for the secondary education, but also for when we are looking for a job in the future.

—**Student**, Van Randwijkschool, Ilpendam, Netherlands

I think that something new has really begun. Now we are focusing on learning by doing. By doing that, we start an investigation: "How do I get my answer to that question?" I found this very refreshing. Together we can face anything, and from collaborating, you become a very social person. So you think before you say or do something. You notice it before you start an action like this, and you also really notice it in daily life.

—**Student**, Van Randwijkschool, Ilpendam, Netherlands

Innovation is really important, especially for education, because we want to teach [learners] the necessary skills, [supporting] them to make the world a more sustainable and better place to live in. And that world—that world keeps changing. It's not only about how to respond to these changes, but also [about] how to reform them.

—**Frank Evers**, Innovation Leader at Turning Learning,
Amsterdam, Netherlands

Deeper learning forms a fluid connection among school, learning, and life. Embedding this connection in the culture of our schools supports learning to happen everywhere and at all times, now and in the future. Since students' deeper learning outcomes may not be explicitly embedded in your local and national curriculums, we've emphasized the importance of forming these curriculum links at the outset of learning experience design. It's common for curriculums in educational systems throughout the United States and globally to emphasize *knowledge* over the other deeper learning outcomes, and the wider learning connections aren't always easy to see. But even within curriculums that are largely content-based, and that may not initially appear to be conducive to deeper learning design, these connections are possible. You just have to make them.

Putting Depth Into Practice

Reflect

Where do self-understanding, competencies, and connection appear (either explicitly or implicitly) in your own curriculum and other standards? Are there instances you hadn't previously seen or considered in which these outcomes are already a focus? How can your understanding of the deeper learning framework help you further solidify these links and connections and better support yourself and your learners to meet these expectations?

We've worked through some examples of student assessment driven by links between student and curriculum—what about links between student and practice? When thinking about student self-assessment and self-measurement, it always helps to begin with the evidence. Teachers already know the importance of evidence—learners may still need guidance to come to terms with it. For example, based on pre-assessment data, learning partners at Derrimut Primary School in Derrimut, Australia (Waites, Ha, & Kapelan, 2017), identified that students

- often made claims with little evidence to support them,
- struggled to articulate their reasoning clearly, and
- needed structured opportunities to support their claims with evidence.

The process for measuring learners' deeper learning outcomes is the same process they'll use to take actions and make decisions for the rest of their lives—it's an important skill to have. You're now equipped with the framework and tools you need to make this measurement a reality, and you know that the practices traditionally associated with "teaching" aren't teachers' responsibility alone. It's important that students develop that same capacity for measurement—designing assessments that foster deeper learning, drawing from a wide range of evidence, and matching that evidence to a learning description or progression—to progress as *deeper learners* both during and after formal education. They have to gather evidence and then use it to determine their own progress and in what areas they need to develop.

In one learning experience at Derrimut Primary, students worked to develop the capacity described earlier while learning the properties of physical force. They began a cycle of research, experimentation, and reflection, in which they engaged in a range of assessments aimed at providing the evidence they needed to support the measurement of their knowledge and competency development. Through continually refined nonlinguistic representations of force, through recordings and reflections in their science journals, and through ongoing experimental testing, students deepened their understanding of force and enabled the self-measurement of learning outcomes with "student-friendly" versions of the Learning Progressions.

After you've engaged learning partners around what really matters for your learners and identified the outcomes you want to develop and measure, *share them with your learners*. Learners need to know the outcomes they're working to develop along with the practices that will develop them. In the same way that you can't assess learners if they don't know the criteria for success, you can't assess their learning outcomes if they don't know what they need in order to be successful—now and for the rest of their lives. Fortunately, with deeper learning, current and future success is one and the same. With all learners, no matter their age or grade level, remember to ensure that learning is celebrated, *not kept secret*, and that your practice is a partnership.

Putting Depth Into Practice

Reflect

What's the value of explicitly and intentionally involving students in each individual inquiry process? Do you ever find your students "exiting" the learning process at times when deeper learning might be enabled by keeping them "in"? How might you support your students to engage with the language of the Learning Progressions to better understand what they're learning, in what ways, and why?

Activity 9.3: Measuring Self-Progression

Student versions of deeper learning progressions have proved valuable at all grade levels not only as a self-measurement tool but as a development exercise as well. These versions of the progressions are designed to maintain the originals' intent while using the language of *self-progression* ("I," "my," etc.). Their impact on students of all ages is the same as that on teachers and other school and school-system leaders—they foster a shared language and understanding around deeper learning and support the measurement and development of its outcomes. If you truly want to enable a deeper learning culture in your classroom, school, or wider system, then *everyone* has to be speaking the same language.

With that in mind, design a "student version" of the Self-Understanding, Connection, or Collaboration progression (Appendix D), repeating with other progressions as helpful. Keeping in mind the intent of the originals, what language choices would better meet the self-measurement and self-assessment needs of your students? When designing any measure for this purpose by yourself or with your change teams, or at any time throughout your learning journey, remember that what you design are *student* tools. Although they lead to valuable assessment evidence that helps inform a complete picture of students' development, for teachers and other professionals that "complete picture" should always be "taken" with the original progression.

The connection between practice, knowledge, and each of the other deeper learning outcomes is an important one, especially considering traditional curriculums' primary emphasis on what students *know*. Even if the curriculum stops there, you don't have to. You have what students need to know—which practices will support them to learn it in a way that also develops their self-understanding, competencies, and connections? The first measurement frames have already provided the foundation for this depth of practice, and it's possible within any system committed to achieving it. Remember that our systems are a reality, but their immovability isn't. Working to move our learners toward deeper learning is working to move our systems toward the same. Let's explore what this can look like within the curriculum areas of literacy, math, science, and technology (Chadwick, 2017).

At Wanaka Primary School in Otago, New Zealand, one of the school's values is *respect*. The value extends beyond respecting peers and members of one's own community, involving respect for all cultures, beliefs, and circumstances and an understanding of the challenges facing different communities throughout the world. Recently, Wanaka students' interest in and engagement with "respect" was piqued by a community partner, who connected with them to share her experiences while in Nepal. The students were determined to learn about children in other parts of the world and to discover opportunities to support them through challenges.

> We looked at children around the world and how they deal with more challenging circumstances, hoping children would then realize the "why" behind our learning about respect. The children became very passionate about what they learned, and we saw this as an ideal opportunity to learn about diverse values and worldviews (citizenship). (Chadwick, 2017)

Their research led them to Purple Cake Day, a charity event that supports learners all over the world to support other learners' education. In order to raise funds for the event, and after a number of meetings to collaboratively determine the best way forward, the learners decided to plan, organize, and facilitate a Soapbox Derby and Gala, inspired by the Rickshaw Run in India. The first step in the implementation journey? Designing soapbox racers.

In planning the designs of their racers, the students realized there was a lot they'd need to learn to make the derby and gala a reality. Collectively, they identified a wide range of workshops to support their learning in the areas of math, science, and technology, which included those related to aerodynamics, braking, building, wheels and axles, and safety. Students developed skills in measurement, scale and 3-D drawing, construction, design and redesign, problem solving, citizenship, character, collaboration, and a number of other curricular and competency domains. The learning continually provided opportunities for further learning, which the students were encouraged and supported to explore as necessary. They decided to create and host a variety of stalls or activities of their choice as a component of the race-day event, which again opened the door to a range of new learning directions and opportunities for assessment. The event was a full-on production that called for a variety of jobs and positions and for additional workshops to support required learning and skills. The workshops focused on each role (e.g., financial manager, advertising coordinator, emcee, crowd control, and health and safety) and were supported by learning partners in students' families and the wider community. As assessments of literacy, students collaborated online to complete Risk Analysis and Management forms, wrote and submitted applications for specific event roles, and created written and video advertisements for event stalls.

If you partner with students in engaging learning experiences that support them to pursue exciting new learning directions as they arise, opportunities for you to gather authentic assessment evidence will create themselves.

> My son came in from school one day with the plans for a go-kart which [he] and his teammates had done, and I was pretty excited because I thought, "What a great project this will be!" And I said, "Can I help with it?" And he said, "Yeah, yeah, yeah, we need parents, anyhow!" The hardest [problem] we had was how [to] attach the wheel to the axle. The plans that the boys had found were great, but [the boys] didn't have any way to do it, so we took what was a bicycle wheel and went . . . to an engineers' firm [to] see how everything worked there, and with them we figured out a way [to] make the axle attach to the wheel and spin, which is quite important at the end of the day! In terms of problem solving, working together, and learning how to use particular tools to actually assemble the go-kart, that was really, really cool. . . . Communication was really important, because they had to talk to each other about . . . what jobs and roles they would have, [and] project management, math, English—the whole lot of it comes together. For me as a parent, it seemed amazing that kids could physically go to this level and do things that we do as adults in the everyday world. Working together with people, solving problems—pretty cool!
>
> —**Parent**, Wanaka Primary School, Otago, New Zealand

What's evidenced here isn't parent participation or support but *real, equitable partnership* among parents, learners, and the school. In another example of partnership in preparing for the derby, two Wanaka students spoke about the role and impact of collaboration throughout the experience, evidencing their collaborative description in the process.

> Doing it as a team, you had to compromise and agree, but it worked out quite well . . . because all these ideas which we'd never have thought of before, with other people [we] collaborated and worked together to give ideas [and] make an all-around better soapbox racer.

So it's kind of like a puzzle. If one person has created this much of the puzzle but they can't figure out how to make the rest of it, but then the other person might have the rest of it but not the bit that this person has, when they bring it together their ideas mingle and mix and they can create a whole idea that is possible to build.

—**Students**, Wanaka Primary School, Otago, New Zealand

Wanaka students developed and applied key curriculum knowledge, showed growth across a range of deeper learning outcomes, raised more than $3,500 for learners in need, and used their respect for and connection to those learners as an opportunity to develop understanding of themselves.

A Recipe for Return: Models of Practice From BESD

Community Workshops

BESD leverages its Citizens Day (see the Chapter 2 case "Deeper Learning Is a Partnership") both as a way to generate community field-experience sponsors and as a way to spark community interest in hosting in-school workshops that support learners' exploration of interests and potential work and career opportunities.

At our high school, we have a "next steps" activity that happens throughout the year, and we have fifty [community members] volunteer to come in and do mini-workshops with our students to [help them] understand how what they're learning now will transfer into a work setting. And that's really powerful in connecting kids with why they're learning, what they're learning, and then what could be possible in the world of college and career.

—**Laurel Browning**, Superintendent, Burlington-Edison School District, United States

Putting Depth Into Practice

Reflect

With the Engaging Learners, Parents, and Communities as Real Partners Capability Rubric (Appendix A.2) in hand, reflect on the capabilities demonstrated in the "Soapbox Derby and Gala" and "Community

Workshops" learning experiences. How might those capabilities translate to your own classroom, school, or wider system? What explicit practices might support your system to further develop them?

Activity 9.4: Assessing Learning—Connection

Refer to the Connection progression (Appendix D.2) and think about how individual assessments might evidence the *conceptual* dimension of the learning experiences at Cygnaeus School and Van Randwijkschool. What evidence do you need to measure a student's progress on the dimension? How could these or similar assessments bring that evidence to life in your own classroom, school, or wider system? Now do the same for the *universal* dimension of the learning experience at Wanaka Primary School.

Activity 9.5: Measuring Practice—Partnerships

Using the Learning Experience Rubric (Appendix G), determine a rating for the *partnerships* dimension of the "Soapbox Derby and Gala" at Wanaka Primary School. What evidence of practice are you using to determine your rating? Where are there evidence gaps, and what's needed to fill them?

After they find a solution to a global challenge, create a work product that reflects their learning outcomes, or develop a message of local or global importance, learners don't want to stop there. They want to know, *how can our learning be shared or communicated to make a lasting and sustainable difference*? Deeper learning constantly creates opportunities for its development. It's learning worth sharing, and the only question is *how*. For students at Springlands School in Blenheim, New Zealand, the answer was *performance* (Springlands School, 2017).

Building on their learning from a previous science and sustainability unit, Springlands students asked, "How can we share an environmental message using visual arts, music, dance, movement, and drama?" They collaborated in groups across grade levels to determine which environmental messages were most important to share with a wider audience, and each group wrote and performed an act in a school-wide play, titled "Kāhore kau he Aorangi B (There Is No Planet B)." In the lead-up to the performance, students advertised their performances online and had a story featured in the local newspaper.

> I had no idea that so much plastic ends up in the oceans each year. We made a difference, as lots of the parents got our main message. It was good to get feedback from mums and dads.
>
> —**Student**, Springlands School, Blenheim, New Zealand

I loved the way children's writing was incorporated into the show. When we returned to the theater to watch the other half of the school perform the following night, my girls whispered to me who had written certain parts of the script. There was ownership and pride, not just for their own production, but for the work of their peers, too. As a parent of children growing up on this planet, I valued the opportunity for them to not only learn about some of the issues facing this planet, but to have a voice to demonstrate their learning through song and dance and to demonstrate what they can do to really make a difference.

—**Parent**, Springlands School, Blenheim, New Zealand

"There Is No Planet B" was flawless. What a wonderful challenge those children presented to the audience. Cherishing our environment, forests, rivers, sea, and creatures, [and] warnings of the dire consequences of the current pollution of land, water, and air, were clearly demonstrated through dance and song. Adults walked away from this concert with the pleas of child advocates for nature ringing in their ears. These young citizens of tomorrow have their priorities right. Let's listen to them and do what we can to ensure that they inherit a healthier planet than we now have.

—**Grandmother**, Springlands School, Blenheim, New Zealand

That's the power of communication in reaching particular audiences in a meaningful way, furthering the breadth and scope of our learning, and using it to contribute back. Don't make students wait to contribute to society—they're ready to make a difference now.

A Recipe for Return: Models of Practice From BESD

The Art of Assessment

While learning about light and sound, BESD students furthered their knowledge by continuing their learning—asking, "How can we create an instrument that generates volume and pitch?" Students partnered with their parents and one another to design and create their very own instruments, formed a "band," and played "live shows" for students at another grade level to showcase what they could do with what they'd learned.

Wherever possible, when you find that the learning is coming to a stop—don't let it.

BESD's "field experience" mindset is translating to powerful learning experiences and partnerships in a range of environments, all because of what might be called the "field flip": shifting the focus from the experience itself to the outcomes it develops.

> We are doing fewer and fewer field trips, and teachers are advocating for fewer. They want field *experiences*. . . . We partner with the Museum of Northwest Art, and they are helping our teachers understand how to leverage art as a way to engage students in critical thinking. They teach a process called "visual thinking strategies," where kids are accessing paintings and accessing sculpture within the setting of the museum and then talking about what they see and defending their understanding of the piece of art and what they believe [it's] trying to convey. That's been really powerful, because you can access that regardless of language; you don't have to be a strong reader. We're watching our special education students engage as deep thinkers in that setting, where[as] before they struggled if they couldn't read well. And then bringing art experts into the classroom [as well] to help teachers leverage art as a way to leverage thinking, expression, and communication.
>
> —**K. C. Knudson**, Executive Director of Teaching and Learning, Burlington-Edison School District, United States

Tools of the Trade

Think back to the "Digital Inquiry" case in Chapter 7, which focuses on the work that BESD put in on the back end to identify needs and build teachers' capacity to leverage digital and other technologies in the direct development of learning outcomes. The shift in thinking in relation to technology mirrors the district's shift from field trips to field experiences: it's not about the technology itself, but about *learning*—"How can we leverage technology to meet the learning needs of our students?" That's the key—with any new technological or other practice, think about how it's directly enabling the measurement and development of deeper learning outcomes. That shift in thinking, and a focus on developing the necessary capabilities, led to powerful shifts in practice, learning experiences, and outcomes in BESD (Wanielista, 2017b, 2017c).

At Bay View Elementary, fifth-grade students engaged with digital technologies as a way to learn about economics *and* provide a valuable service to their community. Leveraging Raspberry Pi devices, students learned the programming skills necessary to design a website, partnered with the Burlington Chamber of Commerce to learn about important economic principles and how they're tied to the operations of a community, and then put their combined learning to use—to demonstrate, further, and share their learning, they designed a website for the chamber of commerce, gaining valuable evaluative feedback from their "client" every step of the way. At Lucille Umbarger Elementary, third-grade students' ongoing environmental inquiry (see Chapter 8, "From Standards to Experiences") included an assessment in which students created digital slideshows to evidence and share what they'd learned, through field and other experiences, about the life cycle of salmon.

> You get to write your own stories on here, and you can have all the pages that you want. How I use technology is making my own unique way of doing things.
>
> —**Student**, Lucille Umbarger Elementary School, Burlington-Edison School District, United States

Fourth-grade students at Lucille Umbarger decided to use their learning about the different forms of energy to write a digital energy textbook (Atkinson, 2017). They each selected the form of energy they were most interested in researching and writing about, and they joined with like-minded classmates to collaborate on a chapter of the textbook. To give you an example, their field experience at the nearby SPARK Museum of Electrical Invention inspired one group to write a chapter about Tesla coils, explaining what these inventions are and why they're important. The creation of the textbook was not only a valuable opportunity to assess learners' knowledge and other outcome development—it will be utilized and expanded on by the school's fourth-grade classes for years to come. Embedding ways in which students' learning can teach others in the classes behind them is a powerful example of leveraging technology to form deeper learning partnerships. BESD's celebration of students' roles as "experts" and "coaches" in relation to technology is supporting students to collaborate, communicate, and share ("trade") their gifts and abilities with one another.

> It's not about the tech; it's about what it helps us do. The kids are being innovative. They're going to share, and they're going to collaborate, and they're going to create.
>
> —**Arie Werder**, Technology Consultant Teacher, Lucille Umbarger Elementary School, Burlington-Edison School District, United States

---

Putting Depth Into Practice

Activity 9.6: Assessing Learning—Collaboration

Consider the *leveraging digital* dimension of the Collaboration progression (Appendix D.3). For the BESD learning experiences described under "The Art of Assessment" and "Tools of the Trade," how might individual assessments evidence this dimension? What evidence do you need to measure a student's progress on the dimension, and how could these or similar assessments bring that evidence to life in your own classroom, school, or school system?

Activity 9.7: Measuring Practice—Inquiry

Think back to the "Kāhore kau he Aorangi B (There Is No Planet B)" learning experience at Springlands School. How would you rate it on the *inquiry* dimension of the Learning Experience Rubric (Appendix G)? What evidence of practice are you using to determine your rating? Where are there evidence gaps, and what's needed to fill them?

Every last detail of the learning experiences described in this chapter represents an opportunity for the assessment of deeper learning. Think back to the list of sample assessments in Figure 8.2—every interaction with your learners and their learning is an opportunity for assessment. Once your measures provide an intentional application for gathered evidence of the outcomes that matter, it's only a matter of matching evidence to measure. Evidence really is everywhere, and we have deeper learning to thank for that. You've seen in the experiences described in these pages that deeper learning never fails to provide additional opportunities for its development—or, therefore, for assessment. How? Because it connects to students' lives and interests, and students are interested in improving the lives of others and the world. That interest knows no limits—we can't let education impose any.

There's unlimited potential for learning when it's treated as a celebration. With what learners throughout the world, as described in our case studies, are accomplishing in their own communities and globally, how could it be treated any other way? They and other learning partners are celebrating who learners are, what they know and can do for one another, how connected we are as a people, and our human capacity for contributing back in meaningful and fulfilling ways. They're making a real difference in their own and others' lives, and we hope their voices and practice will continue to make a difference as their learning continues to spread. Something worth celebrating is something worth sharing—celebrate learning, share it with others, and watch as it spreads.

No Interrupting the Flow

There's so much we can learn from the cases in this chapter alone, and they represent only a fraction of the deeper learning happening around the world. It goes by any number of names and lives in any number of experiences. What's important is the *learning*, as well as the *learning partners* who make it possible. The cases in this chapter have similar elements, but they all demonstrate something unique about practice and learning, and together they give life to the concepts, frameworks, and processes we've been talking about all throughout these pages. Collectively, they show us what deeper learning outcomes, system capabilities, and the elements of authentic practice look like when they all come together in those "deeper learning moments" between students and their learning partners.

The promise of examining learning experiences in this way isn't just that you'll have ideas for new assessments to roll out, but, better still, that you'll identify the practices you need to make deeper learning a reality—no matter the learning at hand. When students have the opportunity to take their learning in the directions they see fit, any assessment can be the spark that sets deeper learning ablaze.

Deeper learning has a characteristic *flow*. It starts with a spark—be it the curriculum content that students need to know or be it any other learning identified as important by learners and their learning partners at any point in time. From there, initial assessment reveals current levels of learning and a glimpse of what will be important to discover along the way, and the necessary curriculum links and connections are formed. Inquiry guides the course of the experience, which never takes a straight-line path but branches to and fro as learners' curiosity and creativity take hold. Explicit attention is paid throughout the learning journey to students' development of deeper learning outcomes, and students are active partners in assessment, along with each of the other elements of inquiry. Students are "teachers"—they leverage partnerships, environments, technology, and inquiry to contribute to the learning of others, understanding the learning process as an active and dynamic partnership between themselves and their learning partners. Assessment evidence informs the measurement of deeper learning outcomes, which in turn informs how the learning moves next. Reflection and change pervade the experience, but those changes never disjoint the learning—*there's no interrupting the flow*.

If deeper learning is the *motion*, then practice is what makes it *move*. With your own learners, remember that meaningful and fulfilling practice isn't just about *instruction*—it's about learning, partnership, and contribution. Your learners aren't the same as the learners in the contexts above, but the deeper learning outcomes, the practices and capabilities that bring them to life, and what those outcomes support us all to do are the same no matter *who* your learners are.

Deeper learning is wide-ranging—students don't naturally learn in the narrow and divided subject or curriculum areas that school systems have constructed for them—but depth isn't contingent on a learning experience's length or the magnitude of its immediate impact. What matters is that each individual assessment be purposeful in connecting to learners and their interests and that the system of assessments collectively work toward every important outcome, every single day. These aren't one-off or disconnected experiences—you can't practice deeper learning one day and traditional learning the next. Deeper learning rides everything, always and everywhere, and any individual assessment can take you deeper. If you're committed to developing deeper learning outcomes, your learners will take care of the rest.

When learning is deeper, you feel that what's happening is worth celebrating and should be shared and that, most importantly, each of your learners should be celebrated, too—for who they are, what they've accomplished, and what's still to come. That sharing is essential—how do we know that the practices embedded in the experiences above develop deeper learning outcomes? Because their effectiveness has been measured in light of learners' outcomes and then shared so that others could reflect on, discuss, and measure the same, in a process called *collaborative moderation*. This process is the subject of the next chapter, and it spreads our practice and learning throughout school systems and the world.

Putting Depth Into Practice

Reflect

Take some time to think about the learning experiences shared throughout this chapter. Did any assessments, practices, or other points of learning especially resonate with you? How might you apply them with your own learners to deepen their learning outcomes? Reflect also on your use of the Learning Progressions and the Learning Experience Rubric. What was successful, challenging, or exciting, and how prepared do you feel to use these measures within your own learning experiences?

Activity 9.8: Authentic Learning Design

Drawing on the cases in this chapter for inspiration, and building on Activity 8.2, "Student Inquiry in Practice" (or heading in a new direction entirely), use your new learning in conjunction with the student design guide (Appendix E.3) to design (or redesign) a deeper learning experience. It could look similar to an assessment described in this chapter; it could be an ongoing project, an out-of-school "field experience," a worksheet, a survey, a question, a conversation starter, or any other way of assessing and further developing your students' outcomes. Whatever the experience, think about how it's connected to your students' lives and interests and how your students' learning might be shared.

For Your Consideration . . .

Ideally, your system will develop into one in which the phrase "deeper learning experience" is redundant—in other words, "deeper learning experience" is synonymous with "learning." The same can be said of

(Continued)

(Continued)

"deeper learning"—the "deeper" qualification is required only when it isn't the norm. Right now, in the United States and globally, deeper learning isn't the norm, so learning is qualified throughout this book and certainly in its manifestations throughout the world (and the result is a bit of a mouthful). We've already talked about the value of engaging with various frameworks and processes as a movement from surface to deeper learning. But the next and ultimate movement is from *deeper learning* to *learning*, where the former's outcomes are synonymous with the latter's, and where every learning experience adds depth to your students and the world. What can you and your learners do, every day, to make depth the norm?

Access the appendices at
resources.corwin.com/MeasuringHumanReturn

CHAPTER 9

Chapter 10

COLLABORATIVE MODERATION

Measuring and Sharing Learning and Practice

Common moderation processes involve grading or scoring students' performance on a particular assessment, using rubrics or another form of scoring guide. The process engages a group of teachers within or often between schools, and its purpose is to ensure consistency in scoring decisions between graders for individual assessments. It's an important professional learning process for a number of reasons, not least of which is the value of directly connecting teachers' professional learning with the examination of students' learning (Darling-Hammond, 2017).

The moderation process we describe in this chapter is slightly different. Rather than working toward grading consistency on a particular assessment, we're interested in measurement consistency in relation to authentic mixed-method assessment. In other words, our focus is on establishing inter-rater reliability in informing Learning Progression and rubric ratings with a range of AMMA evidence. The shift makes sense—AMMA takes the focus off individual assessments and places it on how the breadth of assessment evidence comes together to evidence intended learning. Furthermore, the collaborative moderation described in this chapter involves measuring the effectiveness of instructional *practice*, within a given learning experience, in developing deeper learning outcomes. Student performance is still paramount, and taking your own learning one step further in the examination of *why* students' learning actually occurred will be invaluable. It'll require fully evidenced *descriptions* of the learning that occurred and how it was enabled or enhanced by authentic instructional practice.

We refer to these descriptions as learning **exemplars**, and they take a number of forms (e.g., slideshow presentations, websites, or collections of documents, videos, and pictures). What's important is that the descriptions they provide are enough to fully evidence the learning that occurred, emphasizing both *what* it looked like and *why* it happened. Exemplars, like the learning they describe, are a celebration.

Exemplar moderation is intended to

- develop a shared language and understanding around deeper learning measures, concepts, and outcomes by engaging teachers and other professionals around the sharing of practice and learning;
- collectively identify (and subsequently popularize) the practices that develop deeper learning outcomes, for application in learning partners' daily practice and experiences;
- build understanding of the current depth of practice and learning, both school-wide and system-wide, supporting the identification of strengths and areas for improvement; and
- establish inter-rater reliability in learning partners' use of measures of deeper learning.

In order to make a difference not only in pockets, but for all learners, after engaging in deeper learning experiences, we have to share what's working. And because deeper learning is "strongest when systemic," whatever learning we push up through the system will find its way back to us in the form of strengthened system capabilities and practices that will enable even greater depth. One of the best vehicles for "moving" that learning throughout our school systems is the change team process, and change team meetings offer ideal opportunities for small-scale moderations in addition to any scheduled moderation sessions that engage the school's wider professional community. Both are valuable—ongoing, regular moderation in change teams ensures that we're developing, spreading, and acting on best practices in real time, and providing formal professional learning opportunities that engage a wider range of teachers and other professionals throughout our schools or districts is equally important. We'll explore what the process looks like in change teams and how it might look as a formal professional learning experience as well.

Because of its deep connection to learners and their learning, and because learners are the central focus of and reason for everything you and your partners do, moderation will play a significant role in illuminating areas in which to focus your efforts. We promised you'd be moving into and out of each measurement frame at will, and moderation will tell you a lot about what you need and where you'll need to "be" to find it. Here's how it works:

1. *Inquire.* Among their focal students (those most in need of improvement, as discussed in Chapter 3), teachers select one student for whom to evidence learning and related practice in their exemplar. Why one? Remember the importance of starting small—once you're comfortable evidencing learning and practice in relation to one student, you'll know how to do it for all of them, at which time your exemplars might focus on anywhere from one to all of your focal students. Gather the evidence required to demonstrate the learning that's occurring and why.

2. *Describe.* Teachers design a learning exemplar that shows *that* intended outcomes developed and *why*. Think about what these exemplars might look like in light of AMMA—they should include a range of indicators that combine to fully evidence teachers' decisions with regard to levels of learning (more on the evidence to come). It helps build out the exemplar as the learning progresses to ensure that the necessary evidence is captured for sharing. Plus, if learners are engaged in every aspect of their learning, shouldn't they be engaged in describing it, too? Their learning descriptions can be included in the exemplar. Evidencing learning is an important opportunity for learning in its own right.

3. *Moderate.* Once the exemplars are completed, you're ready to moderate them within change teams or schools. Using online file sharing (or in whatever way is most suited to your context or most suited to an individual exemplar), make the exemplars available to all participants—a group that should include teachers, principals or other school leaders, and any other staff members whose experience or expertise will add value to the process. Both individually and collaboratively, moderation participants should examine each exemplar, reflect on and discuss the evidence provided, measure learning using the Learning Progressions, and measure the effectiveness of embedded practices using the Learning Experience Rubric. Moderation processes may last a couple hours (e.g., during change team meetings), or they may be spread across a day or more—depending, for example, on the number of exemplars and participants. As you've seen, there's always efficacy in going slow to go deeper. Doing so ensures that your intended outcomes will become a reality and that participants will complete the process ready to make positive changes that will deepen learning everywhere and for everyone.

4. *Change.* This seemingly little element of inquiry makes all the difference—it's the reason the inquiry process is continuous, and it's the source of its transformative power. Changes in practice are integral to the inquiry process, and, therefore, your school or wider system's success with deeper learning overall. What you learn from moderation has to be put right back into the system to focus your efforts on developing the outcomes and capabilities in need of improvement, as well as the practices that will bring them to life.

As you learned in Chapter 9, the Learning Experience Rubric measures the depth of practice embedded in each experience. It's what teachers and other learning partners use to measure their own individual experiences, and it's a tool for collective use in the process of moderation. When thinking about new practices to implement and measure in your own school or wider system, the practices illustrated in the previous chapter are a good place to start. *You have the tools, language, and frames to bring these practices to life.* But new practices are and will be emerging all the time, and it's up to you not only to identify them, but to share them as well. Discover and embed them throughout the learning process, evidence them in learning exemplars, and spread them throughout your system through the process of collaborative moderation.

We noted that moderation will tell you a lot about where you need to be in the ongoing measurement process, as well as what you need from each frame (i.e., engagement, development, clarity, inquiry, or depth) at any particular time. As an example, let's say your school's collaborative moderation process reveals challenges surrounding the engagement of parents as real partners in their children's learning, an important aspect of learning partnerships and one of the system capabilities. You've (1) identified this as your top instructional priority and are ready to design solutions. Your (2) professional learning strategy will involve (3) working with parents to jointly understand learners' interests and needs and (4) supporting them to partner in every aspect of the inquiry process. You'll work on (5) supporting, valuing, and utilizing insights gathered through the engagement of learning partners and (6) fostering parent leaders. Throughout the professional learning process, your focus will be on (7) facilitating deeper learning experiences and teaching for 100 percent success and (8) gathering evidence in the system and the community by (9) conducting assessment that provides a complete picture of parent engagement and its impact on students' learning, as monitored and measured using the Learning Progressions. By the time you and your learning partners gather again to (10) moderate these exemplars and identify best practices, you'll have a wealth of new evidence and learning to share and then spread throughout your school or wider system, along with new priorities and professional learning focuses to keep your system in motion.

Each of the numbered elements above represents a dimension of the Capability Rubrics, which work together to support the breadth of activity in your school system. This narrative makes it easy to see how moderation brings everything—from the use of deeper learning tools to the ongoing inquiry required at all levels of the system—together as a whole. Whether you're redesigning assessments, redeveloping measures, or engaging in any other professional learning effort aimed at adding depth to learning experiences, *it's all about the learner*, and it can all be accelerated by moderation.

Putting Depth Into Practice

Reflect

Think about the value and importance of collaborative moderation in professional learning and overall inquiry processes. What might collaborative moderation look like in your system? Would you and your learning partners be comfortable describing, sharing, discussing, and learning from one another's learning experiences? What would it take to embed collaborative moderation in your system's professional learning strategy, and what would it take for it to be successful?

Exemplars, Evidence, and Inter-Rater Reliability

As with all measurement, the strength and ensuing impact of the moderation process is dependent on one primary element—*evidence*. In the same way that a range of AMMA evidence is required to measure students' development of deeper learning outcomes, a range of evidence is required to demonstrate both that and why the development occurred. It's been one of the main questions and considerations to come out of moderation experiences we've witnessed thus far: moderators, including other teachers, may not have witnessed the learning described in teachers' exemplars, so what does the exemplar have to include to allow for fully informed measurement?

To address this issue, when designing exemplars, teachers should try to include the following information:

Context. Why did you focus on evidencing learning with this particular learner? What curriculum areas are you working in, and what are the explicit curriculum links? What outcomes and elements of authentic practice are you focusing on, respectively? Framing the experience in this way will provide the learning context necessary for anchoring the evidence to come.

Ratings. Provide progression ratings for the student's development of the outcomes (or individual dimensions of the outcomes) you're focusing on. Remember that it's okay to focus on a single outcome, or even a single dimension, and that doing so greatly develops your inquiry practice. Also provide ratings of your own practice using the Learning Experience Rubric—again, only for the dimensions you're focusing on. As you know, providing ratings isn't enough. The main objective of any exemplar should be to provide evidence of *why* those ratings were made.

Evidence. Evidence of practice and outcomes makes up the meat of any effective exemplar, and the two are necessarily linked. What practices are developing what outcomes, and to what extent? You already mapped assessment evidence against the Learning Progressions to measure learners' outcomes, so that same evidence—whether it's full or partial classwork, conversations with students or parents, observations, test scores, survey results, or any other AMMA evidence—should be displayed or described in the exemplar alongside your ratings. The goal is for moderators to be able to use the evidence provided in the exemplar to come to the same conclusions about student learning. Similarly, you have to provide the evidence to demonstrate that particular practices, or a combination of practices, led to particular outcomes. If you used the Authentic Inquiry Guides to design, track, and measure the learning, they're valuable evidence sources to include. What did you do, how did you do it, and why did it work? That's what's worth sharing, and as long as you can effectively evidence that practice, it'll make a big difference for your learners and other learning partners.

Reflection. Your own reflections and mid- or post-implementation changes are important conversation starters and discussion pieces for moderation—what were the major successes, what changes were made or will have to be made, and what challenges were met with along the way? When describing and discussing challenges, focus on what was or will be needed to take learning deeper. Doing so will tell your audience a lot about where you are as a system and what needs to happen next to further support the ongoing process of deepening learning.

The common theme—and what eventually will determine the success of moderation—is evidence. It has to anchor you at all times. When making any claim about practices, the learning that occurred, or anything else related to a given exemplar, refer to the evidence. If there's a disagreement between moderation participants, refer to the evidence. Everywhere and at all times, in order to accurately represent the learning described and understand its impact, *refer to the evidence.* And if evidence isn't available, constructively share that feedback with learning partners so that the necessary evidence can either be provided on the spot or be gathered during future iterations and other experiences.

Teachers, students, and others won't all be in the same place at the same time with regard to their learning. That's okay—remember that moderation is a *learning experience*, not a high-stakes system accountability practice. Its purpose is improvement and keeping teachers, school leaders, and other learning partners accountable to students and their needs. *Those* stakes are high, and that's why you should moderate.

You can see how important the evidence is and that teachers and other learning partners will likely need some time to figure out what evidence to include—let alone how best to format, structure, and describe it—in exemplars. We've noted the benefits of starting small to go deeper, and focusing on a single learner will significantly lessen potential challenges. All learners are different, but practice applies—once you learn how to evidence deeper learning for even a single student, it'll become "what you do" with them all. In addition, schools or wider systems may choose to provide a template for exemplar design, which may include a recommended format along with prompts or questions to get learning partners thinking within the content structure outlined earlier. But what you ask of your students throughout the learning process is what you should ask of learning partners here—we're talking about *creativity*. Exemplars should be designed in the way that best demonstrates the learning that occurred. Although a template is a helpful guide and a way of ensuring consistency with a format that works well, learning partners should be supported to get creative in how they showcase and celebrate their learning. No matter the format, what matters is the capacity to clearly and successfully link evidence of deeper learning with evidence of the practices that help bring it to life.

Putting Depth Into Practice

Activity 10.1: Design an Exemplar

Leveraging the experience you designed in Activity 9.8, "Authentic Learning Design," or any learning experience implemented or currently transpiring in your classroom, school, or wider system, describe and evidence the learning that has taken or is taking place for an individual student. In other words, *design an exemplar*. Remember to get creative and to focus on the evidence required to demonstrate *that* (measured outcomes) and *why* (measured practice) learning occurred. Describing learning in this way is a valuable exercise in and of itself, but that value compounds when you share your learning with others. You've engaged your learners and used deeper learning tools and implemented an experience that has deepened students' outcomes. You now have the opportunity to describe and share it in a way that celebrates everything that you, your learners, and your other partners have accomplished.

If your role doesn't involve working directly with students, or if you don't have the evidence you need to describe learning and practice in this way, think about what an exemplar might look like in your context. Is there an exemplar format that might be suited to implementing moderation processes in your schools or districts? What kind of support might your teachers and schools need to kick off and sustain moderation activity?

Because it incorporates all deeper learning tools in one way or another, moderation will greatly increase your capacity to use any measure of deeper learning. It will also help to ensure that your use of these measures is consistent throughout your school or wider system. This consistency is called **inter-rater reliability**, and it must be established in order for any measure or measurement to be valid. If measures (1) work as they should and (2) are used as they should be, then a learning partner presented with the same measure and the same evidence of learning should arrive at a similar rating or measurement decision.

Since moderation requires that you come to collective ratings with regard to the exemplar provided, it's a great opportunity to assess and further establish inter-rater reliability within and across schools. Referring back to the two premises noted earlier, you can determine whether measures are being used as they should be by—you guessed it—referring to the evidence. Differences in measurement can often be explained and worked through by filling in gaps in one or another moderator's evidence bank. But if you've agreed on the evidence and are sure that all moderators are on the same page regarding what's available, and you're still unable to arrive at the same or a very similar decision (say, within two levels of progress), there may be an issue with the measure itself. Go back to the drawing board (i.e., the development frame) and refine the measure based on your collective understanding of what needs to change.

Inter-rater reliability often carries valid concerns for school systems that are considering the systematic measurement and subsequent reporting of deeper learning outcomes. One of the most common initial concerns is that taking the time to establish inter-rater reliability will take the focus away from instruction. *Moderation of the type described earlier places the focus on both.* By engaging in the moderation of exemplars, you can establish inter-rater reliability in the use of measures, further develop your capacity for instruction, and provide valuable evidence to your school or wider system about what's working and what additional support to provide.

In order to continue the learning between moderations, it's useful to set up and continue to add to an online (or otherwise made available) exemplar bank through which teachers and other learning partners can access moderated exemplars and refer to what was presented and discussed during moderation. Similar *assessment* banks are useful in providing examples of assessments that can be implemented in individual schools or classrooms (see the Performance Assessment Resource Bank, www.performanceassessmentresourcebank.org), but exemplars designed and shared with the intentions described previously provide not only assessment designs, but descriptions and evidence of practice and learning as well. Assessment banks are one thing—AMMA banks are another. Although design is important, it's only one of the considerations for authentic practice.

We've framed this discussion around moderation within individual schools, but moderating across schools, districts, and even countries can also be incredibly valuable in deepening each system's collective capacity and the outcomes of its students. Coming together around a diversity of schools' best examples of practice and learning never fails to add depth in any context. Here's one approach to and description of the impact of inter-school moderation, as practiced and experienced by a group of schools in New Zealand.

> The exemplar moderation process has been central to the way we have engaged with schools in New Zealand. Rather than work through the planning process toward moderation as the end point, we've chosen to begin with a moderation activity using an exemplar (often more than one) to engage staff in "thinking backwards" through the planning process, leading to more in-depth and focused understandings of the significance of each of the [elements of authentic practice] in making learning deeper.
>
> We've found this a hugely successful approach, resulting in the leads within each school feeling more empowered in the way they work with their staff and [feeling] confident in terms of their understanding of the process and subsequent ability to respond to questions.

By starting off with the exemplar moderation process, we have been able to address directly some of the challenges around deep versus shallow learning and identify strategically the sorts of things that need to be worked on in each school context (and in each individual teacher context) to achieve the deep learning goals.

—**Derek Wenmoth and Margot McKeegan,**
CORE Education, New Zealand

The notion of "thinking backward" is an important consideration in all work with deeper learning, and it's an especially relevant one as we near the end of this book. If you're planning to engage with deeper learning in your classroom, school, or wider system, you have the complete picture—you know what you're working toward, and you have what you need to get there. Look to the Exemplar Moderation tool in Appendix C.8 when setting up and facilitating moderations in your own change teams, your own schools, or beyond, and use the learning you've added along the way to think backward, engage deeply with what's been presented, and connect the dots from where you want to be back to where you are now. It's a journey, but that's deeper learning—an ongoing process of learning, depth, and discovery.

Putting Depth Into Practice

Reflect

"Think backward" through everything you've read and learned to this point, and reflect on the buildup of learning that comprises your current understanding of your learners, your system, and your and other learning partners' roles and development in relation to depth. How do you feel about what's been presented, and what does it mean for your learners and your practice?

Assess your understanding of the five frames of measurement and then of the role that measurement plays in bringing deeper learning to life. How confident are you in your capacity to *measure human return*? Do you have what you need to make deeper learning a reality? If not, what do you need, and what can you do to get it?

For Your Consideration . . .

What's learning if not a celebration? In short, it isn't *learning*—at least not learning that's *deep*, *meaningful*, and *fulfilling*. If learning in and for school isn't exciting, engaging, and worth celebrating and sharing, then we aren't doing what's right for our learners. When we do what's right

(Continued)

(Continued)

for them, they'll do even more for others and the world. Our students already contribute in so many ways and can contribute in so many more if they're encouraged and supported to learn with and for others. If our schools are places of learning, they'll be driven by contribution. If, to you, the idea of measuring the outcomes that enable that contribution once seemed distant and out of reach, hopefully that's no longer the case—you can teach and learn deeply with what you have now, and you can spread deeper learning to others. Build on the depth you've put into practice all throughout these pages, go back to go deeper, and continue to make a difference in the lives of your learners. The deeper you dive, the deeper the difference you'll make.

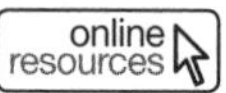

Access the appendices at
resources.corwin.com/MeasuringHumanReturn

Final Reflections on Part III

The inquiry process proves a pleasant and steadfast travel companion. You'll get to know it well—it won't ever leave your side. And it won't be the only companion keeping you company along the way—you'll be working with and for others at every point in the journey. Celebrate yourself and your learning partners and what makes you all who you are. It's bound to make the journey all the better and its outcomes all the deeper. Remember to frame all your activity within the inquiry process and overall measurement framework, and keep in mind that every engagement with your students and within your systems is an opportunity to gather evidence. AMMA will come naturally into focus when you realize how much of the evidence you need is right in front of you and how the tools come together to help you gather and synthesize the rest of it.

The emphasis of education has to change from *acquisition* to *return*. The time for that change is now. With the understandings you've gained by engaging with this book, you know and have what it takes to make it happen—mindsets, frames, processes, tools, and, most important, *depth*.

Conclusion

HOW DEEP ARE YOU?

Very. We all are. Our capacity for self-understanding, knowledge, competency, and connection is extraordinary. It's exciting—and every movement toward deepening any one of those outcomes is something worth celebrating. Deeper learning is cause for celebration because it's collective. If we're learning deeply, it's because we're being supported by others and because we're supporting others to do the same. Nobody wants to celebrate alone. With deeper learning, we never have to. Each outcome leads us to every other—and one another—and they all lead to contribution. It's a beautiful system—it's *meaningful*, and it's *fulfilling*.

It's likely your school system is lagging behind you in the depth department, and that's okay. You're not alone. Our systems have been bringing us "up" to their level for years, and they'll surely resist our efforts to reverse that trend. The difference is that now, maybe for the first time, we're discovering what we need to pull back—the measures and other tools (better yet, *the capacity to develop them*), the language and processes, and the collective strength and desire to move our systems in the right direction. We can resist their pull to the surface, and it starts and continues with a celebration of our and our learners' humanity. If we as students, teachers, parents, school leaders, wider-system leaders, community members, and all learning partners truly want our school systems to make a difference for learners and the world, *we can't leave our depth at the door*.

You've made it to the final frame of measurement, and, really, as you've seen throughout our descriptions of each of the other frames, it's been there all along. Everything that educators do within the interconnected system we're advocating for is framed around adding and working toward greater depth. You know about deeper learning and have seen it in action, in both practice and outcome, so how should we think about "depth" in relation to all of us, every school system, and the world? As should be clear by now, depth is the intersection of learning and contribution. Moving forward, whenever we think or talk about "learning," we should be using that term to embody the breadth of deeper learning outcomes. When we ask students, "What did you learn today?" we should want to know more than what they learned in math, literature, science, history, and other traditional academic subjects. We should want to know what students learned and are learning about (a) themselves and others, (b) what they're capable of doing, and (c) their relationships with others and the world (of course, deeper learning also begs the question,

"What will you learn *tonight*?"). Once all learning partners know what we're looking for and what learning actually involves, what comes next couldn't be more intuitive: "How will you use that learning to make a difference?" That is, how will students contribute back—within their classes, their schools, their families, and their local or global communities? And while these are the questions that are important to ask, depth ensures we'll no longer have to ask them. Their "answers" will be evident, in the form of contributions. As you've seen, learning that's truly engaging—that supports learners to make a difference and leads to lifetimes of meaning and fulfillment for all—is learning worth sharing. It will be shared—*and widely*—and what's shared will make the world a better place.

Depth is the intersection of learning and contribution; *humanity is the force that brings them together*. Why else would we want who we are, what we know and can do, and how we connect with others to make a positive and lasting difference in their lives? The humanity we share is the reason we share. To say that humanity brings learning and contribution together is to say that it brings *us* together, at depths we'd never reach on our own. Our depth allows us to see what makes others who they are and support one another to see the world in new ways. Depth is where and why we connect—it's about discovering what's beautiful about others and the world, about celebrating it together, and about identifying what needs to change and making changes together, too. We can always do better—for ourselves, our families, our learners, and the world—and strengthening our school systems is a powerful way to better us all. Any step, big or small, in the right direction for our systems and our learners is a step in the right direction for the world. Celebrate the beauty in the *movement*.

When learning and contribution come together in this way, so, too, do learning and teaching. We've had the actors right all along—we all need to learn, and we need teachers capable of facilitating and supporting that learning. But we've gone wrong in conceiving of *divisions*—among learner, teacher, and school leader and among school, community, and world—divisions that make our educational systems mere fractions of the places they could be if those walls were to come down: places where everybody learns, teaches, and leads, anywhere and at any time. That's the fluidity our learners need. They want to teach and lead, too, and they have no reason to be alone in their learning.

Similarly, there's a tendency to separate our educational systems' operations into two categories: (1) what we want to do (deeper learning) and (2) what we have to do (everything else). *Deeper learning doesn't do division*. We have to go "all in," and it starts by connecting everything we do to its impact on learners' outcomes. Your school or wider system may not adopt this measurement framework or a focus on deeper learning outcomes right away, but there's no limit to what you can do with what you already have. Use your knowledge of your learners to develop and measure the outcomes that matter, and share your own learning as it develops. *If you share it, it will spread*. Instead of fractionalizing by division, it's time for adding by contribution.

There's a lot that goes into depth, and just thinking about learning and humanity in this way and using this language can go a long way toward changing our thoughts and behaviors in relation to others, our school systems, and our places within them. In the same way that we track students' learning progress, there's invaluable opportunity in understanding our own practice and behaviors as a progression from surface to deep. With the help of this book, you've started by getting to know a little about yourself and your own system, and you've explored the continuous process of setting up and working within a comprehensive measurement framework. You've seen and know what it looks like to move through and "live within" each frame, and you have a developing picture of the measurement process to continue to dive into and fill out at every step of your journey.

So, what's in frame?

Deeper learning begins, always and everywhere, with shifts in thinking. If we don't change the way we see our students and our systems, we'll never make lasting changes in our relationships with them—we won't change our behavior, so we won't change learners' outcomes. In Chapter 1, we reflected on seven **assumption-shatterers** and their importance in our systems, and hopefully we shattered additional assumptions along the way with regard to your own and others' roles, assessment evidence and how to gather it, and why teaching and learning are so important in the first place. What other assumptions were shattered over the course of your reading, *and in what other ways will you shift*?

The beliefs of educators reflect the cultural conditions of our schools and wider systems, which, in turn, say a lot about the **system capabilities** we collectively value and take shared ownership in developing. In Chapter 2, we explored the importance of each capability and illuminated their descriptions with examples from Burlington-Edison School District (BESD) and other systems around the world. All activity within our systems is an opportunity to gather valuable assessment evidence to inform our use of the Capability Rubrics and the Learning Development Rubric, and the most effective way to capture and act on that evidence is the **change team process** described in Chapter 3. Guided by **inquiry**, multilevel change teams keep a finger on the pulse of our systems' capabilities and our learners' outcomes, ensure that what's working in one area of our systems can make a difference in other areas, and provide wider-system learning partners with the evidence they need to remove barriers and provide necessary support.

What really gets deeper learning going are our learners and their outcomes. As introduced in Part II of this book, we can bring them into focus using the lens of *measurement* and the **five frames** that make its authentic practice a reality. Whenever we think about any one of these processes, we have to think about how it's framing our measurement and development of deeper learning outcomes. *We have to think about the learner*. The measurement *lens* and its five connected *frames* will make sure we're "seeing" our students clearly—and responding to what we see—every step of the way. The Capability Rubrics will support us in every frame of measurement, through *engaging* learning partners (Chapter 4); providing the language and process for identifying or *developing* deeper learning measures (Chapter 5); and establishing *clarity* of language, understanding, alignment, and use (Chapter 6). They'll support us to assess, design, implement, measure, and reflect and change, and that process of *inquiry* (Part III) will frame our use of the rubrics. There's no measurement without each of the other inquiry processes, and without measurement, we'll have no way to know how we're tracking in relation to *depth*.

Change teams should engage with the Capability Rubrics every step of the way, in order to identify any areas in need of improvement and to shape priorities at the school, district, and wider-system levels. The only way to know whether our development of system capabilities is actually making a difference is to measure changes in students' outcomes. Our tools for the measurement of student learning are the Learning Progressions, and in Part II we took a detailed look at their development, starting with identifying the outcomes that matter and ending with fully realized measures of self-understanding, connection, and collaboration.

As you and your learning partners work with the Authentic Inquiry Guides to support the development and measurement of capabilities and outcomes, the embedded practices that make both a reality will be found in the **elements of authentic practice** (Chapter 4). Try to embed their underlying practices in all systems-level activity and in students' **deeper learning experiences** (Chapter 9), and measure the effects on learners' outcomes with the Learning Experience Rubric, both in regular practice and for the process of **collaborative moderation** (Chapter 10). Engage learning partners around the measurement and sharing of both learning and practice, in order to (a) establish inter-rater reliability in the use of measures without diverting the focus from instruction, (b) inform the measurement of capabilities and the identification of priorities, and (c) develop practice and outcomes in the process.

The only way to gather the evidence we need to inform our use of measures of outcomes, capability, and practice is **authentic mixed-method assessment (AMMA)**. We have to understand every moment in our interaction with students and their learning as an opportunity to evidence learning—our own, our students', and our systems'—and that whenever we gather evidence, we're assessing. AMMA supports us to capture, measure, and act on the important evidence that's always been around us and to fill evidence gaps in formative ways that further learning in the process. AMMA gives us the opportunity to measure our learners as they really are (and, hopefully, as we've always *seen* them).

We need to treat learning as a deeper learning experience—*it has to become "what we do."* And as students, parents, educators, and other learning partners, it's what we've always wanted to do. Deeper learning isn't daunting; *it's exciting*. We've all seen learners' excitement when they discover something that's interesting and meaningful to their lives—that excitement isn't limited to students. Everybody's a learner, and we demonstrate our learning at all levels of the system through our fortunate inability to keep it to ourselves. It's visible in the stories and experiences shared by learning partners throughout the world and described in these pages, as well as in countless other contexts. Sharing couldn't be more important for the spread and advancement of deeper learning. Fortunately, by its very nature, deeper learning is designed to be shared—*sharing is contributing back.*

A continuous commitment to greater depth requires a continuous commitment to change. Use this book as an ongoing resource in your continuing (and, hopefully, *expanding*) deeper learning journey, because if it works as we intended, *it'll change with you.* We've talked about the importance of taking learning off of a linear plane—we tried to take this book off it, too, by looking forward and back; repeating, retreading, expanding, and building on previous learning; and connecting what we have with what we're learning and where we're headed. *That's deeper learning*, and it won't come together in a linear way. The intent of the reflections and other activities is to shift the focus of education from its contents to their application and to how that application makes a difference in learners' lives and the world. Refer back to, reread, and continue to use this book as a learning tool throughout your journey, drawing from and creating new ideas and learning as your thinking and engagement reach new levels of depth. Measuring as you go will help you see, communicate, and develop learning in unique ways made possible by learning *together*. Deeper learning outcomes are human outcomes. They connect us to one another, and they're what we need to improve our world.

Even in systems already engaging with deeper learning, the focus is often on how deeper learning experiences *prepare* learners for the "real world"—how they'll use their learning in the future or to someday make a difference. But it's all *real*, and whenever we feel the need to draw a distinction between "school" and "world," something's gone wrong. It's instinctive for students who are developing the outcomes that matter to want to take their learning further, and that "further" naturally involves contributing back. For all of us, regardless of age or position, learning is more meaningful when it's connected to something—or someone—outside ourselves. There's a reason many of the learning experiences described in these pages extend beyond school walls, in terms of both impact and scope. When we follow learning to its natural "conclusion," we're using it to make a difference in others' lives and the world. Whether it's a group of learners sharing their own and other cultures with families and other members of the community, connecting with others and their environments to share and create new knowledge, or working collaboratively in any way to deepen one another's learning, we all want who we are and what we know and can do to improve people's lives and "put good into" the world. Of course, with learning like this, there is no conclusion—only outcomes. Those outcomes are global, deep, and ever deepening.

Deeper learning is never ending—we can continuously strive for greater depth in our systems and our world. The challenge of this conclusion—"*How deep are you?*"—doesn't call into question your capacity for self-understanding, knowledge, competency, connection, or contribution, or your capacity for leading a life of meaning and fulfillment. There's incredible depth in the humanity we share, and the challenge is to ensure that depth is felt in your school, your school systems, your every interaction, and the world. You'll know you've succeeded when you're able to measure it. You'll know you've succeeded when "deeper learning" is *learning*.

This book has introduced *human return* as the driving force behind contribution, meaning, fulfillment, and our advancement as a people. Return, in this sense—*the human one*—isn't about what we *get* in return for our actions or from others. It's about what we *give* in return for what others gave us and how what we give makes a difference in the world. Our humanity is a gift so good it's worth celebrating. What will we give in return?

Glossary

Assessment (authentic mixed-method assessment, or AMMA): The specific indicators, *evidence*, and learning experiences that, together, provide the complete picture of performance used to inform the *measurement* of learning, along with the process of gathering that evidence. Assessment lies always underneath the process of measurement, forming the diverse and expansive evidence base without which meaningful measurement is impossible.

Assumption-shatterers: Statements designed to support *learning partners* to question their beliefs and values and ensure that personal and *system*-level interests are aligned to learners' needs.

Capability: The capacity of a school *system* and its professionals to prioritize what matters most for learners and develop the culture and behaviors that will make those student *outcomes* a reality for every learner (see the *system capabilities*).

Capability Rubrics: Measures of each of the five *system capabilities.*

Change team: A connected community of *learning partners* at school, district, and school-system levels designed to most effectively share and spread learning and best practices, communicate challenges and respond to identified needs, and lead the *deeper learning* change process at and between different levels of the school *system.*

Character: Learning to deep learn; possessing the essential character traits of grit, tenacity, perseverance, and resilience; and the ability to make learning an integral part of living (one of the 6Cs; see *competency*).

Citizenship: Thinking like global citizens, considering global issues based on a deep understanding of diverse values and worldviews, and demonstrating a genuine interest in and ability to solve ambiguous and complex problems that impact human and environmental sustainability (one of the 6Cs; see *competency*).

Clarity: Taking time to develop a shared language and understanding of *deeper learning* among all *learning partners*, as well as alignment between the *deeper learning* framework and the school or wider *system* (one of the *five frames of measurement*).

Collaboration: Working interdependently and synergistically in teams with strong interpersonal and team-related skills, including effective management of team dynamics and challenges, making substantive decisions together, and learning from and contributing to the learning of others (one of the 6Cs; see *competency*).

Collective cognition: Leveraging *learning partners'* combined experience, learning, and expertise to determine actions, decisions, and ways forward that will best develop *deeper learning outcomes.*

Communication: Communicating effectively using a variety of styles, modes, and digital and other tools tailored for a range of audiences (one of the 6Cs; see *competency*).

Competency: Leveraging *self-understanding, knowledge,* and connections with others and the world to make a difference in one's own and others' lives and the world (one of the *deeper learning outcomes*). The *deeper learning* competencies are the New Pedagogies for Deep Learning (NPDL) global partnership's 6Cs: *character, citizenship, collaboration, communication, creativity,* and *critical thinking.*

Connection: Connecting with others, one's *environments,* one's learning, and the world in meaningful and fulfilling ways (one of the *deeper learning outcomes*).

Creating a culture of learning, belonging, and high expectations for all: Fostering an environment in which everyone is learning and in which every learner is genuinely known, celebrated, and expected to succeed (one of the *system capabilities*).

Creativity: Having an "entrepreneurial eye" for economic and social opportunities, asking the right questions to generate novel ideas, and possessing the leadership to pursue those ideas and turn them into action (one of the 6Cs; see *competency*).

Critical thinking: Evaluating information and arguments, seeing patterns and connections, constructing meaningful *knowledge,* and applying it in the world (one of the 6Cs; see *competency*).

Cultural iceberg: A *tool* for thinking about and comparing *system* policies and programs, actual norms and behaviors, and the beliefs, values, and assumptions of individuals within systems. The *assumption-shatterers* support *learning partners* to ensure that each level of the iceberg is aligned and focused on what matters for learners.

Deeper learning: Developing the *outcomes* that support learners to make a real and sustainable difference, both now and in the future (see the *deeper learning outcomes*). It's learning that's used to contribute back.

Deeper learning experience: Any learning experience that successfully develops or assesses *deeper learning outcomes*; an assignment, a discussion, a test, a project, or any other activity through which deeper learning outcomes are demonstrated, assessed, or developed.

Deeper learning outcomes: *Self-understanding, knowledge, competency,* and *connection*—the outcomes that support learners to contribute back to the lives of others and the world in meaningful and fulfilling ways.

Depth: The intersection of learning and contribution, found in a focus on *deeper learning outcomes* (one of the *five frames of measurement*). When depth is the intersection of learning and contribution, humanity is the force that brings them together.

Design: The process of crafting or generating assessments that capture evidence of learning and/or develop intended learning *outcomes*, *capabilities*, or *practices*. We design solutions to address evidenced needs.

Development: Using a collective understanding of what matters for learners to fill existing measurement gaps by developing *rubrics*, learning progressions, guides, or other *measures* and *tools* that, collectively, measure and develop *deeper learning outcomes* and *enablers* (one of the *five frames of measurement*).

Dimension: The underlying *outcomes*, *capabilities*, and *practices* that collectively embody the overarching *deeper learning outcomes*, *system capabilities*, and *elements of authentic practice* (e.g., identity, place, capacity, and purpose, which are the dimensions of *self-understanding*). These dimensions are represented in each *Learning Progression* and *rubric*.

Dimension rating: A rating on each of the dimensions of a given *Learning Progression* or *rubric* (see *dimension*).

Elements of authentic practice: *Partnerships*, *environments*, *technology*, and *inquiry*, which encompass the *practices* that make *deeper learning outcomes* a reality for students and make *system capabilities* a reality for professionals.

Enablers: The capabilities (see *system capabilities*) and practices (see *elements of authentic practice*) that enable the development of *deeper learning outcomes*.

Engagement: Engaging *learning partners* to identify and describe what's actually important for learners and what contributes to their success (one of the *five frames of measurement*).

Engaging learners, parents, and communities as real partners: Connecting with students, parents, educators, and communities (*learning partners*) around who learners are and how they can contribute back (one of the *system capabilities*).

Environments: Leveraging where, why, and how we learn in a range of natural and built environments to enable and deepen learning (one of the *elements of authentic practice*).

Evaluative snapshot: Forming a complete, overall picture of the educational *system*, its learners, and what's important in individual contexts, using the *Capability Rubrics* to identify the strengths and needs that lay the foundation for change plans aimed at greater *depth* and improvement.

Evidence (assessment evidence): Data points or indicators of learning or development gathered throughout the assessment process and synthesized during the *measurement* process to inform an overall understanding of learning or development.

Exemplar: A slideshow presentation; a collection of other documents, videos, and pictures; a website; or any other means of describing and evidencing *learning* and why it occurred. Exemplars are used during the process of *exemplar moderation.*

Exemplar moderation: A professional learning experience designed to connect educators and other *learning partners* around describing, sharing, and discussing the *assessment* and *measurement* of student *learning* and professional *practice*, along with the *design* and *implementation* of *deeper learning experiences.* Teachers share their own and a student's learning through the design of a learning *exemplar.*

Five frames of measurement: *Engagement, development, clarity, inquiry,* and *depth*—the frames of thinking, action, and being that focus *systems* on the *measurement* and development of *deeper learning outcomes* through the lens of a comprehensive measurement framework.

Human return: The human capacity for contributing back to the lives of others and the world, fully realized at the intersection of *deeper learning outcomes.*

Identifying and measuring what's important: Setting up a system of *measurement* rooted in *learning-partner* engagement and reliable, *evidence*-based *practice* (one of the *system capabilities*).

Implementation: The process of facilitating designed assessments aimed at developing an intended *outcome, capability,* or *practice.*

Inquiry: The fluid and continuous process of *assessment, design, implementation, measurement,* and *reflection and change* that focuses all our actions and decisions on students and their *outcomes.* Inquiry is an investigation: we inquire into student outcomes and into professional capabilities and *practice.* Inquiry is one of the *elements of authentic practice* and one of the *five frames of measurement.*

Inter-rater reliability: Ensuring that *learning partners* presented with the same *measure* and the same *evidence* of *learning* arrive at the same or a similar *rating* or *measurement* decision. Moderation is a valuable process for establishing inter-rater reliability throughout *systems.*

Knowledge: The factual, conceptual, or content-based understanding that contributes to who we are, what we can do, and how we can contribute back (one of the *deeper learning outcomes*).

Leading for deep and sustainable change: Achieving real and sustainable *outcomes* with a continuous focus on learners and their needs and commitment to collective leadership and change (one of the *system capabilities*).

Learning Development Rubric: A *measure* of a *system*'s overall levels of *development* in relation to each of the *deeper learning outcomes.*

Learning Experience Rubric: A *measure* of the effectiveness of an implemented learning experience's embedded instructional practices.

Learning partners: Students, teachers, parents, school and school-system leaders, community members, and any others who play a role in developing and are committed to collectively improving learners' *outcomes.*

Learning Progression (or, "progression"): A *measure* of student learning (e.g., *self-understanding, connection* and *competency* progressions) written along a continuum that describes students' learning levels at multiple stages of progression.

Measure (*n.*): A tool (e.g., *Learning Progression* or *rubric*) used for the *measurement* of an intended *outcome* or other aim.

Measurement: The measurement of *deeper learning* combines the breadth of available assessment *evidence* to determine current levels of learning; identify areas of strength and areas for improvement; and deepen, through the shared language and understanding provided by the *measures* themselves, the process of teaching and learning in order to further develop student *outcomes.* It provides the overall picture of performance in relation to intended outcomes.

Outcome: Any result of the learning process as experienced by learners (see the *deeper learning outcomes*).

Overall rating: A *rating* that takes into account each individual *dimension rating* to arrive at a fully informed and *evidence*-based understanding of overall levels of learning or development on a given *rubric* or *progression.*

Partnerships: Leveraging student, teacher, parent, community member, and other *learning partner* engagement to enable and deepen learning (one of the *elements of authentic practice*).

Practice: The strategies or approaches that bring the *system capabilities* and *deeper learning outcomes* to life in our school *systems* (see the *elements of authentic practice.*) Practice is a partnership between teachers, students, parents, school leaders, community members, and others.

Rating: The quantifiable result of the *measurement* process that indicates current levels of learning or development. *Learning Progressions* and *rubrics* are used to make *ratings* of student and professional learning or development, respectively (see *dimension rating* and *overall rating.*)

Rating scale: On *Learning Progressions* and *rubrics*, the rating scale refers to the levels of the continuum described in the *measures* (i.e., substantially off track, getting started, looking promising, well on track, geared for success). The measures developed in this book use a five-point rating scale to provide the precision we need to accurately determine how well approaches are working in accelerating ourselves or our learners toward an *outcome* or target.

Reflection and change: Continuously thinking about how to strengthen *practice* in ways that better develop intended *outcomes* and then acting on opportunities for improvement.

Rubric: A measure of *system* and professional *capability* or *practice* (e.g., the *System Capability Rubrics*, the *Learning Development Rubric*, and the *Learning Experience Rubric*).

Self-understanding: Understanding who we are, what we're capable of, how we impact and fit into others' lives and the world, and how we can make a difference (one of the *deeper learning outcomes*).

System: A complex and connected body working, at its best, clearly and cohesively toward shared *outcomes* or ends. Classes, schools, districts, state school systems, national school systems, and other groupings are all systems responsible for developing the outcomes that matter for students, and they can all shift in ways that will better develop those outcomes.

System capabilities: The capabilities all *systems* need to develop to best support students' *development* of *deeper learning outcomes*. In this book, we identify the five system capabilities as (1) *understanding your system*; (2) *engaging learners, parents, and communities as real partners*; (3) *identifying and measuring what's important*; (4) *leading for deep and sustainable change*; and (5) *creating a culture of learning, belonging, and high expectations for all.*

Technology: Leveraging digital *tools* and other technologies to connect learners, expand learning environments, and otherwise enable and deepen learning (one of the *elements of authentic practice*).

Tool: Any *measure*, guide, or other instrument that supports professional or student learning.

Understanding your system: Developing a deeper, *evidence*-based understanding of your *system*, its learners, and the *capabilities* and conditions that enable valued *outcomes* (one of the *system capabilities*).

References

Atkinson, Wendy. (2017). Forms of Energy Textbook. Learning exemplar shared by Wendy Atkinson, fourth-grade teacher at Lucille Umbarger Elementary School. BESD. Burlington, WA.

Bellanca, James, & Ron Brandt. (2010). *21st Century Skills: Rethinking How Students Learn*. Bloomington, IN: Solution Tree.

Cauvel, Kimberly. (2017, June 12). New school program gets third-graders outdoors. *Skagit Valley Herald*. Retrieved from https://www.goskagit.com/news/local_news/new-school-program-gets-third-graders-outdoors/article_84239644-9006-5824-b518-e7d23b29677b.html

Chadwick, Kelly. (2017). Soap Box Racer Derby and Gala. Learning exemplar shared by teacher Kelly Chadwick, in partnership with teachers Jennie Croxford and Anne Jenkins, associate principal Annie McCambridge, and principal Wendy Bamford of Wanaka Primary School in New Zealand.

Chappuis, Stephen, Carol Commodore, & Rick Stiggins. (2017). *Balanced Assessment Systems: Leadership, Quality, and the Role of Classroom Assessment*. Thousand Oaks, CA: Corwin.

Darling-Hammond, Linda. (2017). Developing and Measuring Higher Order Skills: Models for State Performance Assessment Systems. Washington, DC: Council of Chief State School Officers.

Davidson, E. Jane, & Joanne McEachen. (2015). *Making the Important Measurable, Not the Measurable Important: How Authentic Mixed Method Assessment Helps Unlock Student Potential—and Tracks What Really Matters*. Seattle, WA: The Learner First.

Erickson, H. Lynn, Lois A. Lanning, & Rachel French. (2017). *Concept-Based Curriculum and Instruction for the Thinking Classroom*. 2nd ed. Thousand Oaks, CA: Corwin.

Fullan, Michael, & Joanne Quinn. (2015). *Coherence: The Right Drivers in Action for Schools, Districts, and Systems*. Thousand Oaks, CA: Corwin.

Fullan, Michael, Joanne Quinn, & Joanne McEachen. (2017). *Deep Learning: Engage the World, Change the World*. Thousand Oaks, CA: Corwin.

Hall, Edward T. (1976). *Beyond Culture*. Garden City, NY: Anchor Press.

Hammond, Zaretta. (2015). *Culturally Responsive Teaching and the Brain: Promoting Authentic Engagement and Rigor Among Culturally and Linguistically Diverse Students*. Thousand Oaks, CA: Corwin.

Kallick, Bena, & Allison Zmuda. (2017). *Students at the Center: Personalized Learning With Habits of Mind*. Alexandria, VA: ASCD.

Koretz, Daniel. (2009). *Measuring Up: What Educational Testing Really Tells Us*. Cambridge, MA: Harvard University Press.

Kotter, John P. (2012). *Leading Change*. Includes new preface by the author. Boston, MA: Harvard Business Review Press.

Lanning, Lois A., & Tiffanee Brown. (In press). *Concept-Based Literacy Lessons: Designing Learning to Ignite Understanding and Transfer*. Thousand Oaks, CA: Corwin.

Larmer, John, John Mergandoller, & Suzie Boss. (2015). *Setting the Standard for Project Based Learning: A Proven Approach to Rigorous Classroom Instruction*. Alexandria, VA: ASCD.

The Learner First. (2016). Evaluation of a network of early childhood schools in Hawaii. https://thelearnerfirst.com/

McEachen, J. (2017). *Assessment for Deep Learning*. Ontario, Canada: Fullan, M., McEachen, J., & Quinn, J. Retrieved from http://npdl.global/wp-content/uploads/2017/09/Assessment-for-Deep-Learning.pdf

Meier, Deborah, & Matthew Knoester. (2017). *Beyond Testing: Seven Assessments of Students and Schools More Effective Than Standardized Tests*. New York, NY: Teachers College Press.

Merrell, Kenneth W., & Barbara A. Gueldner. (2010). *Social and Emotional Learning in the Classroom: Promoting Mental Health and Academic Success*. New York, NY: Guilford Press.

Morris, Laura. (2016). Personal interview with Laura Morris, principal at Cesar Chavez Elementary, Oklahoma City Public Schools, USA.

Muallim, Minna. (2017). Deep Learning . . . ME! Learning exemplar shared by Minna Muallim, teacher at Cygnaeus Skola in Finland, and translated from Finnish by Tessa Westerstråhle.

New Pedagogies for Deep Learning. (2016). *NPDL Global Report*. Ontario, Canada: Fullan, M., McEachen, J., & Quinn, J. Retrieved from http://npdl.global/wp-content/uploads/2016/12/npdl-global-report-2016.pdf

New Zealand Qualifications Authority (NZQA). (n.d.) *Te Hono o Te Kahurangi: Mātauranga Māori Evaluative Quality Assurance (EER)* (Supplement to NZQA External Evaluation and Review Guidelines). Retrieved from https://www.nzqa.govt.nz/assets/Maori/MMEQA/MM-EQA-EER-Tools.pdf

Paniagua, A., & D. Istance. (2018). *Teachers as Designers of Learning Environments: The Importance of Innovative Pedagogies*. Paris: OECD Centre for Educational Research and Innovation. Retrieved from http://dx.doi.org/10.1787/9789264085374-en

Pickles, Susan. (2016). Speed Dating with the Pollies. Learning exemplar shared by Susan Pickles, teacher at Bendigo Secondary College in Australia.

Ravitch, Diane. (2011). *The Death and Life of the Great American School System: How Testing and Choice Are Undermining Education*. New York, NY: Basic Books.

Schein, Edgar H. (2010). *Organizational Culture and Leadership*. 4th ed. San Francisco, CA: Jossey-Bass.

Spencer, Michelle, et al. (2017). Cultures and Festivals. Learning exemplar shared by principal Michelle Spencer and teachers Trish Weaver, Erin McPhail, Giselle Otway, Honour Welbourn, Phil Funnell, Chris Valli, & Julia Lambie of Rapaura School in New Zealand.

Springlands School. (2017). Kāhore kau he Aorangi B (There Is No Planet B). Learning exemplar shared by Springlands School in Rapaura, New Zealand.

Timperley, Helen. (2011, May). *Using Student Assessment for Professional Learning: Focusing on Students' Outcomes to Identify Teachers' Needs*. Paper No. 21. Melbourne: State of Victoria Department of Education and Early Childhood Development. Retrieved from http://www.education.vic.gov.au/Documents/about/research/timperleyassessment.pdf

Turning Learning. (2017). *Turning Learning NPDL op Harpoen en Van Randwijk*. https://www.youtube.com/watch?v=M7_fN0jYKyc

Waites, Rachael, Olivia Ha, & Jacinta Kapelan. (2017). Chain Reaction. Learning exemplar shared by Rachael Waites, Olivia Ha, & Jacinta Kapelan, teachers at Derrimut Primary School in Australia.

Wanielista, Kera. (2017a, January 26). Elementary school students create dual-language newspaper. *Skagit Valley Herald*. Retrieved from https://www.goskagit

.com/news/elementary-school-students-create-dual-language-newspaper/article_450a9e30-d5f0-5d5b-b722-a91cc164c1f8.html

Wanielista, Kera. (2017b, February 13). Bay View Elementary students learn economics for 21st century. *Skagit Valley Herald*. Retrieved from https://www.goskagit.com/news/local_news/bay-view-elementary-students-learn-economics-for-st-century/article_94cded43-ea0f-530b-a3de-a5f996b5cc9b.html

Wanielista, Kera. (2017c, December 26). Burlington-Edison working to match technology with student needs. *Skagit Valley Herald*. Retrieved from https://www.goskagit.com/news/burlington-edison-working-to-match-technology-with-student-needs/article_1722be68-6b89-5b41-9d97-64b6bc164674.html

Wolk, Ronald A. (2011). *Wasting Minds: Why Our Education System Is Failing and What We Can Do About It*. Alexandria, VA: ASCD.

Index

Acknowledgments

Deeper learning is a partnership. *Sharing it is, too.* To—

Our core team at The Learner First: Andrew Boyd, Max Drummy, Leslie Conery, Jennifer Mersman, Catie Schuster, and Nolan Hellyer;

Learning partners at Burlington-Edison School District who shared their developing "recipe for return," including Don Beazizo, Brenda Booth, Tiffanee Brown, superintendent Laurel Browning, Grant Burwash, Tracy Dabbs, Bryan Jones, K. C. Knudson, Jim Logan, Amy Reisner, and Erica Tolf;

Our collaborators past and present: Steve Arnold, Gavin Beere, Baukje Bemener, Charisse Berner, Diane Chambers, Young Whan Choi, E. Jane Davidson, Cecilia de la Paz, Leslie Decker, Pam Estvold, Michael Fullan, Mag Gardner, Elizabeth Hamming, Rodney Hopson, Janet Levinger, Terry Macaluso, Karin Manns, Rob Neu, Jeff Petty, Joanne Quinn, Aparna Rae, Jacqueline Roebuck Sakho, Adrienne Rossiter, Alejandro Torres, and the brilliant staff at Corwin;

All other students, teachers, leaders, parents, and community members whose learning and examples illuminate these pages; and

Our wonderful families and friends in Seattle, New Zealand, and around the world—

Thank you for sharing yourselves and your learning with us so that we could share them again with others.

Publisher's Acknowledgments

Corwin gratefully acknowledges the contributions of the following reviewers:

Jeff Beaudry, Educational Leadership
University of Southern Maine
Portland, ME

Charisse Berner, Director of Teaching and Learning, Curriculum
Bellingham, WA

Clint Heitz, Instructional Coach
Bettendorf, IA

Susan Kessler, Executive Principal
Nashville, TN

Karen L. Tichy, Assistant Professor of Educational Leadership
Saint Louis University
St. Louis, MO

About the Authors

Joanne McEachen is founder and CEO of The Learner First (thelearnerfirst.com), an international education consultancy based in Seattle, Washington. She leads a team of dedicated education and evaluation specialists who support school systems through the processes of assessment, measurement, and whole-system change. Her methodology interrogates systems through the eyes of their least-served learners, supporting them to embrace and celebrate students' cultural identities and individual interests and needs. Joanne also serves as the Global New Measures Director for New Pedagogies for Deep Learning (NPDL), an international partnership focused on measuring and developing six global competencies of deep learning (the "6Cs"), where she works alongside and in partnership with Michael Fullan, Joanne Quinn, and other educators and system leaders worldwide. With her NPDL cofounders, Joanne coauthored *Deep Learning: Engage the World, Change the World*, which shares and celebrates the learning emerging from throughout NPDL.

Joanne's expertise spans every level of the educational system. She has been a teacher, principal, superintendent, and national-school-system leader in her home country of New Zealand and around the world, and she has worked with multiple large and diverse school districts in the United States to bring deeper learning to life. Drawing from rich and varied experiences tackling the issues faced by schools, districts, education departments, and the individuals within them, Joanne shares measures, tools, approaches, and insights that deepen learning for every learner.

Matthew Kane is the Director of Research and Writing at The Learner First, where he focuses on the role and experiences of school systems in developing the learning outcomes that contribute to lifelong success, connect us with one another, and make a difference in our communities. He has partnered with diverse schools and school systems globally to develop deeper learning tools, language, and practices, and he works as a senior project manager with the New Pedagogies for Deep Learning (NPDL) global partnership. Matthew graduated from the University of Notre Dame and lives in Seattle, Washington.

Helping educators make the greatest impact

CORWIN HAS ONE MISSION: to enhance education through intentional professional learning.

We build long-term relationships with our authors, educators, clients, and associations who partner with us to develop and continuously improve the best evidence-based practices that establish and support lifelong learning.

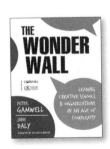

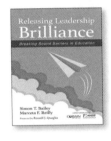

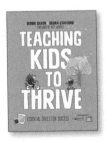

Leadership That Makes an Impact

Also Available

Steven Katz, Lisa Ain Dack, & John Malloy
Leverage the oppositional forces of top-down expectations and bottom-up experience to create an intelligent, responsive school.

Peter M. DeWitt
Centered on staff efficacy, these resources present discussion questions, vignettes, strategies, and action steps to improve school climate, leadership collaboration, and student growth.

Eric Sheninger
Harness digital resources to create a new school culture, increase communication and student engagement, facilitate real-time professional growth, and access new opportunities for your school.

Russell J. Quaglia, Kristine Fox, Deborah Young, Michael J. Corso, & Lisa L. Lande
Listen to your school's voice to see how you can increase engagement, involvement, and academic motivation.

Michael Fullan, Joanne Quinn, & Joanne McEachen
Learn the right drivers to mobilize complex, coherent, whole-system change and transform learning for all students.